**SAGE** was founded in 1965 by Sara Miller McCune to support the dissemination of usable knowledge by publishing innovative and high-quality research and teaching content. Today, we publish over 900 journals, including those of more than 400 learned societies, more than 800 new books per year, and a growing range of library products including archives, data, case studies, reports, and video. SAGE remains majority-owned by our founder, and after Sara's lifetime will become owned by a charitable trust that secures our continued independence.

Los Angeles | London | New Delhi | Singapore | Washington DC | Melbourne

# INFLUENCE
## OF
# ENGLISH
# ON INDIAN
## WOMEN WRITERS

# INFLUENCE
## OF
# ENGLISH
# ON INDIAN
## WOMEN WRITERS

*Voices from Regional Languages*

*Edited by*
## K. SUNEETHA RANI

Los Angeles | London | New Delhi
Singapore | Washington DC | Melbourne

*First published in 2017 by*

**SAGE Publications India Pvt Ltd**
B1/I-1 Mohan Cooperative Industrial Area
Mathura Road, New Delhi 110 044, India
*www.sagepub.in*

**STREE**
16 Southern Avenue
Kolkata 700 026
*www.stree-samyabooks.com*

**SAGE Publications Inc**
2455 Teller Road
Thousand Oaks, California 91320, USA

**SAGE Publications Ltd**
1 Oliver's Yard, 55 City Road
London EC1Y 1SP, United Kingdom

**SAGE Publications Asia-Pacific Pte Ltd**
3 Church Street
#10-04 Samsung Hub
Singapore 049483

Published by Vivek Mehra for SAGE Publications India Pvt Ltd, typeset in 11/13 pt Baskerville Old Face by Zaza Eunice, Hosur, Tamil Nadu, India and printed at Saurabh Printers Pvt Ltd, Greater Noida.

**Library of Congress Cataloging-in-Publication Data**

Name: Suneetha Rani, editor.
Title: Influence of English on Indian women writers: voices from regional
  languages/edited by K. Suneetha Rani.
Description: New Delhi; Thousand Oaks, California: SAGE Publications India
  Pvt Ltd., 2017. | Includes bibliographical references.
Identifiers: LCCN 2017036269 | ISBN 9789381345153 (print (pb): alk. paper) |
  ISBN 9789381345344 (e pub 2.0) | ISBN 9789381345351 (e book)
Subjects: LCSH: Indic literature (English)—Women authors—History and
  criticism. | English language—India. | Women and literature—India.
Classification: LCC PR9488 .I57 2017 | DDC 820.9/92870954—dc23
LC record available at https://lccn.loc.gov/2017036269

**ISBN:** 978-93-81345-15-3 (PB)

**SAGE Stree Team:** Shambhobi Ghosh, Amrita Dutta and Guneet Kaur Gulati

*To my beloved mother
who raised me on letters*

Thank you for choosing a SAGE product!
If you have any comment, observation or feedback,
I would like to personally hear from you.
Please write to me at **contactceo@sagepub.in**

**Vivek Mehra,** Managing Director and CEO, SAGE India.

## Bulk Sales

SAGE India offers special discounts
for purchase of books in bulk.
We also make available special imprints
and excerpts from our books on demand.

*For orders and enquiries, write to us at*

Marketing Department
SAGE Publications India Pvt Ltd
B1/I-1, Mohan Cooperative Industrial Area
Mathura Road, Post Bag 7
New Delhi 110044, India

*E-mail us at* **marketing@sagepub.in**

## Get to know more about SAGE

Be invited to SAGE events, get on our mailing list.
*Write today to* **marketing@sagepub.in**

This book is also available as an e-book.

# Contents

# Introduction

## K. Suneetha Rani

KAMALA DAS, a well-known woman writer in English and Malayalam, proclaims in her poem 'An Introduction':

> I speak three languages, write in
> Two, dream in one.
> Don't write in English, they said, English is
> Not your mother-tongue. Why not leave
> Me alone, critics, friends, visiting cousins,
> Every one of you? Why not let me speak in
> Any language I like? The language I speak,
> Becomes mine, its distortions, its queernesses
> All mine, mine alone. (2004: 62)

This proclamation of choice and condemnation of restrictions on writing in English marks an inheritance of a long history of debates around English in India, especially in the context of women's voices and issues. English was not just a language, a medium of instruction and a colonial heritage but it also signified manners, lifestyle, politics and modernity. Rajeswari Sundar Rajan, in her introduction to her book *The Lie of the Land* (1993: 8) says, 'the disciplinary formation of English in India therefore needs to be contextualized within at least three broad areas: its history, language politics, and the socio-cultural scene of education. By framing it within these larger issues—which, in a sense, provide the fixes for its location—we are also enabled to see from where resistance to it is mounted, and what forms it takes'. While it is true that the disciplinary formation of English in India, as Sundar Rajan observes, needs to be contextualized within at least three broad areas of its history, language politics, and the socio-cultural scene of education, the non-academic/popular (people's) field of English also needs to be contextualized at least within the above three broad areas. In the academic as well as the non-academic forms/fields of English, gender played a crucial role literally and metaphorically. The beginnings of the English discourse in India in the nineteenth and the early twentieth centuries, as many critics have observed and argued, seems to have been built majorly around the category of gender. Such discourse also presented contradictory approaches to the English argument, but they were all intricately connected. English helped in moulding better family women; English provided a garb of modernity to reiterate traditional gender stereotypes; English contributed to the creation of the world of dichotomies but English also created a hope for the outcastes deprived of entry, education and employment.

Kumkum Sangari and Sudesh Vaid in *Recasting Women* (2010: Introduction) discuss the differentiation of language patterns by referring to William Carey, the Baptist missionary who was involved in the Orientalist restoration project. He produced with the help of Indians a reader in 1801 for the students of Fort William College. It was a compendium of sketches of various castes and classes and depicted the idiomatic language, manners and customs of women, merchants, fishermen, beggars, labourers and attempted to reproduce their speech patterns. According to this compendium, linguistic sophistication was proportionate to social status. Women were identified as low caste through the vulgarity of their speech while the vocabulary of higher caste women was represented as a mixture of refinement and vulgarity. The difference between vernacular and the genteel Bengali extended/represented women and men also in terms of their status even within the same family (ibid.: 12–13).

The 1801 compendium not only tried to depict the linguistic scenario but also tried to define and describe the low-caste and the high-caste women based on the language that they used. Such descriptions extended to gender identities as well. It clearly made a statement about gender when it said the upper-caste women used language that was a mixture of refinement and vulgarity. Probably refinement represented their class while vulgarity represented their gender, which was common between the women of lower castes as well as the higher castes according to the compendium. The conflict between English and the Indian languages or the co-relation between the two, given their political and other statuses, began to be identified in terms of gender. As Shefali Chandra observes in her article 'Gendering English' (2007: 289), the masculinity of English was being constantly accompanied by the feminization of the vernacular. This article focuses on the representation and regulation that shaped the context and reach of Indian English, which is the process forming its own language of gender. The author says that 'this gendered English created new codes of signification to support the matrix of colonial-national and heterosexual gender'.

English was viewed as a colonial legacy, which it was. It was also looked upon as an endorsement of colonization and the anti-English stand was considered decolonizing. People questioned, debated, adopted, manipulated and mastered over English but on the other hand admired it, followed it and owned it. English as language, education and culture was inevitably connected to education in the case of women. Jasodhara Bagchi (1993) goes a step forward to understand how the emphasis was shifted to *sishukanya*, the girl child, to mould women. She writes that education for and of girls became a recurrent theme in the writings of the nineteenth century. There was a steady growth of women's education in Bengal from the time of Vidyasagar. Education was considered to be a social space that could provide status and empowerment for women. On the other hand, there was resistance to school education for girls due to the deep rooted fear of early widowhood. Western education became a characteristic feature of the men of the rising middle classes while the girls had to face number of hurdles. Added to that, English/western education was supposed to be encouraging women to become immodest, undisciplined and un-controllable.

Education, particularly women's education, was, and still is, a major issue in India. Modern Indian literatures have discussed this issue from various perspectives. While some voices argued for women's education, some others argued against it for various reasons. In all these debates, English education became the central focus, for not only was it perceived as a colonial heritage but also it was believed to corrupt Indian women and thus lead to the collapse of moral values and the institution of the family in India. Although we could discuss women's education as education for women and English education for women, the two were closely associated as education in the nineteenth century meant education in the English model if not in the English medium.

The initial debates about English in nineteenth-century India directly affected women because of various reasons. Firstly, English as a rule, policy and learning became the crucial spirit of the reform movement. Women's reform was one of the major agendas of the reform movement. Reform of women's conditions quite often targeted, apart from being patronizing, women as the to-be-reformed sections. English became the carving stone in the search for creation of new models for women. Some models were carved out as educated, family women better equipped to shoulder the familial responsibilities and some others, to the contrary, juxtaposed educated women as corrupted against the virtuous family women untouched by English education and manners.

On the other hand, the onus was on the women to access the benefits of modernity and also to prove themselves. This proving was not limited to their capability in education but extended to their loyalties and roles. So, women started to debate English as education and as lifestyle, grounded in their context and crisis. English as modernity was understood and adopted by women as a means to come out of seclusion, invisibility and economic dependence. English as modernity was interpreted by nationalists/anti-colonialists as reiteration of colonization and westernization of women. English as modernity was understood by the traditionalists as a blow to Indian values and the family system, and the modesty and virtue of women. English stood for colonial modernity prior to independence while it represented development and transformation in the post-independence era and it has become a symbol of globalization and westernization in contemporary times with a promise of achievement of aspirations and upward mobility.

Partha Chatterjee (1989a) discusses in detail as to how women's education was a project of making ideal women. He says that the threat to women's education was seen to lie in the fear that the early schools and arrangements for teaching women at home were organized by Christian missionaries and thus the fear of proselytization and exposure of women to harmful western influence. He continues to say that the threat was removed when Indians themselves began to open schools for girls. It might not be such a clear division between schools run by the Christian missionaries and the schools run by the Indians themselves that generated or removed the fear of education corrupting or converting women. This was because the design of the education also played an equally important role in changing the ideologies of women or students in general whether the schools were run by the missionaries or the Indians. However, to reiterate, one of the major threats anticipated by the Indians of the English education was conversion to Christianity. The nineteenth century is one period that frequently brings the issues of education, gender, caste and conversion together; like Pandita Ramabai (1858–1922) who chose to break the restrictions of the Hindu religion by converting into Christianity and re-marrying. Apart from getting education, we come across writers who also focus on conversion to Christianity to access education. *Saraswati Vijayam*, a novel originally written in Malayalam by Potheri Kunhambu in the late nineteenth century and translated into English in the late twentieth century, depicts a lower-caste man and an upper caste-woman, both oppressed by tradition, both running away from home, both getting converted into Christianity to access education, both getting educated, both transgressing the boundaries of casteist and patriarchal society.

While who ran the school became one of the important questions, it was also important to examine the curriculum as it was believed to have the potential to corrupt especially women students. From deciding the status of women based on the language that they used through feminizing regional languages in order to masculinize English or the other way round, we reach the point of administering the proper 'feminine curriculum' that was crucial for women. Shefali Chandra argues that English was repeatedly invoked to signify the very opposite of normative culture, motherhood and femininity.

Native girls were being educated into the ideals of conduct and comportment that defined the lives of 'English young ladies', ideals that had to be *performed* for the interested gaze of an elite, largely male, native and European audience. The social organisation of perceived sexual differences was achieved through the selective display of particular codes and behaviours. This standard of upper-class deportment borrowed heavily from an idealised notion of English feminine accomplishments. And English eased this transnational fashioning of the feminine–domestic. At the heart of the production of mid-nineteenth-century bourgeois gender in Britain was the requirement of domesticity, the separate spheres of male and female influence, knowledge and activity and the elevation of domestic comfort, home and family life. Supported by a companionate understanding between husband and wife, the harmonious domestic ideal required a mutual, cosmopolitan awareness of the larger world. But in the case of India, the selective Anglicisation, performed for and supported by the European and native philanthropists present, compulsorily maintained a requisite quota of 'indigenous' culture in its elaboration (Chandra 2007: 289).

Partha Chatterjee also argues that this context that brought together colonialism, nationalism and women, or rather centred colonialism and nationalism around women, led to the dichotomy of the material-spiritual; home-world and feminine-masculine. This dichotomy led to the emergence of a new woman with traditional feminine virtues as a new patriarchy started to dictate the nationalist Indian woman in a colonial set up. The new patriarchy advocated by nationalism conferred upon women the honour of a new social representation:

For a colonized people, the world was a distressing constraint, forced upon it by the fact of its material weakness. It was a place of oppression and daily humiliation, a place where the norms of the colonizer had perforce to be accepted. It was also the place, as nationalists were soon to argue, where the battle would be waged for national independence. This required that the subjugated learn from the West the modern sciences and arts of the material world. Then their strength would be matched and ultimately the colonizer overthrown. But in the entire phase of the national struggle, the crucial need was to protect, preserve and strengthen the inner core of the national culture, its spiritual essence. No encroachments by the colonizer must be allowed in that inner sanctum, in the world, imitation and adaptation to Western norms was a necessity: at home, they were tantamount to one's very identity.

Once we match this new meaning of the home/world dichotomy with the identification of social roles by gender, we get the ideological framework within which nationalism answered the women's question (1989b: 624–25).

Partha Chatterjee also explains how the nationalist paradigm did not dismiss modernity but rather made an attempt to make modernity consistent with the nationalist project and how the nationalist construction of reform functioned as a project of both emancipation and self-emancipation of women (and hence a project in which both men and women must participate). The late nineteenth century witnessed the emergence of women writers in different Indian languages as well as in English. While Savitribai Phule established schools for girls and lower-caste children, the other major women writers such as Krupabai Sattianadhan, Pandita Ramabai Saraswati and Tarabai Shinde connected English with the issues of caste, class and religion as well. Cornelia Sorabjee was another Indian woman who could access English education and went on to become a lawyer but was not allowed to enrol in the bar council for 20 years for being a woman. This instance proves how English education did not drastically change women's status and eliminate the social evils and prejudices working against women. However, it did open up new areas of expertise and paved way for the professional achievement of women. The reform movement had voices that were raised for and against English. However, the domain that was targeted by both the strands was the domestic sphere, that is, the domesticity of women. The initial concern was to motivate women to make their private sphere better. The private sphere was emphasized as that was considered to be the primary and the sole space and commitment for women and also that they had and they were allowed no concept of the public sphere.

Susie Tharu's analysis (1989: 261–62) takes forward this discussion on the nationalist project in the guise of modernity by interestingly choosing examples of women writing in English. She argues that Toru Dutt and Sarojini Naidu were spreading the ideal of Indian womanhood in English and in the model of Victorian values but to support the national movement. She says, 'If Toru Dutt, in the anxiety to present a pure, uncorrupted India transforms the Indian landscape morally into a western one, and her heroines into virtuous Victorians, Naidu composes a land and a people that fits into a different, more exotic area in the western imagination. She feeds essentially feudal, Vedic and Islamic cultural formations into what was the structure of Victorian sentiment. And where women were concerned, these diverse patriarchal cultures were surprisingly accommodative and reinforcing of each other.' Condemning the western influence on women strongly depended on glorification of indigenous tradition. On one hand the westernized woman was being presented as a deviation of the normal, that is, traditional woman and on the other hand the traditional woman was strongly being invoked to support the nationalist agenda. Partha Chatterjee's concept of dichotomies becomes more intense when we examine how a dichotomy is created within the domain of women's education by using it in two ways with two purposes, that is, denying education for women in the belief that they will be corrupted if they accessed education, especially modern education, and on the other hand, using the same education as a strategy to educate women in order to make them better wives, daughters and daughters-in-law.

Nita Kumar's essay 'Mothers and Non-Mothers' (2005) discusses the opposing binaries of mothers and non-mothers and mothering and non-mothering as an important discourse in the making of nation, gender and education in the nineteenth century. It also argues that mothers, biological or the mentoring, played a crucial role not only in the reform movement led by men, but they also played an instrumental role in inspiring and moulding the intelligentsia who actively took the initiative in the reform movement. Nita Kumar subverts the stereotypical representation of passive women by saying, 'A gendered history of education reveals that there are multiple discourses: women were formed by men through a discourse of reform and the "private", and men were formed by women through a discourse of motherhood and family'. But, interestingly, she says that these women who could form men were doing so through a discourse of motherhood and family, thus reiterating the spaces to which women were confined in the reform movement.

In this design of traditionalizing Indian women with the help of the modernity discourse, women's voices were also extensively heard as Susie Tharu quotes from Toru Dutt and Sarojni Naidu. Women, like the lower castes, however, could understand the importance of education, especially English education. They were not mere passive agents of the agenda of preserving tradition and not all women were a party to this spread of the ideology of tradition in the guise of modernity. While society and the state were trying to employ English education to teach them Victorian models and morals, women also took to English to equip themselves and to use that equipment as a weapon against prejudices and as a means towards change. English education represented modernity in a positive sense for women while Indian society kept debating for a long time, and still continues to debate, if English education for women was the worst consequence of colonization and globalization.

As English and education or English education were associated with class, gender, language, nation and modernity, they were also creating discomfort to the savarna castes and were also unveiling a ray of hope for the others. People who responded to English diversely had diverse identities as well. The royal tongue was employed by the rulers to lure the ruled and to train them in serving the rulers. Thus, English became a means for the aspirants to ascend the ladder of education and career. While English is confined to the questions of colonization and achievement in the context of the 'mainstream', it acquired other connotations and agendas when it is studied in the context of the people who are not traditionally allowed access to knowledge and success. It became expression, emancipation, and empowerment for some. Lower-caste people, for instance, strongly believed that education, English education in that, was the sole blessing for them to come out of centuries of toil and exploitation. It was an effective means of subverting the hegemonic structures (Alladi Uma et al. 2014). It was a landmark in the history of education in

India when Jyotirao Phule and Savitribai Phule established schools for the lower castes and girls with an emphasis on 'modern' education in English. Savitribai Phule vociferously argues in her poetry for education for the underprivileged sections. Education did not mean only English education for her. But her concept of education was deconstruction of the traditional exclusionist education. She has overtly given a call to the marginalized sections to learn English in her poem 'Learn English':

> Throw away the authority
> Of the Brahmin and his teachings,
> Break the shackles of caste,
> By learning English.[1]

When we re-visit Partha Chatterjee's discussion (1989 a, b) of the dichotomies of the home and the world, spiritual and material, man and woman that the nationalist agenda created, we notice another significant dichotomy that in a sense decided or transformed the politics of English in India, that is, the dichotomy of purity and pollution. Chatterjee's dichotomies, like the purity-pollution dichotomy, acquire multiple dimensions and branch out into complexities based on the specific contexts and identities. Mythily Sivaraman's *Fragments of a Life* presents an example for the debatable relationship among gender, caste, education and purity. Subbalakshmi, Mythily Sivaraman's grandmother, was not sent to school in 1908 as 'the caste purity of the "twice born" could not be sullied by contact with such trivialities as school education' (2013: 19). The men in her family became her sources to access education as she was not sent to school. She had no direct access to education, particularly English education. Her entry into this space was through the male members of her family, as an aide or as a surreptitious reader. Her responsibility of having to read the *Hindu* newspaper to her grandfather whose eyesight was failing gave her the first opportunity to familiarize herself with letters while the books that her college-going elder brother borrowed from library introduced her to the world of knowledge in print. English, for Subbalakshmi, was not just education/medium, but politics, a means to know and comment on the political affairs.

Subbalakshmi's story repeated in her daughter's case when she found to her astonishment that her husband did not want to send their daughter to school as his elder brother thought it was unbecoming for a Brahmin girl to attend school and learn English. The space deprived to Subbalakshmi became a revelation/shock for her daughter when Pankajam saw her servants' children not as servants in inheritance but as her co-students in the school.

This argument/aspect unveils another angle when we look at it from the perspective of the others whose entry was banned into school not due to fear of losing purity as it was in the case of Subbalakshmi but because of the social stigma of pollution that was attached to them. The threat was not to their purity which could be polluted if they went to school as it was in the case of ritually pure women but the threat was to others' purity that could be polluted by the inherently polluted and capable of polluting lower-caste women. Subbalakshmi's encounter with schooling can be contrasted with Dalit women not allowed to and not affording it but wanting to enter the school.

The narratives of Kumud Pawde (1992) and Urmila Pawar (2011), both Dalit women from Maharashtra, precisely address this issue at various levels. Kumud Pawde's 'The Story of My Sanskrit' traces the trajectory of a Dalit woman, twice-prohibited, based on her caste and gender, mastering the language that was considered to be the domain of the twice-born. While the prohibition inflicted on her is multi-fold and her achievement in accessing it is at many levels, the backlash that she faces also happens in different forms. While her teachers and classmates refuse to acknowledge her learning, her colleagues and students refuse to accept her teaching. As she is accused, she not only pollutes the classroom, discipline, language, knowledge but also pollutes the condescension of the excluding hierarchies. She looks towards English in her attempt to get a job. Although this attempt also fails her, it is significant that she thinks English can get her a job while Sanskrit has failed her. It is neither her Sanskrit, nor her English but her husband's backward caste surname that she makes part of her name that 'tradition' considers the eligibility criterion for Kumud Pawde's candidature.

Similarly, Urmila Pawar (2011) depicts how her childhood encountered the hegemony of caste, gender and learning. She could enter the space of the school. But as a lower-caste girl, the teacher thought the best that she could do was to clean the school. In order to justify his decision, he shifted the blame onto the cow that her family owned which he thought could have dirtied the school premises. The dichotomy becomes even more specific and focused here as within the school we can see the space, function and identity-divided. School provides the space for learning (though it created a space of possible pollution for women like Subbalakshmi) for students while it provided the space for cleaning for Urmila Pawar, reiterating her identity as a Dalit woman and re-inflicting the traditional occupation that the society has allotted to her people. Thus, this creates another dichotomy of tradition and modernity or tradition in the guise of modernity as it happened in the case of women in the nationalist agenda as argued by Partha Chatterjee, Jasodhara Bagchi, Shefali Chandra, Susie Tharu and others.

Subbalakshmi, who was never allowed to study English or never allowed to go to school, had written her diary in English which was kept a secret by her only to be re-discovered and documented by her granddaughter Mythily Sivaraman much later. She chose a language that she never used in her life to write her diary. Her politics, her diary and her English prove a combination that she kept a secret that was close to her heart as this combination could subvert the confinement that she was subjected to by her people, by tradition and by her own health conditions. A parallel can be found in Kumud Pawde when she accesses the language that has always been used as an agency by the other to hegemonize knowledge and deprive people like her of mobility—social, cultural, economic, and, especially, intellectual. Both the 'pure' *savarna* woman and the 'polluted/polluting' *avarna* woman were engaging with the politics of language that was being manipulated by tradition whether it was Sanskrit or English.

Another dimension of the discourse of English and the Indian women is revealed in Antoinette Burton's essay (1996) from a very different perspective but about the nationalist obligation. She refers to Pandita Ramabai's testimony before the Hunter Commission in 1882 about the need for women doctors in India, thus arguing that Indian women were both directly and indirectly responsible for the organized interest in supplying women doctors for India in the late Victorian period. She also argues that the Indian woman was imagined as imprisoned and awaiting liberation at the hands of Englishwomen's benevolence. In order to unveil the domestic institutions that were bound up with the empire and its projects in nineteenth-century Britain, she chooses the example of the origins of the London School of Medicine for Women and its concern for Indian women in the zenana. She states that the conviction that Indian women were trapped in the allegedly unhygienic Oriental zenana motivated the institutionalization of women's medicine and was crucial to the professionalization of women doctors in Victorian Britain. So, according to her, it became nothing short of national and imperial obligation to offer services in India and other parts of the East, where native customs made it practically impossible for women to be attended by medical men.

There seems to be a close parallel between the nationalist reform agenda and the imperialist reform agenda, not only because both were majorly focusing on Indian women, but also because both were exclusively focusing on the privileged women, either in terms of caste and class, or the 'normal' woman (the normative family woman) and completely excluding the lower-caste, lower-class and the other women. The excluded women might have identities in different combinations. Similarly, the designs to exclude them from the reform debate also chose different combinations. While the anti-nautch movement branded the courtesan woman as the corrupting force and pushed her to the fringes, the lower-caste woman never came into the discussions and hence remained invisible in the fringes.

The debate had caught the imagination of the writers and thinkers in regional languages as it affected them the most and challenged them the most. There were writers who opposed English and there were writers who supported it but there were also writers who used English as a language and as a discourse to strengthen the tradition in a new guise as it was happening in the nationalist discourse. In the Telugu language context, the best example for this in the nineteenth century is the life, activism and writings of Kandukuri

Veeresalingam (Suneetha Rani 2015), a renowned thinker, writer and social reformer from the Telugu-speaking region who vociferously argued for English education for women as he strongly believed that it would teach women the art of making perfect homes.[2] Veeresalingam hailed the English language for the treasure house of knowledge it was and British rule as the blessing from heaven. He chose to write about the Englishwomen who could provide models for Indian women. Many of his writings echoed the English writings in style and message. Thus, English functioned as a treasure house and as a tool for the spread of a code of conduct in colonial India for ideal new women to mould them into better wives in order to enable them to make better homes.

Magazines became the most important platforms to discuss these ideas and convey the 'message' to the target groups. A considerable number of women's magazines emerged in the late nineteenth century, some run by men and some by women. Some of them had descriptive names such *Satihitabodhini*, the one run by Kandukuri Veeresalingam, while some others had suggestive names such as *Savitri, Anasuya, Hindu Sundari, Grihalakshmi* and so on. It is interesting to note that most Indian languages had women's magazines, those that addressed women and those that addressed issues about women, that had similar names referring to the ideal women and domesticity. Mytheli Sreenivas (2003) argues that the print culture of the nineteenth century was part of a broader history of middle-class identity as it developed under the conditions of colonial modernity. The article also explains that early women's magazines in Tamil were part of an urban print culture that centred on the south-eastern city of Madras (Chennai) which was the British administrative centre for peninsular India. The article provides important information that though the magazines included articles that reflected the colonial context, some magazines included articles in English as well. Such bilingual magazines provide clues to understand the target readership especially in the case of women's magazines that they also addressed the English-knowing gentlemen apart from speaking to the home-making, 'vernacular'-speaking women. The author divides the history of women's magazines in Tamil under the heads of 'Educating Wives' (1850–1920); 'Visions of Companionship' (1920–1940), 'Desire and Pleasure in Marriage' (1936–1939) (ibid.). This comes very close to the women's magazines in Telugu as well.

Another significant feature of the Telugu writings was the code-switching between Telugu and English. Either the titles of the books had English titles as well or the Preface/Introduction was written in English. It requires an extensive discussion as to why and how the Telugu books had English titles and introductions. However, this experimentation clearly shows the way the writers were playing with languages and reaching out to the English-knowing readers as well. This could be an attempt to show how tradition and modernity were being brought together by mastering the colonial language.[3] Some of Veeresalingam's books have chunks of writing in English as well shifting between English and Telugu even in his essays. This code-switching was happening while there were vociferous arguments happening for the use of common people's language in literature and other writings. So, the journey seems to be from the *granthika* (language used in writing books) through *vyavaharika* (colloquial language) to English which resulted in the use of all the three together sometimes. It was a Telugu nation that was being constructed while being part of the Madras state politically, publishing also from Madras and catering to the readers in more than one language.

The regional languages, thus, became vibrant platforms for the discourse around the English question, closely connecting it with the questions of tradition, modernity, colonialism, nation and especially gender. English became an agency for women to express themselves and to explore the domains of knowledge that they were not allowed to access earlier. Such women's voices are heard more extensively and powerfully in regional languages in their fiction, personal narratives, essays, columns and editorials of the journals. The articles in this volume examine the English debate from various angles as debated by women in their articles, speeches, fiction, biographies and letters.

The essays in this volume rightly take the identities and specificities into consideration instead of essentializing the debates around English. They also pay attention to the parallel movements and contexts which directly and indirectly influenced and worked together with women's issues. They attempt to unmask the politics behind the arguments for saving of languages as marks of the glorious culture. The collection of articles in this volume select issues from the vast field of the above mentioned discourse, while some address the regional contexts, some others address the English-English context where English is being debated in English. Most of the essays locate their discussion in the late nineteenth century or/and early twentieth century as this was the time when English was being interpreted, adopted and protested as a discourse that was crucial for the larger movements. The aim of this book is to record the different ways in which women responded to the debates around English in different languages and different genres. Some articles discuss how English education was considered as a mark of modernity and was juxtaposed against traditions and patriotism, some others present the conflict that women had to face when they were compelled to take a firm stand, sometimes even against their own people, to access English education.

Although most of the articles discuss how the English debate is centred on domesticity, in the case of women their concerns extend to the fundamental questions such as writing women and their choice of language. This book brings into discussion Indian women's choice of writing or not writing in English in the context of identity movements. While English may not be an issue for some as they inherit it from their families and communities, it is a hard hurdle for the majority of Indians who are forced to learn it while many of them fear English as a belittling burden.

The articles have chosen specific locations—ideological, geographical, cultural, linguistic and the time period—to speak from and to speak about. As all of them more or less address similar questions related to the English discourse and the woman question, it is difficult to divide them under sections. However, they can be organized in a way that one leads to the other in one's attempt to understand and interpret the gendered politics of English.

Chapter 1, C. Vijayasree, 'Language, Reform and Nationalism: Indian Women's Writing in the Nineteenth Century' argues that the intersecting sites of English education, rhetoric of reform and nationalist discourse provided a larger context within which the literary production of Indian women writers took shape in the nineteenth century. These writers engaged critically with both Orientalist and nationalist discourses of reform and articulated their views on the politics of language and gender. This article probes the subtexts in women's writing and examines the interventions made by women writers into the dominant discourses of the nineteenth century. This investigation exposes the many contradictions involved in the making of the nation and point to the impossibility of conceiving nationalist thought as monolithic.

Chapter 2, Alladi Uma, 'Women and "Reform",' introduces the woman question in terms of reform and the nautch question, focusing on the late nineteenth and early twentieth centuries. The author chooses three women writers who wrote in English, Tamil and Telugu to address the questions of education and reform or education as reform that became the underlying ideology of women's reform. This article discusses education and movement from private to public as modernity and raises questions about patriarchal modernity. It also argues how education was not only intended to make housewives better but was also perceived as a boon to courtesan women to release themselves from institutionalized slavery and exploitation. However, one cannot miss the point in this discussion that reforming the other woman was taken up by mainstream patriarchy to save the man and the family woman. Attempts were also made to push the other woman into domesticity and appropriate and brahminize the art forms that were the domain of the other woman traditionally.

In Chapter 3, Sanjukta Dasgupta presents 'Colonized: The Bengali Woman Writer in British India', drawing our attention to an interesting anti-colonial notion in the nineteenth century that women's education, their ability to read and write and publish their writing in regional and English languages were considered serious subversive acts. It focuses on the anxieties of authorship and the career graph of the writers Rokeya Sakhawat Hossain and Swarnakumari Devi among others. It concentrates on women's education and women's writing. It interestingly compares the women writers in Britain and in British India in the early twentieth century

in terms of their demand for gender equality. This chapter also
states how English education was looked upon as de-nationalizing
for women by some nationalists who said that they were not against
women's education but were against colonial education.

Chapter 4, Somdatta Bhattacharya, 'Rokeya's Dream: Feminist
Interventions and Utopias', attempts to locate the Bengali Muslim
educator and feminist writer Rokeya Sakhawat Hossain in the larger
context of women's education in colonial Bengal and India in the
1900s. We can witness the conflict between two languages, that is,
Bengali and Urdu, that Begum Rokeya encountered. She wanted
to start a Bengali-medium section in her school but could not as
the parents wanted their children to be educated in Urdu. English
for Begum Rokeya was a means and a medium to achieve her aim
to run her educational institution successfully. The chapter interestingly presents how her two works *Sultana's Dream* and *Padmarag*
depict women as agents of change. But Hossain's choice of utopias
to depict the change in terms of reversal of gender roles and education also raises questions about the fulfilment of such hopes.

Chapter 5, Meera Kosambi, 'Marathi Women Novelists and
Colonial Modernity: Kashibai Kanitkar and Indirabai Sahasrabuddhe',
argues how reform in nineteenth-century western India was a direct
result of English education and was a male project with women
presented as passive recipients of benefits of the reform movement.
But, there were women whose writings launched a parallel discourse.
English education was part of the colonial modernity which went on
to become a crucial tool for the reformist movement. While women's
reform movement was propagated by men as upliftment of women,
there are also women who took charge of the movement gradually.
While some carried the male, mainstream, Hindu, upper-caste
agendas forward, some others paved a different way for themselves,
questioning the patterns associated with gender, such as caste, class,
religion, language, region and political affiliations.

Chapter 6, Omprakash Kamble, 'Mukta Salve: The Early
Emergence of a Protest Voice in Mid-Nineteenth-Century Bombay
Presidency, 1855,' in a way continues the discussion on the discourse of women and English in Marathi by focusing on a very
important voice from the nineteenth century. Mukta Salve's essay

'*Mang Maharanchya Dukkha Wishayi Nibandh*' published in 1855 discusses the pain and suffering of Dalits. This article rightly brings in the voice of Savitribai Phule who vociferously argued for English education for Dalits. Similar to the situation discussed by Yogitha Shetty in Chapter 11 also discusses how anti-English was considered as anti-colonial and pro-English was considered anti-national. English education opened up a space and an opportunity especially for the people of the marginalized sections. So these sections embraced English education as a means of emancipation and subversion of hierarchy and discrimination. Dalits, tribals, minorities and women took to English as they found the traditional/mainstream oppressive and exclusive.

Alladi Uma's discussion of reform as visualized and carried out by the women writers in their writings is taken forward by Paromita Bose in Chapter 7, 'Writing Self: Writing for Others' by choosing to discuss personal histories, identity politics and their close connection with women's movements. This article attempts to analyse Muthulakshmi Reddi's autobiographies from the perspective of English education that is considered synonymous with modernity and the discourse of health. When education was still not easily accessible to women, Muthulakshmi Reddi one of the first women doctors in India, not only accessed the English education, that too professional education, but also went abroad for education. Her specialization in diseases concerning women and children and her passionate involvement in the Anti-Nautch movement that began in Madras in 1892 are closely connected with her English education that instructed and constructed the ideal womanhood in the model of the Victorian morality. Around this time, attempts were being made to build an interesting sisterhood between the Indian women and the British ladies, as this article explains, not only for Indian women to follow Victorian womanhood but also for the British women to avoid any contact with the the nautch girls. Interestingly, this entire debate, from the Indian as well as the British perspectives was centred on the man, the Indian man who has to be rescued from the vicious, greedy nautch girl and the housewife had to play a major role in this by moulding herself as the new woman. Muthulakshmi Reddi's multiple and intersecting locations and identities as an insider of the Nautch community and as a doctor and a legislator simultaneously present her as the affected, the healer and the policy maker. The medium that she chooses to write her life stories, that is English, not only reflects on her access to English education but also extends the debate of the local and the cultural to the larger political contexts and domains.

Chapter 8, Jinju S., 'Reconfiguring Boundaries: Education, Modernity and Conjugality in Lalithambika Antharjanam's *Agnisakshi* and Zeenuth Futehally's *Zohra*' shifts the focus of this anthology from the late nineteenth century and early twentieth century to the first half of the twentieth century, to be precise, to pre-independence India. Also, it has chosen two novels from different contexts and regions and languages as its major focus. Similarly, it combines the issues of English education and writing. Interestingly, one of these novels is written in English by a Muslim woman thus debating the English question in English.

Nikhila H. in Chapter 9 'Securing Pass Marks: Education for Women in the Early Modern Kannada Novel' focuses on the changing meanings of education, especially women's education and educated women, in the Kannada context during the twentieth century. She chooses four early novels in Kannada for analysis to map the changing debates and connotations of education and modernity. Chapter 10, Sowmya Dechamma C.C., 'Women and English Education in Coorg/Kodagu: A Discussion of Alternate Modernities during 1834–1882' discusses how Coorgs/Kodavas as a community volunteered to educate their children, especially daughters. It also debates how modernities are understood and adopted differently by different communities. Modernity in the form of English education was a negative development for the mainstream, dominant sections while the same modernity in the form of English education became desirable for the sections that are pushed to the margins. It would be interesting to juxtapose this situation where a community/a culture/ a nation like Kodagu looked upon English education as means of building a nation for themselves while the Indian nation was looking upon English education as anti-national. It proves once again how colonial modernity reached people differently.

Chapter 11, Yogitha Shetty, 'Nation, Ideal Womanhood and English Education: Revisiting the First Tulu Novel, *Sati Kamale*' is focused on the first Tulu novel *Sati Kamale* by S. U. Paniyadi. The novel criticises colonial modernity brought in the form of English education, presenting a binary of man (husband)/woman (wife) who fight the battle against colonial modernity outside in the world and at home respectively. It argues how there were divided voices and opinions in Tulunad with regard to English as a tool of forced colonial modernity. In passing Shetty refers to the issue that becomes the focus of Sowmya Dechamma C.C.'s piece on the dawn of Kodava modernity (Chapter 10) through English and the Kodava representation to the higher authorities for English education.

Chapter 12, Jasbir Jain, 'Between Language and Parole: The Forked Road to Development' touches upon language in the context of education, pedagogy and culture. While it endorses the multiple ways in which language is used, it also states that any language has a divided access to people or that there is a divide among people who access language. It provides a good introduction to language and education in a critical manner by raising various crucial questions but not really referring to gender alone. One of the vital questions is about employment and the language skills that people acquire as required by the job. Here, English is not a matter of excellence and sophistication, but a matter of survival and quick-learning skill. This article raises fundamental questions about the focus of this book such as why English, why women and why marginalized women in that, and attempts to connect the threads spread all over, It emphatically states that language plays a major role in identity politics and nation-building. It debates issues ranging from classroom to globalization with a focus on English and concludes that education is never a simple task. It presents a general review of English in India without confining to any one particular period.

In examining Indian women's writing in English, some writers like Toru Dutt form the background to a discussion on influence of English on Indian women writers. The beginnings of Indian women's writing in English got strengthened in the twentieth century. However, it is only in post-independence India that the number of writers is gradually increasing. English probably lost some of its connotations such as a colonial legacy and pro-colonial stand. Women writers have also started to own and acknowledge English as the best medium to express themselves. They are also very clear about the target audience. They were debating domesticity as well as the nation, the two diverse and as oppositional as possible locations for women, in English. They publish fiction, poetry, auto-biographies, drama and articles in English. It has helped the women to debate their identity as third-world women and also to reach the global audience. Debates around teaching English and writing in English became more prominent. But, one cannot, in the Indian context, forget that there are many women writers in India who are still fighting for access to English. On the other hand, there are also women writers who are demanding a kind of English that can belong to everyone and that can be as flexible as possible to accommodate the expressions and aspirations of every language. This is probably an attempt to subjugate a long subduing colonial legacy appropriated by the privileged sections of the Indian society. To conclude, I quote Meena Kandasamy's wish for an English that brings her 'Mulligawtanny Dreams' true (2008).

> I dream of an English
> full of the words of my language.

I take this opportunity to thank all those who supported me on my way to publish this book. This anthology of articles on women and English is a revised collection, with essays selected, of the proceedings of the National Seminar on Women and English organized by UGC-DSA programme of the Department of English, University of Hyderabad in January 2012. My thanks to the UGC-DSA programme, Department of English, University of Hyderabad, Coordinator of the Programme at the time of the seminar, Professor M. Sridhar, my colleague and friend Alladi Uma, Heads of the Department of English in 2012, and now my PhD, scholar Meenu, contributors and all those who stood by me with discussions. My special thanks to Stree-Samya for their sustained support.

## NOTES

1. See https://drambedkarbooks.com/2015/01/03/few-poems-by-savitribai-phule/k%20the%20shackles%20of%20caste, accessed 3 August 2017.
2. I have discussed Kandukuri Veeresalingam's admiration and emulation in detail in my paper titled 'Translations in Telugu' that I was invited to present in IIAS, Shimla, as part of a project seminar on translations in Indian languages held in August 2015, forthcoming.
3. Telugu adapted novel as *navala* which stands of course for the indigenization of the form and the word 'novel'. But, navala also means a woman in Telugu. So, intentionally or unintentionally, feminization of writing took place in the early nineteenth century, which, interestingly, also decided the politics of the woman question as reflected in the Telugu writing scenario.

## REFERENCES

Alladi Uma, K. Suneetha Rani and D. Murali Manohar, eds., 2014. *English in the Dalit Context*, Delhi: Orient Blackswan.

Bagchi, Jasodhara. 1993. 'Socialising the Girl Child in Colonial Bengal', *Economic and Political Weekly* (henceforth *EPW*) 28, 41 (Oct. 9): 2214–19.

Bannerji, Himani. 1991. 'Fashioning a Self: Educational Proposals for and by Women in Popular Magazines in Colonial Bengal', *EPW* 26, 43 (Oct. 26): WS50–WS62.

Burton, Antoinette. 1996. 'Contesting the Zenana: The Mission to Make "Lady Doctors for India" 1874–1885', *Journal of British Studies* 35, 3 (Jul.): 368–97.

Chanda, Shefali. 2007. 'Gendering English: Sexuality, Gender and the Language of Desire in Western India 1850–1940', *Gender and History* 19, 2 (August): 284–304.

Chatterjee, Partha 1989a. 'The Nationalist Resolution of the Women's Question', in *Recasting Women: Essays in Indian Colonial History*, edited by Kumkum Sangari and Sudesh Vaid, Delhi: Kali for Women: 233–53.

Chatterjee, Partha. 1989b. 'Colonialism, Nationalism, and Colonialized Women: The Contest in India', *American Ethnologist* 16, 4 (Nov.): 624–25.

Das, Kamala. [1965] 2004. *Summer in Calcutta*, Kottayam: DC Books: 62.

Jain, Jasbir. 1997. *Feminising Political Discourse: Women and the Novel in India 1857–1905*, Jaipur and Delhi, Rawat.

Kamat, A. R. 1976. 'Women's Education and Social Change in India', *Social Scientist* 5, 1 (Aug.): 3–27.

Kandasamy, Meena. 2008. http://meenakandasamy.wordpress.com/2008 /06/01/mulligatawny-dreams accessed on 2nd December 2016.

Kent, Eliza F. 2004. *Converting Women: Gender and Protestant Christianity in Colonial South India*, Delhi: Oxford University Press.

Kumar, Nita. 2005. 'Mothers and Non-Mothers: Gendering the Discourse of Education in South Asia', *Gender & History* 17, 1 (April): 154–82.

Pawar, Urmila. 2011. 'My Four Enemies', *in Patriarchy: Cross Cultural Readings*, edited by Jasbir Jain, Delhi: Rawat.

Pawde, Kumud. 1992. 'The Story of My Sanskrit', in *Poisoned Bread: Translations from Modern Marathi Dalit Literature*, edited by Arjun Dangle, Hyderabad: Orient Longman.

Phule, Savitribai. 2016. https://drambedkarbooks.com/2015/01/03/few-poems-by-savitribai-phule accessed on 2nd December.

Rajan, Rajeswari Sunder. 1993. *The Lie of the Land: English Literary Studies in India*, Delhi: Oxford University Press.

Sangari, Kumkum and Sudesh Vaid, eds. [1989]. 2010. *Recasting Women: Essays in Colonial History*, Delhi: Zubaan.

Sarkar, Sumit. 1997. *Writing Social History*, New York: Oxford University Press.

Sarkar, Sumit, and Tanika Sarkar. 2008. *Women and Social Reform in India: A Reader*, Bloomington, IN: Indiana: Indiana University Press, 2008.

Sen, Indrani. 2014. 'Writing English, Writing Reform: Two Indian Women's Novels of the 19th Century', *Indian Journal of Gender Studies* 21, 1 (Feb.): 1–26.

Sivaraman, Mythily. 2013. *Haunted by Fire. Essays on Caste, Class, Exploitation and Emancipation*. Delhi: Left Word.

———. 2007. *Fragments of a Life: A Family Archive*, Delhi: Zubaan.

Sreenivas, Mytheli. 2003. 'Emotion, Identity and the Female Subject: Tamil Women's Magazines in Colonial India, 1890–1940', *Journal of Women's History* 14, 4 (Winter): 59–82.

Sridhar, M., ed. 2008. *Reception of English Cultural Responses in Telugu Documents*, Delhi: Cambridge University Press.

Suleri Sara. 2004. *The Rhetoric of English India*, Delhi: Penguin.

Viswanathan, Gauri. 2007. 'Literacy and Conversion in the Discourse of Hindu Nationalism', *The Crisis of Secularism in India*, edited by Anuradha Dingwaney and Rajeswari Sunder Rajan, Durham, NC: Duke University Press: 333–55.

———. 1987. 'The Beginnings of English Literary Study in British India', *Oxford Literary Review* 9(1–2): 376–80.

Walsh, Judith E. 2004. *Domesticity in Colonial India: What Women Learned When Men Gave Them Advice*, New York: Rowman & Littlefield.

# 1

# Language, Reform and Nationalism

## INDIAN WOMEN'S WRITING IN THE NINETEENTH CENTURY

C. Vijayasree

INDIAN WOMEN writing in the nineteenth century wrote about their lives and the society they lived in, deploying a variety of forms— fictional and non-fictional. They addressed all the urgent concerns of their times—colonialism, nationalism, reform and the woman question. These texts are pertinent since they not only address the overlapping domains of caste, class, gender, colonialism and nationalism but also offer subtle but sharp critiques of the dominant discourses of the time—imperialist as well as nationalist— exposing their patriarchal imperatives. When I make a reference to nineteenth-century women writers I am not referring only to the better known names such as Toru Dutt and Sarojini Naidu. In this essay I am concerned with writers whose work has not been given enough critical attention or to date has remained largely ignored.

The work of Indian women writers of the nineteenth century is a sizeable archive of immense significance for those who wish to understand the complex socio-cultural reality of those times.

Even a random recall brings to our mind the works of writers like Pandita Ramabai, Krupabai Satthianadhan, Cornelia Sorabjee, Shevantibai Nikambe, Sunity Devi, Swarnakumari Ghosal (better known as Swarnakumari Devi) and Dosebai Cowasjee Jussewalla among others. Some of these voices were almost forgotten and histories of Indian Writing in English made no reference to them. Such omissions, as we know, result in distorted histories, and recovery of these voices is important for rectification of these anomalies. I am not only talking about histories of literature but histories of culture and ideas as well. How can debates on nineteenth-century reform, or nationalism, or politics of language and education ignore the views articulated in these texts? How can the history of English in India be either complete or coherent without a critical appreciation of the contribution of these writers to Indian English writing? But for the path-breaking work of Susie Tharu and K. Lalita many of these writers would not have been restored. The neglect of these voices was partially ameliorated by the publication of some of the nineteenth-century texts by Sahitya Akademi in its 'Rare Books' series and later by the classics reissue series of Oxford University Press. Now the texts are available for us to read; but what I am making a case for is the inscription of these texts into the various histories—be it the history of colonialism, national consciousness, reform, or English in India. When we do this not only does history get rewritten but it reveals dimensions of Indian life and experience under colonialism in the nineteenth century unravelled hitherto. When voices of women writers like Swarnakumari and Shevantibai are reinstated into the historical narrative of the period, we will be able to understand the nuances of many of those ongoing discourses that give the nineteenth century its particular dynamism.

The women I am referring to are not only writers but pioneers in many ways. Krupabai Satthianadhan authored the first autobiographical novel in English; Swarnakumari made a name for herself in the Bangla literary scene when she was barely fifteen, translated her own work into English, edited *Bharati*, a distinguished journal, for more than thirty years, and promoted circulation of women's views on a range of contemporary issues.; Dosebai Cowasjee as she herself claims in her autobiography, *The Story of My Life*, 'the first Indian girl to receive the benefits of an English education' (de Souza and Pereira 2002); Shevantibai Nikambe is a writer and reformist in the manner of Pandita Ramabai and dedicated her work and writing to the cause of women's education.

Now let me contextualize the work of these writers. The intersecting sites of English education, rhetoric of reform and nationalist discourse provided a larger context within which the literary production of these Indian women writers took shape in the nineteenth century. Apparently writing simple and straightforward narratives that were often life stories of their protagonists, these writers engaged critically with both Orientalist and nationalist discourses of reform and articulated their views on the politics of language and gender. These often constitute the subtexts of these women's texts and get glossed over in general critical readings. The purpose of this essay is to probe these subtexts and examine the interventions made by women writers into the dominant discourses of the nineteenth century. This investigation exposes the many contradictions involved in the making of the nation and point to the impossibility of conceiving nationalist thought as monolithic. Furthermore, it will also demonstrate how the issues of language, gender and nationalism get inextricably interlinked in the ideological configurations embedded in these texts. I shall also show how these texts engage with the creation of a new kind of subjectivity for a certain section of Indian women—middle-class, upper-caste women born in the families where men were engaged with social reform. In this new subjectivity, education (read 'English' education) becomes an important aspect.

# I

Swarnakumari Devi was born into the illustrious Tagore family of Calcutta's Jorasanko, the tenth child of Debendernath Tagore and Sarada Devi. Swarnakumari's father, Debendernath Tagore, was among the earliest to accept the Brahmo faith and he played an important role in the reform movements of the time—this is known history. Growing up in the Tagore household, Swarnakumari absorbed a variety of influences—her father's spiritual engagements and penchant for reform, her mother's religiosity, her family's nationalistic zeal as well as appreciation for the English language and western culture. She also absorbed the rich culture of the family enlivened by stimulating intellectual and literary debates. Besides music, painting and drama, writing and editing were commonplace activities in the Tagore family. Growing up among her accomplished brothers who secured celebrity status like Dwijendranath, Satyendranath, Jyotirindranath and Rabindranath must have been both an enabling and inhibiting experience for Swarnakumari. She went to a Zenana school and her education was typical of the kind of education given to girl students of affluent families, except that an educated Vaishnavi came into the andarmahal to teach the girls and women, and her father had made arrangements for a fine scholar, Ajodhyanath Pakrashi, to teach her at home. She writes about this in 'Sekaler Katha', *Bharati,* Chaitra 1916.[1] But in addition she received training from her father which she acknowledges (1899): 'It was my father, Debendernath Tagore, who had prepared me for my life's career by giving me an education unusual for Hindu girls of those days.' This unusual education included English and science. When she took over the family journal *Bharati*, she could run it successfully and turn it into a forum for lively discussions of contemporary concerns such as the spirit of rationalism, need for developing a scientific temper, women's education, and so on. She won wide acclaim early in life with the publication of her first novel at fifteen. This was followed by more than ten novels, scores of short stories in Bangla and 'she became in her own life time as popular as Bankimchandra' as Susie Tharu and Lalita claim (1993). But then like most other women writers of her own time she receded into oblivion until feminist scholarship retrieved her work and showcased its prominence. What is of concern for me here is her own translation of her novel *Kahake*, written in 1898, which appeared under the title *An Unfinished Song* (1913; 2008). The novel was originally written in Bengali and translated into English by the author fifteen years after its publication. What motivated her to undertake this project?

The translation was obviously meant for western readers as she herself states in her brief preface (ibid.: 3): 'I trust it will give the western reader some insight into the Hindu nature.' The novel is primarily a love story narrated from the perspective of the female protagonist, Moni. Moni represents Swarnakumari's version of the new woman—intelligent, educated, English-speaking, talented, accomplished, freedom-loving and independent. In forging such a woman at the centre of her narrative, Swarnakumari was offering a corrective to the colonialist images of an ignorant, illiterate and much abused Indian woman which formed an important component of the white man's justification for colonization. In 1913, Swarnakumari perhaps thought it would be appropriate to take her text into wider circulation by rendering it into English. Her western reader, she hoped, might be able to understand India and particularly Hindus better by reading her work. In her preface to the English translation of another novel: *Fatal Garland* (1915), she made this objective quite clear: 'We feel today that it is of the greatest importance that Europe—more specially England—should understand India. And this understanding can, I think, only be brought about by a study of our literature.' Here we find a total inversion of Macaulay's mission. Swarnakumari finds English—the language of the colonizer—a suitable vehicle for educating the English about the richness of Indian tradition. The role she envisaged for herself is not that of a native informant providing the western reader with anthropological detail but of an interpreter who could give the foreign reader, especially the colonial ruler, insights into Indian culture he proposed to 'civilize' out of ignorance of the intrinsic richness of this culture.

'This is the story of the Reformed Party of Bengal, the members of which have to some extent adopted western customs'—this is how Swarnakumari describes the milieu of her novel. The lifestyle of men and women in this novel clearly reflects the anglicizing impact of English education. They have tennis parties, quote spontaneously from English poets—Byron, Gray and Shelley among others—indulge in lengthy debates on literature, admire the freedom offered by England, follow the rules of etiquette popularized by English schooling. Even as Swarnakumari narrates the story of this section of the Bengali elite, she refers to Moni's suitor Ramanath.

His letter breathes love and humility and melts Moni's heart; but Moni articulating her maker's views remarks: 'Needless to say the letter was written in English. That the love letters of a Bengali youth, whose whole life is one great imitation, should be written in his native tongue—this preposterous idea would not occur to anyone.' Moni tries to write a reply in English. Moni had all the training necessary for such a task. She sums up her credentials thus:

> I was reputed to be well grounded in that language. I had received my education at one of the best English schools in Calcutta. My correspondence was conducted almost entirely in English. The letters to my aunt and father were the only ones written in Bengali. I seldom even spoke in my mother tongue with my friends and as to the English poems and novels that I had read, their number was legion. To tell the truth I was a little vain of the command I had acquired over the English language, yet however hard I might try I could not make this letter a success.

This brings home to Moni the realization that an alien tongue will always remains alien. She genuinely feels, 'If we would bestow half the care on our own language that we do on an alien tongue we might carry its literary merit to the highest perfection.' This incident and this remark acquire significance in the context of the nationalist agenda for the restoration of a respectable place to Indian languages. Swarnakumari fought for vernacular education through the columns of her journal as well.

The subtexts of this textual incident are important to note: even as the writer accepts English as the language of power and communication with the colonial master, she underscores the need for limiting its deployment to the public arena and highlights the fact that English can never/should never be a substitute for one's mother tongue. She is writing from within the social segment of the community—the educated elite of Bengal—and yet critiques the slavish imitation of this anglophile-group. She advocates an eclectic approach to the West. Indians should choose what is 'good' in the West. Swarnakumari's Moni will also remain an important configuration in the complex process of construction of female subjectivity occurring in nineteenth-century Indian women's writing.

## II

On 24 August 1884, a Marathi-language article titled 'Strishikshan' published in a weekly, *Poona Vaibhav,* warned Marathi people of the dangers of imparting English education to their daughters. The article's primary purpose was to critique the inauguration of the Poona Indian Girls High School. The school provoked strong reactions even from those reformers who were in favour of female education on account of its 'radical' agenda of bringing the language of the colonial modern to Indian women. This was the first native-managed enterprise in British India to teach Indian girls in the English language and through the stage of matriculation. The major argument of the article was to emphasize that the English education would turn them into women of loose morals in the manner of Englishwomen who were worse than Indian prostitutes in their sexual behaviour. This argument reveals multiple alliances between race, caste, language and sexuality in nineteenth-century India.

I have quoted this incident in order to read Shevantibai Nikambe's 1895 novel: *Ratanbai: A Sketch of a Bombay High Caste Hindu Young Wife* against this background. Shevantibai was an Indian Christian born in Poona in 1865. She matriculated from St. Peter's Girls High School, Bombay. She played a vital role in the promotion of women's education as the first headmistress of the students' literary and scientific societies, a staff member at Ramabai's Sarada Sadan High School, as the proprietor and headmistress of an English school for Indian girls and Inspector of Girls' Primary schools in Bombay. Widely travelled, she studied Christian work and methods in Europe and America. She also revisited Europe to study education and social work. She successfully ran The Married Women's School for more than two decades.

Her novel *Ratanbai* (2004) reflects her lifelong passion of promoting women's education. The novel was published in London by Marshall Brothers and the text was primarily intended to promote women's education. Apparently the book was meant to serve two purposes: *(i)* to offer an account of Hindu life to its British readers and also to show native appreciation of English education; the greatest boon provided by British imperialism; *(ii)* to convince her

Indian readers—the educated elite of the Hindu society—of the need to educate their daughters. The novel is dedicated to 'Her Gracious Majesty the Queen, our beloved Empress for so graciously granting me the permission to dedicate this small work to Her Majesty, whose happy rule in my dear native land is bringing [*sic*] and enlightening the lives and homes of many Hindu women'. Although not explicitly stated, the enlightening factor in the lives and homes of Hindu women is clearly education.

Though there are several interesting strands in this text, I am going to focus on the enlightening impact of English education. The story narrates the trials and tribulations faced by a high-caste Hindu child wife in pursuing her dream of education. So it is primarily a novel of reform and like in other reform novels, certain men who had the good fortune of English education act as facilitators in promoting Ratanbai's pursuit and certain women who have no exposure to education act as antagonists and obstructers. Superseding all obstacles, Ratanbai succeeds in her pursuit and becomes a companionate wife to her England-returned husband. This slender text which appears to be nothing more than a propaganda tale contains what Gilbert and Gubar call 'submerged meanings, meanings hidden within or behind the more accessible or public content' (1979; 1965; 1987; 1989). In the discussion that follows I shall highlight these substructures, particularly the ones that refer to education, English language and reform.

Ratanbai is a child wife who is still staying with her parents, awaiting attainment of maturity and her eventual migration to her in-laws. Her father, a liberal male of the Reform party, is keen on sending her to school and manages to do so with the permission of her in-laws. The novel opens with Ratan in standard III where she is revealed to be an avid learner passionate about reading and writing. Her education is constantly hampered by her mother who insists on taking Ratan to all celebrations, rituals and women's get-togethers in the homes of relatives and friends. All these functions are described in vivid detail for the benefit of non-Indian readers. An older relative at her father-in-law's place, having failed in every way to stop Ratan's education, flings the final threat at her: 'Wait, let Pratap Rao come this evening. I will tell him I saw you looking at the gardener with an evil eye, and after your mother-in-law comes to know of it we shall see how you go to school' (54). The old woman here is using the popular misgiving about English education to manipulate the situation and get Ratan out of school. But the narrative demonstrates how in reality English education refines Ratan's personality and makes her a fit wife to her educated husband.

Now to the details of the 'English' education Ratan receives: There are two brief references to what Ratan read at school. She reads 'Casabianca' by Felicia Hemans and the poem is all about a little boy's faith in and unquestioning obedience to his father. On another occasion Ratan recites 'Meddlesome Matty' by Ann Taylor which warns little girls against being inquisitive and meddlesome. These two references may appear casual but they clearly indicate that English literature has a lot to offer for refining the behaviour of young people. Again the school chooses the material wisely so that the English instruction offered will also inculcate moral values among the learners. Once again Nikambe is dispelling the popular fears about English education. The novel thus makes a solid case for not only education for girls but English education. When Ratan is finally taken out from school, she regretfully thinks 'I wish I had known how to converse in English. Sasubai should have kept me at school till then (43).' To be able to speak English or write in English is considered an accomplishment for young ladies and Ratan's regretful remark conjures up this image which acts as the inspiration to her. Here once again we see an instance of shaping a particular kind of subjectivity for women in the nineteenth century.

I would also like to make references to subtle acts of subversion performed in the text: While her account like the typical reformist narratives projects the role of male reformers in redeeming womankind, she suggests that this refinement in men is totally on account of western education and its attendant value system they were exposed to. Talking about Ratan's husband, Nikambe says: 'Pratap Rao attended Wilson College, and here the sound education he received and the exemplary lives he came in contact with day after day, made great impression on his young heart and prepared him for the life before him.'

The popular notions about English education which were deeply gendered were hinted in the comments of Kakubai, an elderly relative of Ratanbai: 'What! Going up for men's examinations! What good are we to get by educating girls?' (23).' As if Nikambe were answering this question, she concludes the narrative thus: 'Pratap Rao Khote claims young Ratanbai as his partner in life. They begin life together, recognizing the responsibilities which lie before them, and which concern not only themselves but their people and their country (59).' The slipping in of this reference to the 'country' is not without significance.

Another such quiet dropping of a hint occurs with regard to religion. Nikambe describes the Hindu rituals, customs and celebrations in minute detail, never being dismissive or critical of these things. She is careful to avoid any reference to Christianity throughout the narrative. But in the very end when Ratan and her husband get together to begin their life together in a companionate relationship, they decide to make the 'beautifully bound gilt-edged Book' their guide in life. It is not hard to guess which Book she is referring to (de Souza and Pereira 2008).

Thus narrating the story of a Hindu child wife she subtly drops in the suggestion that the ultimate guidance can only come from the Book. Having dedicated the book to the Queen and paid tribute to her golden rule, Nikambe envisages educated couples working together for their people and their country, which reveals her vision of her nation's future; she views English education as an important accomplishment for the new woman who would take her place as the companion of man and 'work for her people and her country'.

NOTE

[1]  Mid-March to mid-April, the last month of the Bengali calendar; translation by Supriya Chaudhuri, in *Talking of Power: Early Writings of Bengali Women,* edited by Malini Bhattacarya and Abhijit Sen (Kolkata: Stree: 2003).

REFERENCES

De Souza, Eunice, and Lindsay Pereira, eds, 2002. *Women's Voices: Selections from Nineteenth and Early Twentieth Century Indian Writing in English,* Delhi: Oxford University Press.

Devi, Swarnakumari. 1919. *The Fatal Garland (Phulermala),* New York: Macmillan.

——. [1899] 1948, 'Amar Grihe Antahpur-Siksha o Tahar Samaskar' (Education of Women in Our Family and Its Reforms); originally published in *Pradeep* (Autumn); reprinted in *Sahitya-Sadhak-Charitmala* (Biographies of Literary Celebrities), edited by Brojendranath Bandyopandhyay, vol. 2, Bangiya Sahitya Parishad. Calcutta.

——. 2008. *An Unfinished Song,* translated by Swarnakumari Devi and edited by C. Vijayasree, Delhi: Oxford University Press.

Gilbert, Sandra, and Susan Gubar. [1987; 1989] 1996. *No Man's Land: The Place of the Woman Writer in the Twentieth Century,* 3 vols., New Haven: Yale University Press.

——. eds, 1985. *The Norton Anthology of Literature by Women: The Traditions in English,* New York: Norton.

——.1979. *The Madwoman in the Attic: The Woman Writer and the Nineteenth Century Literary Imagination,* New Haven: Yale.

Nikambe, Shevantibai. 2004. *Ratanbai: A Sketch of a Bombay High Caste Hindu Young Wife,* edited by Chandani Lokuge, Delhi: Oxford University Press.

Tharu, Susie J, and K. Lalita, eds, 1993. *Women Writing in India: The Twentieth Century,* Delhi: Oxford University Press.

# 2

# Women and 'Reform'

Alladi Uma

THE DISCUSSIONS on the interface between women and English in India are centred on English as a language, English as a 'trope' denoting culture, religion, social values, education and more.[1] We wonder at the number of texts by women that came out in the 1930s. We may debate if there were men who had supported and argued for reform concerning women. My endeavour here is to negotiate these issues with reference to texts in Telugu with special focus on two significant texts written in the 1930s in English and in Tamil. I use a variety of genres in an attempt to understand the larger literary and socio-cultural scenario.

As early as 1902, Bhandaru Acchamamba wrote what can be considered one of the earliest short stories in Telugu, 'Strividya' (Women's Education) in the form of a dialogue where the husband urges his wife to learn the alphabet so she can write to him, be supportive of him, look after the accounts, and be of help to the children, while the wife is apprehensive that education may be the cause of decrease in the lifespan of the husband, among many other evils associated with the education of women. It is the man who says that scriptures are not against women's education so long as she does not shun domestic chores. It is an ingenious way in which the woman writer seeks reform but voices it through the man. By making the woman argue against education, she does not merely reiterate the orthodoxy of the woman but uses her as a 'devil's advocate' who can counter-argue in order to elicit the significance of education from the mouth of a man, even though he may have fixed notions of the duty of a woman.

Let us move on to a writer like Kanuparti Varalakshmamma. The short story, 'Ottu' (Promise) (1933) seems a simple enough story. The husband, Professor Jagannadham, M.A., L.T. (Masters in Arts and Licentiate to Teach), is a member of the Society for the Promotion of Dramatic Arts in Bandar. He along with the other members wants women to perform the roles of women in plays, something unheard of till then. Jagannadham moves the resolution which is tied and it gets passed only because the President casts his vote in favour of the resolution. They feel it would be best initially for their wives to act the roles. None of the members are able to convince their wives, but Jagannadham makes his wife, Janaki, agree through a trick he plays on her—by making her promise to do what he wants and if she reneges, it will be his death. Janaki can do nothing but concede. She agrees to perform the plays but on three conditions—she wouldn't go for rehearsals, wouldn't act in their town and wouldn't go to other towns without her husband and children. She is to act in three plays, *Savitri*, *Paduka Pattabhisekham* and *Sarangadhara*. Playing *Savitri* may sound simple enough but how could a *pativrata* like her allow a man to lie on her lap? But not to do it would mean the death of the husband and doesn't the play talk of a character who fights with the God of Death to save her husband?

How could she take on the role of Kaika who 'ranks first among the women who have been blamed by society' (68)? The three promises Kaika asks of her husband need to be viewed alongside the conditions Janaki places on her husband. Is the writer also asking the readers to view the 'courage/power' of Kaika who saved Dasaratha from death? Wasn't Janaki too saving her husband from humiliation of a rash promise on behalf of someone else? Janaki wonders how she could take on the role of a 'seductress', Chitrangi, who desires

Sarangadhara and wants to lure him. Janaki can't be Chitrangi. She cannot 'perform'. The mob jeers. The husband who is unable to take care of the children comes to the venue, fumes at her 'wanton' behaviour and both leave the venue.

This short summary raises many questions: How does a woman writer deal with the issue of modernity? Why does she have a character like Jagannadham who has modern education—M.A., L.T.? What are the author's views on the role of a society such as the Society for the Promotion of Dramatic Arts? Can one usher in 'reform' in the theatre by ensuring that women 'perform'? If the notion of 'modernity' involves the issue of freedom, what are her views about 'patriarchal modernity'? Who decides on the significance of the 'public' over the 'private'? In writing such a 'simple' story, is the writer also bringing up questions regarding the genre of the short story itself, which some have argued is a 'new' boon of the West? This brings to mind a discussion between a husband and wife in 'Katha Etlaa Undaale.' (The Charm of a Cherished Story) (Varalakshamma 2005) where the wife argues that the short story is not a foreign but an indigenous form and that stories must have 'creativity, which is the form, description, which is its colour, *rasa,* the smell, and the message that's the honey' and stresses the significance of the moral value of a story and bemoans the lack of it in the modern stories by men.

What happens when a Dalit woman writer raises issues of nationalism, of women's involvement in the struggle and her taking on a westernized Indian 'gentleman'? The result is 'One Kiss' by Thadi Nagamma in 1939 (Suneetha Rani 2012). The story announces in a simple but vigorous manner the Swadeshi movement and the Non-Cooperation movement. There is an awareness of world history. There is an awareness of the stories from the *Puranas* that speak of the significant achievements of great women like Anasuya, Savitri, Sita and Draupadi; of historical figures like the Rani of Jhansi, and achievers of the world like the pioneering woman pilot Amy Johnson. The young woman protagonist urging people to banish foreign goods in Andhra is contrasted with 'a young lad…in a Ford motorcar…[buying] foreign clothes' (27). The lad 'was wearing a British suit, a French hat, a Belgium tie, Vienna spectacles and German hair oil. He was holding a Swedish hand stick, Virginia cigarette and was chewing Kakinada spicy pan. It looked as if he was under an illusion that the entire modern civilization was dancing on his face alone as he exhibited western tricks and latest tantrums' (ibid.). This is almost a caricature of a 'WOG' (Westernized Oriental Gentleman) who assumes that everything 'foreign' is wonderful (ibid.: 28). To the request by the young woman to give up foreign clothes, he asks for a kiss in return. He is stunned at her response: 'Can't I give a kiss to rescue a brother like you who has become a prey to the poison of foreign goods?'(ibid.). Here is a woman writer who critiques the so-called modernity of the West while at the same time voicing the freedom and determination of the woman who moves beyond the private to the public sphere. We will find this again in Madhuravani in *Kanyasulkam* (Rao 2002).

Even before the now (in)famous Macaulay's 'Minute', Telugus like Vennelacunty Soob Row, in the early part of the nineteenth century, have discussed the impact and influence of English education on Indians. As has been mentioned earlier, to several Telugu intellectuals like Kandukuri Veeresalingam, Gidugu Ramamurthy, and Jayanti Ramayya Pantulu, English did not mean just the English language but also the social and cultural values associated with it. Even while some opposed British rule, they accepted certain scientific and rationalist discourses that were taking place in Britain. One such person was Gurajada Appa Rao who started his literary career by writing in English and then went on to write *Kanyasulkam* in Telugu, in 1897, a play that is acclaimed as a milestone in Telugu literary history.

The play works at many levels. Gurajada avowedly says in his 'Preface' written in English that he wrote the play to comment on the evil practice of child marriage; that too with an older man for a bride price. The play was to be performed, not just to be read and critiqued. It was to serve a social purpose. It is significant to note that he goes beyond just the issue of bride price to discuss various other issues related to women like the plight of widows, their sexuality and widow remarriage (a consequence of child marriage with an older man) and the 'nautch' question, and the role of English education in Indian society. Of course each of these is not an independent entity, but all are interrelated issues.

Let us look at Girisam, an English-educated youth, at the beginning of the play. Advocating widow remarriage, he says, 'When the essence of "civilization" is "widow remarriage", "civilization" comes to a "halt" in the absence of "infant marriages". There won't be any progress, and therefore, infant marriages must be encouraged' (Rao 34). The explanation is very logical and ludicrous at the same time. Obviously, Gurajada is critiquing characters like Girisam who pretend to be progressive through their knowledge of English and their 'rationality' that English education is supposed to provide.

In contrast to him is Saujanya Rao Pantulu, a lawyer, clearly a product of English education and one who needs to be logical to be able to argue well and be well respected in his vocation as a lawyer. His argument against child marriage is simple yet solid: 'My argument [is] that old men shouldn't marry young girls and that *kanyasulkam* is an offence… I earnestly advise you to send your daughter to a widow's home' (202). He is not only against child marriage but against prostitution, which to him is immoral. In the words of Karataka Sastrulu, a character in the play, 'Some of our English-educated men entertain these [anti-nautch] funny notions. But there are many types among them…. Saujanya Rao is "anti-nautch" in thought, word and deed' (208).

What according to a 'reasonable' person are the options available to women like Madhuravani who decide to leave the profession? What about marriage, even to a person like Girisam? Here's Saujanya Rao's response: 'What a terrible thing you've said! He is going to marry a pious widow in a day or two; do you think he'll marry a prostitute?' (252). How does one reconcile the supposed rationality of an individual who advocates the abolition of the practice of prostitution with the irrational prejudice against prostitutes? It may be pertinent to quote Volga (2010) here

> If great people deride prostitutes and reject them, how will those prostitutes who wish to marry find bridegrooms? Should they then reconcile themselves and marry anyone, even a thoroughly useless one?
>
> There is no scope for this in the widow remarriages that Veeresalingam (a late nineteenth century social reformer who

opened homes for widows and advocated widow remarriage) conducted. Later, people like Gurajada and Chalam Gudipati Venkata Chalam [a writer who is acknowledged by many Telugu women writers as a pioneer of women's freedom, particularly the right to one's own body] debated on this. It is but natural that such great people become the target of criticism. We cannot progress without criticism. Even if one has a lot of regard for Veeresalingam, if one cannot accept the criticism by Gurajada, widows and prostitutes cannot find another way out except to find themselves in another bog (20).

But Saujanya Rao is Gurajada's creation. One would have assumed that a man of Saujanya Rao's standing would have shown no caste prejudice. But consider the following two statements by Saujanya Rao to Madhuravani:
'After all, Lubdhavadhanlu is an old Brahmin, and if you come to his rescue, you'll indeed be doing a virtuous deed' (Rao: 229) and 'You are a good woman. You must be the offspring of a virtuous man's moral lapse' (ibid.: 261).

Should one think that he is good enough to realize her goodness, ask her to opt out of her profession and turn to God—Krishna—via the book he gives her, the Bhagavad Gita? While Volga reads the message of the Gita thus, 'The very direct message—even if *adharma* is committed by one's own people it is one's duty to combat it' (25), I am not sure how to deconstruct the picture of Krishna that goes with it. How does one view Krishna bereft of his *rasalilas* (love play of Krishna with many women)? What does it tell us of Saujanya Rao?—that even when he advocates the message of the Gita to her, he cannot forget her background? Maybe I am reading too much into it. But then the whole play does talk about Madhuravani's sensuality.

Let us move a little further and try to understand Madhuravani in all her complexity. Lubdhavadhanlu may be a traditionalist (evident from his qualified praise of Madhuravani) but he gives her credit for her knowledge and wisdom: 'This Madhuravani, though a prostitute, knows many things. If our housewives had half her sense, we would be better off (105).' There may be occasions where Madhuravani seems to fit into the 'stereotyped' notion of a prostitute. But if we were to read her statements closely, we realise her astuteness; she knows her situation in life; she knows she has to make the best of it: 'It's true, there is nothing like education—except one. What's that? Wealth. Education that doesn't bring money is the cause of poverty' (47), and

> Have you heard the saying, 'A sweet vendor's desire for sweets and a dancing girl's love should always remain suppressed'? Our life depends on youth, which is transient; and so our love is fixed on one thing [gold] alone (211).

But she will not tolerate injustice, especially against a woman: 'You [Ramappantulu] raise your hand on a woman? What chivalry! Instead of lying, stand by what you promised. Caste, good looks—why, what does she lack? You've ruined her life anyway, now marry her and make amends. I'll open the door only after you marry her' (186).

She is after all a product of society and of her times, and therefore would have imbibed values of caste superiority, feminine attributes, and so on. This may be the reason why she thinks that Meenakshi's positive attributes are her Brahmin caste and her 'good looks'. But she moves beyond it, even if she needed a catalyst like Saujanya Rao to catapult her into action: 'I am quite aware of the heinous nature of my profession. Now that I am blessed with the kindness of a virtuous man like you, why will I continue in that wretched profession?' (261). Madhuravani's assertion of leading a 'virtuous' life when read along with her acts of courage and generosity, makes us agree with Volga that 'she [Madhuravani] is not a woman without morals and that she is not one who lives coveting money alone' (Volga: 11). Madhuravani also seems to score over Saujanya Rao when she rejects his kiss, a gesture that Volga reads 'as a victory over him' and a reflection of 'self-respect' (22). Volga further says that Madhuravani 'does not desire to be a pativrata. She does not desire to be motherhood incarnate…. She feels that only by hard work can one have security in life' (24). While Madhuravani's rejection of the kiss shows her authority over herself and rejection of stereotypes, the nationalist's willingness to give a kiss in Thadi Nagamma's 'One Kiss' also shows her authority over herself by making the kiss asexual (affectionate kiss to a brother). In both cases the women assert the right over their bodies.

Why does Gurajada end the play with Girisam, an unrepentant Girisam, saying, 'The story has somersaulted' (Rao: 263)? Maybe the somersault is necessary, the world that the characters lived in had to be turned upside down. Maybe, it is Gurajada's dig at the pseudo-English educated who can never come to terms with reality and the changing world.

Gurajada's play was originally written in 1897 and later revised in 1909. Muvalur Ramamirthammal was born in 1883 and Muthulakshmi Reddi in 1886. Ramamirthammal (1938/2003) was born in a non-devadasi family but was forced into prostitution. Muthulakshmi Reddi (1964) was born of a devadasi mother and a Brahmin father. While Ramamirthammal talks openly about the fact that she was forced into prostitution and later becomes a staunch advocate for the abolition of the system, Muthulakshmi Reddi never openly admits her mother's lineage in her autobiography. She goes on to become a well-known doctor caring for the health of women, a legislator and an activist fighting for the abolition of the devadasi system. Ramamirthammal wrote *Dasigal Mosavalai (Web of Deceit)* in Tamil in 1938. Muthulakshmi Reddi wrote *My Experience as a Legislator* in 1930 and *Autobiography* in 1964, both in English (see Chapter 7). I was interested in viewing how the devadasi question that is such a preoccupation in these two writers would compare with the presentation of Gurajada, a Brahmin, male writer interested in social reform. I am aware that all three used different genres—Gurajada, a play, Ramamirthammal, a novel of 'lived lives', and Muthulakshmi Reddi, an autobiography. Nevertheless, I venture into the comparison because the aim of all three writers was social reform.

Ramamirthammal's *Web of Deceit* is a text that seems to argue for the importance of English education. She pits two zamindars, one of Dharmapuri who is steeped in traditional values and Sanskrit education and the other of Sornapuri who stands for modernity, who has brought in many reforms and has educated his daughter, Gnanasundari, in Tamil and English. Like Girisam in *Kanyasulkam*, we have Somasekaran, the son of the zamindar of Dharmapuri, who does not use the benefits of modern education but instead gets involved with prostitutes. Unlike in the play, Ramamirthammal makes Gnanasundari (one endowed with the beauty of knowledge) take the lead in converting her husband and making her father who, though progressive, had never considered the significance of the abolition of the devadasi system, move in the direction of the abolition of the system. If Gnanasundari plays a major role in this move towards abolition, it is the reformed devadasi, Gunabusani (one who is adorned with virtue) who converts the minor, is vocal and advocates the demand for abolition in the Tiruchi Social Reform Conference. She is aware that a law against prostitution alone cannot change the situation and places the problem in its socio-cultural and religious context:

> Bringing the law against prostitution into effect and getting rid of prostitutes has only resulted in the incomes of devadasis shooting up. Is it not because of this religion, God and Brahminism, that they are spared by the law? That is why these must be wiped out first. … Declare that all devadasi women should be married (2003: 202–203).

She too sees marriage as a way out for the devadasis. One can see here an inability to explore any other possibility than marriage for women. Or are we looking at this from a position based on today and being unfair to Ramamirthammal?

Among the important resolutions taken at that conference are:

> Dedicating girls in the name of God should stop and this meaningless and shameful devadasi system should be abolished completely.
> Hereafter all devadasis should be married.
> All men and women in the devadasi caste should be provided access to primary and higher education (207).

It is interesting to note here the primacy given to education. It is perhaps this lack of education that makes devadasis like Kantha indulge in subterfuge and deceit to make a living. The likes of Kantha in this novel are portrayed as only sensual, thereby denying them the kind of wit that Madhuravani possesses. But in Gunabusani, a reformed devadasi, and in Vivekavati (the wise one) we see the merging of intellect and sensuality. Kalpana Kannabiran and Vasanth Kannabiran in their introduction to the book, 'Framing the *Web of Deceit*' write:

This reduction of the attraction to dasis as purely sexual and divorced from any nuance of admiration for their artistic ability, wit, charm, capacity for informed, intelligent conversation is accompanied by a critique of existing forms of conjugality as traditional and repelling to the young male, driving him to temptation and evil (2003: 16).

At the end of the novel, Kantha is able to analyse her own situation, in effect the situation of all the devadasis in this manner: 'Mothers fear that their self-interest will suffer if we develop love for any man…. And so through frightening and coaxing they mould our minds (212).' Her mother, Boga Chintamani, too seems to realize her own negative role. This view of Kantha seems to differ from that of Madhuravani who seems to see a positive role played by her mother and is appreciative of the advice given to her by her mother, that of being good to people who are good and bad to those who are bad.

Even while one may be wary of the reformist zeal in the novel and even while one may question certain stereotypical representations in the novel, one cannot miss out on the agency given to women in them. While the rich elitist woman, Gnanasundari, may seem to take the lead in organizing the conference, one cannot miss Gunabusani's voice, the voice of one who has experienced and chosen the way out. Let us then move to another activist, Muthulakshmi Reddi. She was an exceptional woman who became a doctor and a legislator. She writes *My Experiences as a Legislator* in 1930, a year after the Act against Dedication of Devadasis was passed in 1929. She very forcefully argued as a legislator for laws that would alleviate the position of the disadvantaged including women. She was aware of the changes that were happening in India and abroad. She was convinced of the role of the government and the legislature in ushering in change. Talking of child abuse, she says:

It is a most painful fact that we possess yet no laws for the protection of minor girls in this twentieth century against the danger of immorality when the whole civilized world is so much advanced in child reform and child legislation. Have we not realised then that only a fully responsible and national government can solve many of these social problems which still await solution at our hands (Reddi 1930: 120).

It is in this spirit that she appreciates the 'native state Mysore', which 'had done away with the system [devadasi] as early as 1909' (ibid.: 109), and that the 'Maharani of Travancore abolished the system with one stroke of the pen' (ibid.: 119). She strove to introduce 'a bill (to abolish the devadasi service in the temples and to prevent the dedication of girls) as an amendment to that act [Hindu Religious Endowment Act] (ibid.: 113).' Appendix B of the book contains the 'Bill to Amend the Madras Hindu Religious Endowments Act, 1926,' Appendix C contains 'Madras Act No. V of 1929,' and Appendix D contains 'A Bill to Prevent the Dedication of Women to Hindu Temples in the Presidency of Madras'. Such was her concern for reform that not only did she discuss the issues in detail in the book, but also provided the Bills in detail at the end to make people conscious of what she considered the ills in society that needed to be addressed. In Appendix B she states:

> In section 44 the following proviso shall be issued:–
>
> Provided that where a grant of land has been made to dancing girls or devadasis for the performance of any service wherever in any temple, such service inam land shall be enfranchised to the present holder thereof and she shall not be required to perform any service in the temple (ibid.: 237).

Reddi was obviously aware of the economic independence of the devadasis and felt that the above would ensure the continuation of the independent status of those already in service as devadasis. She advocated marriage for such women and becoming one with the mainstream. While one may not doubt the conviction of Muthulakshmi Reddi to abolish the system as she saw it as a violation of the body and a wrecker of health of women, one would like to know how she would have envisaged the women retaining their economic independence.

Even in her *Autobiography* written in 1964, the devadasi question seems to be uppermost in her mind. Here too she is quite vocal about the need for a legislation to abolish the devadasi system:

This practice of dedicating young girls or young women to temples for immoral purposes is a slur on Indian womanhood... that in the cause of humanity and justice, we can no longer delay this piece of legislation, a reform by which we can rescue thousands of young innocent children from a life of immorality and vice, from life-long invalidism, suffering, disease and death resulting from infection with venereal disease (ibid.:138).

When Muthulakshmi Reddi says this practice is a 'slur on Indian womanhood', she seems to view a very homogeneous 'Indian womanhood' with a universal and unquestioned notion of 'virtue', with no possibility for plurality. While we may question such an essentialist tendency on the part of Muthulakshmi Reddi we cannot miss her genuine concern for the health and well-being of all those involved in this system.

What is clear from the passage quoted above is her concern for not only justice but also for the physical and moral health of the young girls and young women. As a doctor she is most definitely concerned with the deterioration of the health of the young girls. Anandhi (2008) expresses quite succinctly:

> First of all she negates the body as embedded in the aesthetics of the self or in the structure of feelings. Instead she medicalises it (as in her extensive description of the medical aspects of her deliveries) or de-eroticizes it by restoring it to certain pure motherhood devoid of sexual desire (Reddi 1964:21–35). But in the context of lower class and uneducated women such as the Devadasis, she presents them as embodied and disenfranchises them from the public domain.

> In short, she legitimises the 'moral authority' of the few educated women like her, who are supposed to be capable of rational thinking, to speak on behalf of the entire womenfolk (ibid.: 12).

It is no doubt true that she, as a member of the educated elite, takes on the role of not just a 'health' keeper but a 'moral' keeper. At one level I am in consonance with Anandhi's reservations:

> Even as the middle-class feminists like Muthulakshmi Reddy challenged the modernity's gendered politics of exclusion,

inescapably they too recuperated a different logic of exclusion in their articulation of a 'new public.' Thus the feminist modern 'remained within the contrary, fractured, modernity' and its politics of exclusion and power (ibid.: 13).

But at another level, I feel we must understand the compulsions under which Reddi was acting. Her own location must have had an effect in the way she reacted to the devadasi issue. She sees the system entrenched in our society primarily because of religion and caste as has been pointed out by Gunabusani in the novel, *Web of Deceit* (Ramamirthammal 2003). Therefore, she sees the difficulty in abolishing such a system in India. Pointing to England, Reddi says:

> The agitation for the enactment of this good measure had been started even as early as 1868. (In this connection it is significant to note that about the same time the campaign against State regulation of vice was started by that eminent Englishwoman Josephine Butler in England and was carried to a successful termination in 1886.) What was easy there has been rendered difficult here because of its association with religion and the existence of caste in this country (Reddi 1964: 142).

Nevertheless, the effort has to go on and this 'evil' practice has to be abolished, for she seems to believe in a glorious and golden Indian past as is evident from the following quote:

> What will be the result of such a reform?
>
> The result will be that the moral tone of the society will be strengthened.
>
> Then are we whose ancestors had practised the highest ideals of sexual purity which human nature is capable of and had attained the utmost height of spirituality to be left behind and pointed out as a morally backward race? (ibid.: 148).

Reddi ends the section on the devadasi question thus:

> I am glad that that this time old Devadasi System in the Hindu Temples as well as Dedication of Girls to Hindu Idols have

been totally abolished by two measures—Act No. 5 of 1929 and Prevention of Dedication Act of 1949 (ibid.:149).

Madhuravani in *Kanyasulkam* says, as we have quoted before: 'I am quite aware of the heinous nature of my profession. Now that I am blessed with the kindness of a virtuous man like you, why will I continue in that wretched profession?' (261). Ramamirthammal in *Web of Deceit* ends with the Tiruchi Conference and the resolution to abolish the devadasi system and emphasizes education, and an educated Muthulakshmi Reddi ends expressing her happiness at the abolishing of the devadasi system. But would all devadasis view the system as evil enough to be abolished? That remains a question.

## NOTE

[1] I am aware of the differences in the historical contexts in which the texts ranging from one written in 1897 (revised in 1909) to the 1930s when the woman question and the question of education were compounded by the question of the nation. The texts I have selected for a detailed analysis have a strong bearing on one or more of these aspects. In addition to these, some of these texts specifically deal with the question of freedom in relation to the social and economic status of the devadasis. The responses of these women to these questions vary precisely because of the caste, class and gender of the writers, and the time period in which they were written.

## REFERENCES

Acchamamba, Bhandaru. 2012. '*Stirvidya*.' Trans. Malathi Nidadavolu. www.thulika.net/2007January/ABstory.htm, accessed on 2 January 2012.

Anandhi, S. 2008. 'The Manifesto and the Modern Self: Reading the Autobiography of Muthulakshmi Reddi', Chennai: MIDS (MIDS Working Paper 204): 3–16.

Nagamma, Thadi. 2012. 'The Kiss', in *Flowering from the Soil: Dalit Women's Writing from Telugu*, translated and edited by K. Suneetha Rani, Delhi: Prestige: 23–28.

Ramamirthammal, Muvalur. 2003. *Web of Deceit: Devadasi Reform in Colonial India*, translated by Kalpana Kannabiran and Vasanth Kannabiran, Delhi: Kali for Women.

Rao, Gurajada Appa. 2002. *Kanyasulkam*, translated by. C. Vijayasree and T. Vijay Kumar, Delhi: Book Review Literary Trust.

Reddi, Muthulakshmi. 1964. *Autobiography*, Madras: MLJ Press.

——. 1930. *My Experience as a Legislator*, Madras: Current Thought Press.

Varalakshmamma, Kanuparthi. 2005. 'The Charm of a Cherished Story'. www.thulika.net/2005April/cherishedstory.html, accessed on 3 January.

——. 2001. 'The Promise', in *Ayoni and Other Stories*, translated and edited by Alladi Uma and M. Sridhar, Delhi: Katha: 57–76.

Volga. 2010. 'Manavatvam Parimalinche Madhuravani', Sahitha: Sahithya Vyasalu. Hyderabad: Author, 9–28.

# 3

## Colonized

### THE BENGALI WOMAN WRITER
### IN BRITISH INDIA

Sanjukta Dasgupta

I

*We can only read our own tongue and write our own language,*
*we who are in fact, members not of the intelligentsia but of the*
*ignorantsia.*

–Virginia Woolf

IF THE above statement had been made by Rassundrari Devi,
Kailashbasini Devi, Krishnabhabini Dasi or even Rokeya Sakhawat
Hossain or Swarnakumari Devi, it would have had the expected
impact—but when this line is an extract from a British text published
in 1938 and written by Virginia Woolf as the third essay of her scathing satire on the education system of Britain in *Three Guineas* (1966:
87) matters seem to be far more complex in terms of confinement
in monolinguality, the hegemonic thrust of the English language, linguistic imperialism and cultural homogenization.

I think it may not be out of place to juxtapose a comparative quantification. According to the literary critic Elaine Showalter in the nineteenth century, there were over 200 women writers in mainland Britain. Interestingly, in British India there were almost 200 Bengali women writers; some well known, others mostly minor writers. However, among them mostly Brahmo and Hindu women writers could read English literature and write in English and even translate into English from the original Bengali texts (Sinha: 238). The critic Ghulam Murshid gives us a more conservative figure of about 83 women writers, many of whom were graduates from Calcutta University and had studied English Honours at the undergraduate level. Because of the hegemony of the power language English and the powerlessness of women, possibly in any location, it indeed a minefield, an engagement with a troubled terrain of social, linguistic and cultural tensions.

Katherine Mayo's much maligned text *Mother India* is a critique of Indians and Indian society and culture in British India, dismissed by Gandhi as the research of a drain-inspector. Mayo had used agricultural images and tools to outline the transformation of Indian education from the prevalent Arabic and Persian language and literature set up by the Mughal administrators for official purposes into the English language. Mayo wrote in 1927, referring to the introduction of the English language in official communication, 'back in the days of the East India Company—that a little seed was sown with whose fruit we now deal. This was the changing of the language of the Courts of Justice from Persian to English. The change took place as a logical part of the westernizing of Indian education. It looked simple. Its results have been simple, like the results of a clean stroke of the axe' (289).

In Part 11 of her book titled *Grand Trunk Road* (1927/1986) Mayo referred to mostly illiterate Indian women who were brought up with the belief that their husbands were earthly gods, and their reason to be born was to become wives and mothers. Mayo described in detail the imprisonment of women in zenanas and purdah, the unhygienic conditions of the confinement of pregnant women, inadequate nourishment and childbirth assisted by untrained mid-wives or *dais* which led to high incidence of maternal and infant mortality.

This part of the book also referred to the plight of widows, widow re-marriage and marriage of widows if they were virgins. The education of women even in the dawn of the twentieth century was limited, and here again religious control of Hindu orthodoxy played an immense role. Mayo used many excerpts from the Calcutta University Commission Reports in order to support her arguments along with references to Cornelia Sorabji's textbook *Between the Twilights* on the misery of Hindu women (1908).

Moreover, in Chapter 10 titled 'Woman the Spinster', Mayo wrote, 'Less than 2 per cent of the women of British India are literate in the sense of being able to write a letter of a few simple phrases, and read its answer, in any one language or dialect... that a century ago literate, save for a few rare stars, were practically unknown in India; and second, that the great body of the peoples, always heavily opposed to female education, still so opposes it, and on religio-social grounds (Mayo: 119). Also, Mayo used an excerpt from the Calcutta University Commission Report (1917–19: vol. 12: 411) where Professor Mohini Mohan Bhattacharjee stated,

> The higher education of Indian Mohammadan women... may almost be said to be beyond the scope of practical reform. No Hindu or Muhammadan woman of the orthodox type has ever joined a college or even read up to the higher classes in a school. The girls who receive university education are either Brahmo or Christian.... The time is far distant when the University will be called upon to make arrangements for the higher education of any large or even a decent number of girls in Bengal (Mayo: 127).

Therefore, it is indeed a matter of curiosity that in 1939, at a time when—as the Second World War threatened—fascism had led to pacifist and anti-imperialist movements, Virginia Woolf would publish *Three Guineas* as a response to women's support to anti-war protests where she lashed out at British gender injustice that denied quality living to British women. In obvious sarcasm Virginia Woolf detailed the misery and subaltern status of the daughters and wives of educated men in the nineteenth century, who were denied higher education in universities, were compelled to undertake unpaid labour—which has always been justified as unconditional labour of love and the stark reality that marriage was the widely promoted profession for women.

Virginia Woolf referred to the fact that though women had been admitted into reading, writing and teaching English literature, this too was limited to the middle school teaching-learning process. Woolf cited an obscure journal by a governess named Miss Weeton, who lamented, 'Oh, how I have burnt to learn Latin, French, the arts, the Sciences, anything rather than the dog trot way of sewing, teaching, writing copies, washing dishes every day... Why are not Females permitted to study physics, divinity, astronomy, etc., etc., with their attendants, chemistry, botany, logic, mathematics etc.?' (Woolf: 75–76). Referring to the nurturance of male and female siblings within a family Woolf stated, 'You shall not learn; you shall not earn; you shall not own; you shall not—such was the society relationship of brother and sister for many centuries' (105).

Interrogating the question about women contributing to culture and intellectual liberty, Woolf argued that women were systematically debarred from enrolment as students in universities and when they could do so, there were innumerable restrictions. Referring to education at home or unpaid-for education, she expressed her despair that such education was extremely limited. Further pointing out that with such unpaid-for education, as the epigraph says, 'we can only read our own tongue and write our own language, we who are in fact, members not of the intelligentsia but of the ignorantsia' (87). Woolf further refers to Whitaker's observation that 'not a single educated man's daughter is thought capable of teaching the literature of her own language at either university' (ibid.).

And yet when Mary Carpenter in her two-volume published journal (1868) referred to the lack of female education in India, we find she was referring to primary and middle school education for females, though the factors of deprivation from knowledge pursuits, marriage, subservience to patriarchal norms seem to be common between the daughters of the colonized and the colonizer's daughters who were even sent to the colonies in search of eligible bachelors.

This is thus a significant factor that women both globally and locally have been deprived of gender equality in terms of training for acquisition of knowledge, empowerment through independent minds, independent income and creative freedom. While identifying the need for female teachers and urging her European sisters to join in philanthropic work of supporting native female education and allaying fears of conversion that English education and Christian missionary school education could enforce through a process of social conditioning, Mary Carpenter however recognized the merit of the native female students. Carpenter stated that she had reservations about the learning ability of native female students 'but the very different condition of the girls in all the Mission Boarding Schools, which were under female teachers, fully convinced me that Hindoo girls wanted only proper instruction to make them in every way equal, and in some respects superior, to those of our country' (143).

The fear of educated women exposed to western education and culture, becoming de-feminized, and transforming themselves into a hybrid weirdo was common, as the translated poem by the popular nineteenth-century poet Iswar Chandra Gupta (1812–1859) bears out:

> In my grandmother's days girls were so pure!
> They lived by the code and the rituals to be sure,
> And then came Bethune and anon
> All these feminine virtues have gone,
> And gone with the wind is the woman demure,
> And jettisoning those old world charms,
> These modern girls with books in their arms
> Must learn their As, Bs and Cs
> To speak like the Feringhees,
> And drive their own four-in-hand,
> To visit the Maidan and listen to the Band,
> Sooner or later, boots will adorn their figures
> And who knows, they may even take to cigars (Ray 2002: 36).

Partha Chatterjee referred to women, home and familial responsibilities in the nineteenth century as sacrosanct, the home being an insular space that preserved national culture and any invasion of its closely guarded practices was ridiculed as the negative influences of westernization that were commonly manifest in women's education, fashion, and food, such as tea drinking. Chatterjee (2010) commented

> But the crucial requirement was to retain the inner spirituality of indigenous social life. The home was the principal site for expressing the spiritual quality of the national culture, and women must take the mail responsibility for protecting and nurturing this quality. No matter what the changes in the external conditions of life for women, they must not lose their essentially spiritual (that is, feminine) virtues; they must not, in other words, become essentially Westernized... There would be a marked difference in the degree and manner of Westernization of women, as distinct from men, in the modern world of the nation' (126).

## II

It is indeed remarkable that women's lack of education or acquiring education was dependent on male preferences and priorities. So Ghulam Murshid (1983) observed that in nineteenth-century Bengal, sometimes described as the Bengal Renaissance, it was men who desired women to acquire some skills in learning, enabling them thereby to play the role of companions. Companionate marriage was an ideal of the times amongst English-educated urban Bengali men, mostly Brahmos, converted Christians and a few Hindus. 'It was the concern of a section of English educated men to give their women some education and thereby modernize them, because they found it impossible either to advance their society or to fulfil their own lives without uplifting their women. They therefore launched a movement which at once aimed to elevate their women and enrich their own lives' (Murshid: 16–17).

Moreover Murshid expressed his scepticism about how much creative freedom women writers enjoyed in this period as they were trapped in the triple bind of being colonized by the British on the socio-political level, colonized as women within the patriarchal system and further colonized as the inferior biological sex. So Murshid commented, 'However, it was not clear how far the opinions expressed in these writings were genuinely their own. Even if they wrote on social problems, they did not expose either their private life or their own views. In any case, these writings of women were highly influenced by male-defined values' (ibid.).

In the journal *Tattvabodhini Patrika* (1843–1883), administered by the Adi Brahmo Samaj of Debendranath Tagore, we find a distinction between what was considered to be feminine education and what led to masculine traits in women if they were exposed to education exclusive to masculinist domains. The essay 'Strisiksha and Striswadhinata' (Nov-Dec 1878: 154–56) states quite categorically,

> We are not against female education… However, we are against the kind of education now being given to women… The books women are asked to read are either translation from English or are English-influenced. Consequently, our women become denationalized. We believe women should read only those books that will help them to become better wives and better mothers. This is an age of luxury. Most of the women are luxurious and indifferent to housekeeping and to the bringing up of their children' (Murshid: 47).

Moreover, Tagore's elder brother Satyendranath urged his wife, Jnanadanandini, to join him in England as he was keen to have his wife as his companion. He even tried to instil in his wife the spirit of social upliftment for the women of Bengal as he urged his wife to join him in England where he was living then. He wrote, 'I am certain you can improve your mind and soul a thousand times if you live in English society. By improving yourself you can help other women of our country, who will find in you an example to follow' (Letter no 5 18.2.1864: 53, Murshid: 210). In the same letter he adds with some impatience, 'If you live in England for only two years after having lived in the zenana for 25 years, you will then realize that two years in England is better than 25 years in the zenana so far as the development of your mind and intellect is concerned' (ibid.: 211).

It is indeed remarkable that women's lack of education or acquiring education was dependent on male preferences and priorities along with conservative casteism and therefore religious affiliations.

It is noteworthy that the first two women graduates of Calcutta University, Chandramukhi Bose (1860–1944) was a Christian who also was the first woman to have an MA degree in English from the same university. She became the principal of Bethune College, the first woman to hold this position in India and perhaps in South Asia. However, due to ill health and other personal reasons she discontinued her job in 1899, settled in Dehradun where she lived for a long time. Kadambini Basu (Ganguly) 1861–1923 graduated in the same year. She was a Brahmo woman who after marriage went to England, trained as a doctor and practised too, despite marriage and five children. Both were direct contemporaries of Tagore (1861–1941) and their extraordinary career graphs indicate that the nineteenth century and the early twentieth century, for some exceptional women in Bengal, were periods of transition from the darkness of ignorance to the light of knowledge.

## III

Who were the Bengali women writers during Tagore's time? We have become increasingly aware that Tagore's contemporaries require an exhaustive compendium that deal with their contribution to the evolution of Bengali culture. Though texts on Tagore's contemporaries do exist, not many deal with aspects of gender and family and their impact and counter-impact on Tagore's discourse. In this connection Rokeya Sakhawat Hossain's position as a younger contemporary of Tagore is significant, not only because she was a self-taught woman but also belonged to the minority Muslim community where opportunities for women's education were even more limited. In her memoirs Rokeya recalled that she had to observe purdah from the age of five. She was introduced to basic English, Urdu, and Bengali education by her elder brother Ibrahim Saber and her married sister Karimunessa.

Born on 9 December 1880, Rokeya was nineteen years younger than Tagore but, remarkably, both were born into distinguished zamindar households and coincidentally both were born when their respective families were experiencing severe financial constraints due to injudicious expenditures. Born in Rangpur, now in

Bangladesh, Rokeya was self-educated. In 1896, at the age of sixteen, she was married to Syed Sakhawat, a 40-year-old talented and liberated widower who provided her with all the support she needed in order to nurture her creative skills. Khan Bahadur Syed Sakhawat Hossain was a deputy magistrate and Urdu was his spoken language, unlike Rokeya who spoke Bengali, though her own father nurtured a marked preference for Urdu language and literature as the areas of preferred formal education. After the death of her husband in 1909, Rokeya set up a school for Muslim girls: the Sakhawat Memorial Girls School. At first the school was set up in Odisha but due to strained relations with her step-daughter she moved to Calcutta and set up her school there. One wonders whether Rokeya's life would have been different if instead of being childless she had been a widowed mother of minor children.

The contrast in the career of the two contemporaries Tagore and Rokeya reminds one of the stark contrast between the nineteenth-century American contemporary writers Mark Twain and Harriet Beecher Stowe. While Mark Twain travelled through the world and even visited Calcutta and became a marketing triumph in his country due to the huge sales figures of his books, Harriet Beecher Stowe was not a commercial success despite being recognized as the key inspiration to the Civil War. Stowe's modest house next door to Mark Twain's mansion is an architectural symbol of juxtaposition of material success and power linked to gender accreditation.

Yet Rokeya wielded a powerful pen and seemed to write more vociferously in Bengali about the exploitation of women than in English. Is this because she was aware that an English write-up could be easily noticed for subversion by the ruling British government whereas a Bengali essay though more strident would not have the same far-reaching impact in terms of reaching the colonial masters? This is how Rokeya argues and concludes her essay in English titled 'Educational Ideals for the Modern Indian Girl', first published in *The Mussalman,* 5 March 1931, (Rouf et al. 2008) just a year before her death:

> We should be all means broaden the outlook of our girls and teach them to modernize themselves. Yet they should be made

to realize that the domestic duties entrusted to them cover a task on which the welfare of the country depends.... The future of India lies in its girls. The development of its educational system on proper lines is therefore a question of permanent importance.... In short, our girls would not only obtain University degrees, but must be ideal daughter, wives and mother—or I may say obedient daughters, loving sisters, dutiful wives and instructive mothers' (502).

In another rather oft-cited Bengali essay, initially titled 'Alankar Na Badge of Slavery' (Not Ornaments but Badge of Slavery), later the revised title for the essay was, 'The Degradation of Womankind' wherein Rokeya began her essay dramatically, 'Women Readers? Have you ever reflected on your pitiable plight? In this twentieth-century civilized world, who are we? Slaves! I've heard that slave trade has been banished from the world, but has our slavery been eradicated? No. Why are we slaves?' (ibid.: 15).

In another essay that was published in *The Mussalman* on 6 December 1927, Rokeya challenged the societal norms almost echoing Virginia Woolf in *A Room of One's Own* and *Three Guineas* as she asked, 'The worst crime that our brothers commit against us is to deprive us of education.... May we challenge such grandfathers, fathers or uncles to show the authority on which they prevent their girls from acquiring education? Can they quote from the Holy Quran or Hadis any injunction prohibiting women from obtaining knowledge?' (ibid.: 497).

We are of course aware of Rokeya's utopian narrative *Sultana's Dream* (1908) which she dedicated to her elder sister Karimunessa from whom she had learnt to read and write English—'To my elder sister who was kind enough to help me in my childhood to commence my ABC of the English language this book is reverently dedicated' (487). When *Sultana's Dream* was published in the *Indian Ladies Magazine,* a Madras-based journal, the District Commissioner of Bhagalpur Mr Macpherson had stated, 'We consider it a most charming little composition. The ideas expressed in it are quite delightful and full of originality and they are written in perfect English' (Syed Rokeya: 22).

In *Motichur* (1904) Rokeya includes some significant remarks about intertextuality, as the essays in *Motichur* were alleged to be similar to the popular British woman writer Marie Corelli's novel *The Murder of Delcia.* Rokeya states that she had heard about Corelli's novel much after the publication of *Motichur.* Then she herself ponders rhetorically how such similarities are created:

> Then the question may arise, why such similarities happen? Bengal, Punjab, Deccan (Hyderabad) Bombay, England–how is it that from everywhere such effusive expressions emerge? In answer one can venture to answer that perhaps it is due to the spiritual unity of all the silent women of the British empire, both women of the mainland and the colonies (Rouf: 7).

She had later translated this novel into Bengali.

## IV

Let us now turn to Tagore's own elder sister Swarnakumari Devi. Born in 1856, that is, twenty-four years before Rokeya, Swarnakumari was self-taught but had the exceptional advantage of being born in the distinguished Tagore family. As a matter of fact, both Rokeya and Swarnakumri were daughters of educated men with significant economic power. But Rabindranath himself voluntarily discontinued institutionalized education, for Swarnakumari there were no such options, she was self-taught, because she chose to learn, learning was not compulsory as in the case of male members of the family The interactions between the members of the Brahmo Samaj that she was exposed to within her family, through her father Debendranath and her elder brothers Dwijendranath, Satyendranath and Jyotirindranath all contributed in fertilizing Swarnakumari's inquisitive and intelligent mind. She was married in 1867 at the age of twelve; her husband Janakinath Ghosal was a 27-year-old liberal man, who did not discourage her from reading and writing. She was the mother of four children by the age of eighteen, that is, by 1874. Her husband died in 1913. Swarnakumari published her first novel in 1876 at the age of twenty, and her last fictional publication was released in 1925. Swarnakumari died at the age of seventy-six, in 1932. Rokeya too died in 1932 at the age of 52. Though Swarnakumari has left behind six volumes of her writings that include novels, plays, essays, and short stories, she was the first woman writer to have produced a trilogy, and had edited for 18 years the literary journal *Bharati,* in which she wrote copiously, including several essays on general science. Along with starting a women's association *Sakhi Samiti* and becoming the first woman representative from Bengal in the Indian National Congress, she was awarded the Jagatarini Medal by Calcutta University; she was the fourth recipient and the first woman recipient of this medal, the third recipient being her younger brother Rabindranath Tagore. Yet Swarnakumari Devi's one hundred and fiftieth birth anniversary in 2007 was scarcely noticed.

Prashanta Kumar Pal, the biographer of Tagore's definitive biography *Rabijibani,* records several excerpts which, in one sense, indicates Tagore's pragmatic views as a literary critic and at the same time Tagore's rather impersonal assessment of his elder sister Swarnakumari's Devi's literary ambitions, which in terms of middle-class culture would seem rather insensitive towards a talented married sister seeking support in finding publishers for the English translations of her novels (vol. 6: 355). On 28 January 1913, Tagore wrote to his sister,

> Your book reached me at the railway station on the day I was leaving for America. You just don't know how difficult it is to get any book published here. Of course It is not difficult if you pay to be published, but no publisher unless he is certain that there is demand from readers for a book will not publish the book at their own expense… I know trying to publish the book here will not be a success. Moreover the translation is not all that good—that is, it has not reached the high standards of English composition.

Pal assumes that Swarnakumari may have sent her own translation of her novel *Kahake* to Tagore.

Around February 1914, after he had received the Nobel Prize, however, Tagore wrote in much harsher terms to his friend Rothenstein about his sister's literary ambitions,

> She is one of those unfortunate beings who have more ambition than abilities but just enough talent to keep her mediocrity alive for a short period of time. Her weakness has been taken advantage of by some unscrupulous literary agents in London and she had her stories translated and published. I have given her no encouragement but I have not been successful in making her see things in their proper light. It is likely that she may go to England and use my name and you may meet her but be merciful [*sic*] to her and never let her harbour in her mind any illusion about her worth and her chance. I am afraid she will be a source of trouble to my friends who I hope will be candid to her for my sake and will not allow her to mistake ordinary politeness for encouragement (ibid.).

Also referring to Swarnakumari writing for support to Trevelyan, Tagore wrote, 'She urged Trevelyan to put forth efforts on her behalf, since it was difficult to attract the attention of literati in England' (ibid.: 655).

In this context it should be mentioned that Swarnakumari's novel *Floral Garland (Phuler Mala)* was translated and published as a serial novel in *The Modern Review* between April–December 1909 and was thereafter published in 1910 as a novel. In 1898, her brother Hemendranath Tagore's daughter Shobhana Devi had translated her Bengali novel *Kahake*. In 1907, Swarnakumari translated the same novel and titled it *An Unfinished Song* and the novel was published in 1913 in England by T. Werner Laurie Ltd. The second reprint of the novel was published in 1914 which, after all, proves its popularity.

To conclude I will allude to issues of gender, woman as creative writer and language that has been integral to this essay as I refer to a sequence in Swarnakumari Devi's novel *Kahake*. In *Kahake,* there is an interesting debate about the literary status of Shakespeare and George Eliot as competitors with an innuendo that George Eliot

alias Mary Evans had to change her own name to a male pseud-
onym in order to write. Interestingly again, the conversation that
Swarnakumari scripts in her Bengali novel is in English. In fact, in
her novel Swarnakumari uses many English words, phrases, and
sentences. For instance, in Chapter 11 we find a discussion about
George Eliot's novel *Middlemarch,* the art of fiction, and the purpose of a novelist to represent her understanding of life in a series of
images. Significantly, the doctor who is a staunch fan of George Eliot
states, 'You forget that the novelist is not a moral instructor' when
he is told that the heroine of *Middlemarch* married twice, which did
not indicate 'self-sacrifice'.

Here is an excerpt as the brother-in-law of the doctor Binay
asks whether they are talking about George Eliot. It must be noticed
that this dialogue is written in the English language:

> Oh, she is a great creator, we must admit that, I am sorry to say.
>
> Doctor: What a reluctant admission. Does not your man's nature
> take delight in glorifying such genius in a woman? What a grand
> intellect she had—combined with sympathetic heart and subtle
> instinct of a true woman?

These lines are in English, followed by some observations in Bengali
that I am translating:

> The quintessential preoccupations of human beings, the direc-
> tions of the profound subjective self emanating from refined
> emotions that she has represented so meticulously, has any male
> novelist been able to do the same?
>
> Brother in law: There I quite disagree. Do you mean to say she is
> as great a genius as Shakespeare, or even modern—
>
> Doctor responded emphatically, 'Of course, why not? Though
> at first I spoke of novelists only—yet if you choose to bring in
> Shakespeare's name, I have not the slightest hesitation in pro-
> nouncing her to be as great in her sphere, as Shakespeare is in his.

While the brother-in-law dismissed it as a 'monstrous proposition',
the doctor said he regarded George Eliot as equal to any renowned

poet or novelist of England. Ultimately, this verbal duel ended on a pleasant reconciliatory tone by both wishing 'three cheers' to Shakespeare and George Eliot, but each prioritizing his preference.

> Brother in law, Three cheers for Shakespeare—three cheers for George Eliot.
>
> Doctor: 'and vice versa. Three cheers for George Eliot—three cheers for Shakespeare? (*Kahake 52–55*).

The above extract, of course, quite unequivocally reveals Swarnakumari's awareness of British literature and the canon, and the systematic marginalization of women writers even in mainland Britain.

Chitra Deb includes in her book *Thakurbarir Andarmahal* two brief reviews of Swarnakumari's novel *Kahake*, or *The Unfinished Song*, which makes Tagore's negative appraisal of his sister's own translation of her novel rather inexplicable and seems almost close to sibling rivalry, though neither Prashanta Kumar Pal nor Chitra Deb as life historians have speculated on this possibility. The editor of the *Westminster Gazette* wrote, 'Mrs Ghoshal, as one of the pioneers of the women movement in Bengal, and fortunate in her upbringing, is well qualified to give this picture of a Hindu maiden's development' (Deb: 36). Also, the *Clarion* stated, 'Remarkable for the picture of Hindu life the story is overshadowed by the personality of the authoress, one of the foremost Bengali writers to-day' (ibid.). About Swarnakumari's contribution to Bengali literature and culture Chitra Deb wrote, 'Except for Rabindranath no one else in Tagore's family had written as much…. Yet Swarnakumari has not yet been given her rightful place in the Bengali literary tradition. With Bankimchandra at one end and Rabindranath at the other, we can refer to Swarnakumari as the bridge between the two' (Deb 32; my translation). Swarnakumari Devi and Rokeya Sakhawat's creative texts script narratives of resistance not just in terms of their aesthetic content but bear ample evidence of their having liberated themselves effectively if not completely, from the social and cultural claustrophobia. In varying degrees they proved their creative freedom and excellence despite male control and phallogocentrism. Both the

*Sanjukta Dasgupta*

Brahmo and Muslim married women who became widows early in life were activist-writers, editors, organizers of political forums for women and proved that education was the liberating and enabling tool that widened their horizons. Though both these women writers were not known for their support of the imperialistic policies of the British colonial rule in India, their ability to read and write in the colonizer's tongue, the English language, empowered them to a significant extent as bi-lingual readers, writers, translators and activists, thereby enabling them to traverse intellectually and linguistically beyond the cultural lines of control.

REFERENCES

Calcutta University Commission. 1917–1919. *Report*, vol. 12, Calcutta: University of Calcutta.

Carpenter, Mary. 1868. *Six Months in India,* London: Longmans, Green and Co.

Chatterjee, Partha. 2010. *The Partha Chatterjee Omnibus*, New Delhi: Oxford University Press.

Deb, Chitra. 2011. *Thakurbarir Andarmahal*, Kolkata: Ananda Publishers.

Devi, Swarnakumari. 2002. *Kahake.* Introduced by Sudakshina Ghosh, Kolkata: Dey's Publishing.

Mayo, Katherine. [1927] 1986. *Mother India*, Delhi: Anmol Publications.

Murshid, Ghulam. 1983. *Reluctant Debutante: Response of Bengali Women to Modernization (1905-1849)*, Rajshahi: Sahitya Samsad, Rajshahi University.

Pal, Prashanta Kumar. 2001. *Rabijibani (Life of Tagore),* vol. 6, Kolkata: Ananda Publishers.

Ray, Bharati. 1994. *Shekaler Narishiksha:* Bamabodhini Patrika, Kolkata: Women's Studies Research Centre.

——. 2002. *Early Feminists of Colonial India*, New Delhi: Oxford University Press.

Rouf, Abdur et al. 2008. *Rokeya Rochona Sangraha* (Collected Writings of Rokeya) Kolkata: Visvakosh Parisad.

Sen, Abhijit, and Anindita Bhaduri, eds, 2000. *Swarnakumari Devi'r Rachana Sankalan* (Collection of Swarnakumari Devi's Writings). Kolkata: Dey's Publishing.

Sinha, Manjusree. 2000. *Unobingsho Shatabdir Sahitya o Sanskritite Bangamahila* (Bengali Women in Nineteenth-Century Literature and Culture) Kolkata: Granthasamput.

Sorabjee, Cornelia. 1908. *Between the Twilights: Being Studies of Indian Women by One of Themselves*, London: Harper and Row: 125–32.

Syed, Abdul Mannan. 1996. *Begum Rokeya*, Dhaka: Abosar.

Woolf, Virginia. [1938] 1966. *Three Guineas*, San Diego: Harvest Book.

# 4

# Rokeya's Dream

## FEMINIST INTERVENTIONS AND UTOPIAS

Somdatta Bhattacharya

*Once we match this new meaning of the home/world dichot-
omy with the identification of social roles by gender, we get the
ideological framework within which nationalism answered the
women's question.*

–Partha Chatterjee 1989

CHATTERJEE'S WELL-KNOWN theorization of the 'contradictory pulls on nationalist ideology in its struggle against the dominance of colonialism' (1989: 237) identifies the social space of
*ghar* (home) into which the women were meant to withdraw. The
woman is the representation of this space untouched by colonial
hegemony—a space where the nation remains unvanquished by the
colonial master or *his* culture. Chatterjee emphasizes that this sepa-
ration was not mere conservatism or a defence of traditional roles.
It was part of the very essence of the anti-colonial movement. This
struggle framed a *new* patriarchy and, importantly, a *new* woman,
who is neither the westernized *memsahib* nor the vulgar *common*
woman. This framework is an interesting backdrop to read the life

and work of Rokeya Sakhawat Hossain (1880–1932), as they present a significant feminist intervention that questions the neat spatial divide that pigeonholes both the activist and her milieu. This essay tries to read Hossain's feminist utopias as interventions that question both the colonial authority and the nationalist deification of the Indian Woman.

Rokeya, or Raku as she was called at home, was born in 1880 in a landowning family at Pairaband, Rangpur District in erstwhile East Bengal, now Bangladesh (see also Chapter 3). Her orthodox father frowned upon the idea of women's education, but an elder sister and an elder brother secretly taught her to read and write English and Bengali respectively. And it was this brother, Ibrahim Saber, who arranged the marriage of the sixteen-year-old Rokeya with the forty-year-old Khan Bahadur Syed Sakhawat Hossain. Sakhawat Hossain was at that time the Deputy Magistrate of Bhagalpur, Bihar. And it was this much older, affectionate and liberated man, under whose influence Rokeya started blooming into the woman she was to become later.

Rokeya was born towards the end of the nineteenth century that was a crucial period for colonial Bengal. What is famously known as the Bengal Renaissance of the early and mid-nineteenth century had concerns for the social position of women at the centre of its ideological matrix. Rammohan Roy and Vidyasagar were iconic Hindu, upper-caste, educated, reformist figures of this period and much of their work revolved around the central issue of the 'women's question'. However, as the nationalist movement gained force, the importance of the 'women's question' began to diminish in Bengal. Popular attitudes towards the West-inspired modernization movement changed and the project was viewed with suspicion and distrust. From this perspective, the moment of nationalist upsurge seems marked by a significant retrogression when it came to considering women's role in the perceived nation's public and private lives, when compared to the zeal that Bengal Renaissance exuded in seeking to liberalise women. In this framework of a linear historical progression/retrogression from the renaissance to nationalism, the women's question became the obvious casualty when nationalism demanded a lionisation of the past and its value systems. However,

Partha Chatterjee, in 'The Nationalist Resolution of the Women's Question', has powerfully critiqued this linear narrative by questioning whether it was at all possible to push a liberal/rationalist agenda in the context of colonialism, and by pointing out that even the renaissance leaders were reluctant liberals when it came to tackling the women's question.

Chatterjee's essay takes its lead from Sumit Sarkar's analysis of the renaissance reformist push as necessitated by the need to realign interpersonal relationships within the family, rather than of any ideological origin. Sarkar analysed the renaissance reformist agenda as 'a limited and controlled emancipation of wives as a personal necessity for survival in a hostile social world' (Sarkar 1973, cited in Mishra 188). While Chatterjee takes Sarkar's analysis as his point of departure—that 'fundamental elements of social conservatism… were conspicuous in the reform movements of the early and mid-nineteenth century' (Chatterjee 235)—he breaks away from Sarkar in formulating that the discourse of nationalism provided an answer to the new and emerging socio-cultural problems that concerned the position of women in 'modern' times. This answer, he claims, 'was posited not on an identity but on a difference with the perceived forms of cultural modernity in the West'. The discourse imagined women who 'must not lose their essential spiritual (i.e. feminine) virtues; they must not become essentially westernized' (243). He gives us the example of the education of women in Bengal, an issue that received much attention from the reformers: the early schools (including home-schooling initiatives) here were organized by Christian missionaries, and that resulted in the perceived threat of women being exposed to harmful western influences as well as the hazard of proselytization; but by the 1850s Indians had started opening schools for girls, and from '95 girls' schools with an attendance of 2,500 in 1863, the figures went up to 2,238 schools in 1890 with a total of more than 80,000 students' (245). Long before Oxford and Cambridge opened their gates to female students, Calcutta University awarded Bachelor of Arts degrees to accomplished Bengali women. The debates at this time over making Bengali as the medium of teaching instead of English also point to the same idea, of creating a 'new woman' of an indigenous variety whose central place was still home, as distinct from the 'western woman' for whom education meant a means of competing with men in the public world of wage-based economy. Textbooks, periodicals and creative works to be consumed by women were written in their mother-tongue Bengali to emphasize the national project of crafting culturally rooted womanhood.

The areas of education approved by the 'new patriarchy' were also significant, inculcating values of thrift, hygiene, accounting and orderliness. As Chatterjee notes, 'the domain where the new idea of womanhood was sought to be actualized was the home' (250), and hence there is little evidence of any autonomous struggle by women in the 'public archives of political affairs'. Efforts of reformist women actively engaged with women's education are hence seen as 'already inscribed into the 'new patriarchy" (Bagchi 2009: 744). If we agree in any absolute sense with this 'resolution' of the extremely complex case of the nineteenth-century 'women's question', we run the risk of erasing the achievements of women who through their writings and activities challenged both the nationalist discourse as well as the colonial hegemony. This essay brings together relevant biographical details of Rokeya Sakhawat Hossain to provide such an instance of feminist intervention and activism. It shall also examine a select sample of her writings on women's education, with special emphasis on *Sultana's Dream* (1905) and *Padmarag* (1924). They amount to a significant moment in the evolution of feminist writing and activism in India, especially in the emphasis they put on education as a means of emancipation: 'The history of education [was] inscribed not merely in the formal school that Rokeya founded, but in her larger career—first, as powerful writer in the literary sphere, and secondly, as builder up of women's associations and institutions furthering informal processes of women's development and education' (ibid.: 746).

During the period when Khan Bahadur Sakhawat Hossain was bedridden with an illness, it was Rokeya who managed his official and personal correspondences in English. Arguably he had the best interest of women's education in his mind, since he bequeathed his wife Rupees 10,000 to set up a girls' school after his death. When he died after thirteen years of marriage, Rokeya tried to use the money to set up a Muslim girls' school at Bhagalpur, where she was staying. The plan failed due to her strained relationship with her in-laws. But she eventually set up the school in a rented house in Calcutta in 1911 with eight students. The curriculum included, among other things, courses in Bengali, English, Urdu, Persian and Arabic. Today, it is a prestigious government-funded institution at the centre of the city, with about 1500 students. In 1916, Rokeya started the Bengal branch of Anjuman-e-Khwatin-e-Islam, an association for Muslim women, which busied itself with welfare and developmental initiatives directed at women. In 1922, Rokeya became the president of two organizations, *Narishilpa Vidyalaya* (Women's Arts and Industry School) and *Naritirtha* (Women's Institution) to rehabilitate destitute women and prostitutes.

Mrs R.S. Hossain, as she was known through her lifetime, had by 1916 become a regular contributor to the Bengali language periodicals. Her status as a polemical, feminist writer did not much help her cause as an educationist, but the greater visibility that she gained through this, in a way, stressed her seriousness of purpose in public imagination. To become and remain acceptable to the parents of her students, Rokeya remained in purdah all her life. The unschooled Rokeya also had a sound grasp over English, and she did not reject the language on grounds of it being 'western' and the language of the colonizers. She wrote long letters in English to the journal *The Mussalman*, charting out the problems her school was facing. In 1911, she wrote asking for funds to augment her husband's legacy. In 1913, she appealed for private funding to establish a school hostel for students from the *mufassils*. In 1917, she lamented her failure to open a Bengali-medium section in her school, largely due to the disapproval of the parents who wanted their wards to be educated in Urdu. At present though, Sakhawat Memorial School has a mix of both Muslim and Hindu students, with Urdu and Bengali run parallel as the medium of instruction.

Rokeya published *Sultana's Dream* in English in 1905 in *The Indian Ladies' Magazine*. This magazine was started by Kamala Satthianadhan, the Tamil Christian writer, in 1901 (see also Chapter 1). This was the first time she was writing in the language her brother had taught her: English. In fact, it was Rokeya's ever-encouraging husband who urged her to publish the funny, witty

*Sultana's Dream*. Although more than a hundred years have passed since its publication, the piece is still widely read and fresh as a successful example of early Indian writing in English. The narrator, Sultana, falls asleep on her easy chair one evening and reaches Ladyland in her dream. She is given a guided tour of the capital city by a woman who resembles her friend Sister Sara. The name 'Sultana' clearly suggests the Muslim lineage of the character, and she is a *purdahnashin* (a veiled woman). The nomenclature of the main protagonist is significant for yet another reason: 'Sultana' literally means 'empress' or 'female political ruler' and the high aspirations that Rokeya had for colonized Indian women are clearly etched out in this choice for a name. When she expresses her discomfort at walking around in broad daylight without a veil, Sister Sara reminds her that in Ladyland men do not often come out on the streets and that she has no reason to feel threatened. Women are in charge of public affairs and men mostly remain in confinement in this antipodal utopia. Sultana cannot help but compare Ladyland to Calcutta (where she has come from) and marvels at the civic amenities Ladyland boasts of. Sister Sara, in a matter of fact manner points out that unlike in Calcutta, the development of Ladyland is completely in the hands of women. The place has a Queen who believes that education holds the key to women's empowerment and progress. Hence the government has founded and funds a number of girls' schools, and prohibits child marriage by law. Women in Ladyland study the sciences while the men of the country engage in meaningless warfare. It was during a war when men could not get the better of the enemy that the women decided to take matters in their hands. The principals of the two women's universities of the place decided to tap solar energy to fight back the enemy. So that *purdahnashin* women could freely move around during this time, the men were ordered by the Queen to retreat into the *zenana* till the war lasted. The enemy was defeated, but the men did not come out of seclusion. In time, they stopped complaining about not being able to go out in public, and now Ladyland has changed the name of zenana to 'mardana'. In this inverted world order, reminiscent of the rabbit hole Alice had tumbled into, Sultana meets the admirable Queen and gets to see some of the scientific inventions made by the women of the place. When she wakes up, Sultana finds herself on her easy chair in her own bedroom. At the centre of *Sultana's Dream* is the need for Indian women's education and abolition of such debilitating social practices as child marriage. The utopian feminist country, Ladyland, with the wise Queen for the leader, succeeded because of the women's education it promoted and propagated. Particular emphasis was placed on the need for women to acquaint themselves with the world of science, hitherto demarcated as male territory. The history of science shows how it has always been a 'male' discipline of study, and women have been conditioned to believing that it is too difficult a pursuit for them. Susanne Sheffield (2006) discusses how men did not include women in the worldview of science 'as a method of investigating the physical world through experimentation, mathematics, and correct reasoning, all reported in an impersonal manner' because of 'the "natural" character of women, which they believed was irrational, emotional, spiritual, and lacking intellectual rigor' (3). Yet, when Sultana asks Sister Sara, how she manages her hobby of embroidery along with her office work, Sara replies rather casually, 'I do not stick to the laboratory all day long. I finish my work in two hours' (Bagchi 2005: 6).

The capital city of Ladyland has two universities where a number of women scientists are engaged in constant scientific research, while the men of the country are busy with military activity. Rokeya perhaps suggests here that men have often used science for military purposes, to create destructive tools, but in the hands of women science ceases to remain the proverbial Frankenstein's monster and becomes the means of developing sustainable well-being. Rokeya, however, complicates the situation further, when the men cannot win the war by themselves, the principal of one of the women's universities along with her two thousand students marches to the battlefield, and 'directed all the rays of the concentrated sunlight and heat towards the enemy' (ibid.: 10). In effect, what the author presents is a race of women, educated and adept in the ways of science, who can use solar energy to both cook food and burn down enemies, if need be. The women have revolutionized transport in the utopian nation, by employing electricity to 'aerial conveyances' and have invented unique measures of harvesting rain-water. Partha Chatterjee has elaborated on how a nationalist imagination divides culture into the spiritual and the material, the 'home' and the 'world', and how the spiritual domain is always inhabited by the woman. But when Sultana asks Sara about the religious practices of the women of Ladyland, Sara tells her that they have no organized religion. Most of their time is spent in honing their science and making nature 'yield as much as she can' (ibid.: 12).

Rokeya's Bengali novella *Padmarag* (The Ruby) (1924) takes the idea of women's education further and creates representations of women as 'agents of social and educational change', according to Barnita Bagchi (2005). Rokeya's administrative and political work has largely been local in nature, just as she preferred to write in Bengali, she based most of her work with Bengal as the centre. *Padmarag* presents an educational and philanthropic utopia. At the centre is Dina-Tarini Sen, a Brahmo woman who runs an institution by the name of Tarini Bhavan. Dina-Tarini is ostracised by the mainstream society for her choice of work. Adult women with tragic pasts of domestic violence or oppression come together at Tarini Bhavan and undertake teaching and other administrative activities related to the school. We can only imagine how Rokeya's own experiences of struggles and successes as a school administrator must have seeped into this narrative about the collaborative efforts put in by a motley group of women to found and run a school. Interestingly, she locates this institution as a space that clearly isolates itself from both the ruling classes—the colonial administration and the native elite that had declared its allegiance to the colonial authority:

> The school did without financial assistance from the govern-
> ment. It was, therefore, under no obligation to include the
> 'government-approved' syllabus.… The students were not forced
> to memorise misleading versions of history and end up despising
> themselves and their fellow Indians…. Special care was taken to
> ensure that handouts were not accepted from the ruling aristoc-
> racy of native Indian states that had declared their allegiance to
> the British empire (Bagchi 2005: 30–31).

I read this gesture as indicating an attempt to free the women's education movement from both the traditional and the colonial ideological inflections. It also points to the author's understanding of the situation of women in colonial India as doubly colonized, fractured subjectivities. The only way to emancipation and liberty is indicated by her in the productive alliances that women can form with other women.

The women inmates of this organization have seen it all—cruel and cunning husbands and in-laws, indifferent parents and scheming relatives and unscrupulous zamindars who have no qualms about duping the women of their property and inheritance. And Tarini Bhavan, their refuge, has a school, a workshop, and a home for the destitute. The school again has both boarders and day-scholars. Some of the inhabitants are called 'sisters' which has the spiritual associations of nuns. A mysterious woman, Siddika/Zainab/Padmarag enters this framework, and Rokeya keeps the readers guessing about her real identity. She is abandoned by her husband due to a misunderstanding. Siddika is not trained in any of the activities the other inhabitants of Tarini Bhavan engage in, but with time, she develops into a strong, independent woman. The novel ends with Siddika rejecting domestic harmony in favour of working for underprivileged women of her community. Interspersed with romance, melodrama and disasters, the novella thrives on coincidences.

Rokeya, an educator and administrator of a school herself, saw emancipation of female colonial subjects as the aim of education. Education is seen as an enabling force for women not just within the private space of domesticity but beyond the thresholds into the public sphere of politics and unrestricted communal life. She creates here a self-sustaining collective of women who survive the injustices of their past by symbiotically gaining comfort from one another. In these female spaces that Rokeya creates in both her works discussed above, the characters break away from social seclusion and communicate with the whole wide world. Again and again, she lashes back at the Islamic system of strict maintenance of purdah, which inevitably secludes women from outsider males, and results in the fracturing of the domestic space into zenana and mardana. In *Sultana's Dream*, Sultana reaches Ladyland, where men are in seclusion and women can walk freely on the streets and in *Padmarag*, Siddika breaks away from the patriarchal structures of power and seeks refuge at Tarini Bhavan, a sanctuary of and for women. The narratives of the inmates—the stories that they tell one another about their past—in *Padmarag* combine comic elements with pathos. The pun hinging on the word '*biye* fail' (where 'biye' is both 'marriage' in Bengali and 'BA', the college-leaving degree) is a clever construction, which plays on the possibilities open to the women. Again, the utopian Tarini Bhavan, is 'a realm of highly syncretic spiritualism with respect for and images drawn from all religions.... Thus, we are introduced to the Brahmo and Hindu women of Tarini Bhavan with whom Siddika [the heroine] instinctively seeks refuge' (ibid.: xviii–xix). The movement here is towards a larger community of women (Sakina, Saudamini and Helen Horace) seeking emancipation through education and agency in the public sphere.

These are not isolated incidents in the literary productions of Rokeya Sakhawat Hossain. The activities of the Bengal chapter of Anjuman-e-Khawatin-e-Islam (Muslim Women's Association) were, as Jahan (1988) notes, 'Related directly to disadvantaged poor women. It offered financial assistance to poor widows, rescued and sheltered battered wives, helped poor families to marry their daughters, and above all helped poor women to achieve literacy' (42). Towards the end of the nineteenth century, such *anjumans* set up by Muslim social workers and *samitis* set up by Brahmo/Hindu reformers were working for the social and legal rights of women. Rokeya, along with the sisters Sarala Ray (1861–1946) and Abala Bose (1864–1951),[1] was also part of the Bengal Women's Education League (BWEL). The league convened the Bengal Educational Conference from 16 to 19 April, 1927, and in this conference Rokeya spoke on the scope of curriculum in primary schools. Two other notable national organizations of the same nature were Women's Indian Organization formed in 1917, and All India Women's Conference formed in 1927 and led by the Indian National Congress. The All India Women's Conference session of 1932 held in Lucknow passed a resolution in favour of Muslim girls' education. The legal rights of the woman was a central issue at this time and women's rights to divorce, and to inherit and control property were being discussed and debated with great fervour. In this context, Rokeya Sakhawat Hossain is a pioneering voice, a precursor of a more organized movement seeking answers to these raging contemporary questions, and a tireless fighter against such debilitating practices as purdah, polygamy and other social evils afflicting especially the Muslim woman. In an article in *The Mussalman* (5 March 1931), Rokeya writes,

> The future of India lies in its girls. The development of its educational system on proper lines is therefore a question of permanent importance. Although India must learn many lessons from the West, to impose on it the western system without modifications to make it suitable to us is a huge mistake (Hossain 2008: 506).

In Rokeya, we hear the articulate voice of a woman educator, protesting against both conservative Indian nationalists and the hegemonic colonial power. In her allegorical political essays, 'Gyan-phal' (The Fruit of Knowledge) and 'Mukti-phal' (The Fruit of Liberty) (both essays included in Hossain 2008), Rokeya draws vital connections between women's education, women's agency and political freedom. In 'The Fruit of Liberty', a mother is cursed for not treating her daughters as equals to her sons. In both these anti-colonial, anti-imperial works, the production and consumption of knowledge are seen as much of a female enterprises as a male vocation, and a way of destabilising the monoliths of both patriarchy and colonialism.

Rokeya's writings and her career as an educationist and school administrator are proof of her anti-patriarchal and anti-colonial ideology. The characters in her fiction (especially in *Padmarag*) are drawn from various religious and social backgrounds, and so were Rokeya's associates and fellow activists—Sarala Ray and Abala Bose, for instance. Her syncretic secular vision is the only way she could have challenged the restrictions that a country of various religious faiths can impose, especially on a woman from a minority religious background. Both West Bengal and erstwhile East Bengal, now Bangladesh, celebrate the legacy left behind by this visionary woman. On 9 December, people of Bangladesh commemorate 'Begum

Rokeya Day' in memory of this versatile woman educationist and writer.

I conclude by coming back to the point where I had started. Mir Monaz Haque (2011) writes about Rokeya Sakhawat Hossain's role in the history of women's education:

> As is often the case, feminist literature is used many times by male leaders not to advance women's causes but to unite both sexes against colonial and imperialistic powers. Unfortunately for women, when their country gains independence and the society reinstates its traditions, their interests once again get relegated to the background. Subsequently, gender oppression, already present in customs, is reinforced.

One can detect here the parallels of the discussion of the problem of women reformers and advocates of women's education of colonial Bengal being inscribed in the new patriarchy of a revivalist nationalist discourse. Someone such as Rokeya is seen as a social activist, divorced from the public and male world of politics. This division between the 'social' and the 'political' is itself located within an alienating gendered discourse. Men and women were designated different spaces of activity; the public world of politics is the reserve of the man and the woman is denied access into this exclusive male realm of politics. The truism of this rather simple equation is questioned when we narrate the life of Rokeya, or when we analyse her written works.

Reading Rokeya's life and works closely and unearthing connections among female activists scattered throughout colonial India is part of the South Asian feminist project of 'writing women back into history'. Eminent feminist scholars such as Bharati Ray (2002) and Barnita Bagchi (2009) have negotiated the various strands of identities that combine in this versatile woman, Rokeya Sakhawat Hossain. An examination of Rokeya Sakhawat Hossain's oeuvre and her life proves to us that the agency of elite colonial Bengali women was more complex and multilayered than what is encoded in the postcolonial readings of the inner/outer binaries, and their work cannot be just relegated to the realm of 'social work'. The insights gleaned

56 *Somdatta Bhattacharya*

from the fictional and non-fictional writings of Rokeya on women's education reveal how the 'woman's question' in nineteenth-century India had a life beyond the tussle between imperial British hegemony and masculinist native nationalism.

## NOTE

[1] Daughters of Brahmo reformer Durga Mohan Das, both Sarala Ray and Abala Bose played significant roles in the furthering the cause of women's education in colonial Bengal. Ray set up a school for girls in Dhaka and Gokhale Memorial Girls' College in Calcutta. Abala Bose, an early feminist and wife of Sir Jagadish Chandra Bose, founded and led the Nari Shiksha Samiti. Both the sisters were leading lights of the Brahmo Balika Shikshalaya.

## REFERENCES

Bagchi, Barnita, ed. and trans. 2005. *Sultana's Dream and Padmarag: Two Feminist Utopias*, New Delhi: Penguin.

——. 2009. 'Towards Ladyland: Rokeya Sakhawat Hossain and the Movement for Women's Education in Bengal, c.1900–c.1932', *Pedagogica Historica* 45.6: 743–55.

Chatterjee, Partha. 1989. 'The Nationalist Resolution of the Women's Question', in *Recasting Women: Essays in Indian Colonial History*, edited by Kumkum Sangari and Sudesh Vaid, Delhi: Kali for Women: 233–53.

Haque, Mir Monaz. 2011. 'Begum Rokeya Sakhwat Hossain: A Pioneer of Women's Liberation Movement in Undivided India', *Bangladeshonline. de*, N.p., n.d. Web. 26 Dec. 2011.

Hossain, Rokeya Sakhawat. 2008. *Rokeya Rachanabali*, edited by Helaluddin Babar, Dhaka: Uttaran.

Jahan, Roushan.1988. *Sultana's Dream and Selections from The Secluded Ones*, New York: Feminist Press at the City University of New York, 1988.

Mishra, Yuthika. 2004. 'The Indian National Movement and Women's Issue: Century of Social Reforms 1850–1950', in *Encyclopaedia of*

*Women Studies: Women's Movements,* edited by S. Channa, Delhi: Cosmo Publications.

Ray, Bharati. 2002. *Early Feminists of Colonial India: Sarala Devi Chaudhurani and Rokeya Sakhawat Hossain,* Delhi: Oxford University Press, 2002.

Sarkar, Sumit. 1973. 'The Complexities of Young Bengal', *Nineteenth Century Studies* 4: 504–34.

Sheffield, Susan. 2006. *Women and Science: Social Impact and Interaction,* Rutgers: Rutgers University Press.

5

# Marathi Women Novelists and Colonial Modernity

## KASHIBAI KANITKAR AND INDIRABAI SAHASRABUDDHE

Meera Kosambi

THAT COLONIAL modernity assumed a variety of forms is self-evident. The relative nature of modernity is equally evident: what was considered 'modern' in a colony such as India was not necessarily modern in Britain, the mother country. Thus, although nineteenth-century Maharashtra's—and India's—route to modernity wended partly through a western-style education and English-language texts, some of these texts (especially novels) were hardly intrinsically modern or emancipatory; it was sometimes only a matter of interpretation.[1] Modernity lay arguably in the eye of the beholder—or rather, the reader.

The dissemination of English education, alongside other elements associated with British colonial rule, sparked off Maharashtra's social reform movement in the mid-nineteenth century; roughly two decades after the East India Company conquered the western part of the region.[2] Significantly, the reform movement

was constructed as an entirely male project, with women recon-
structed as passive recipients of ameliorative benefits (in terms of
marriage-related issues and education) gifted to them by reformist
men in confrontation with the conservative majority.

Although women were muted as far as the mainstream reform
discourse was concerned, a few literate and articulate women
deployed fiction and non-fiction writings in a manner that can be
collectively read as a women's parallel discourse, as I have argued
elsewhere (Kosambi 2012). These were individual initiatives rather
than a well-orchestrated movement. As iconic examples, I have
selected Kashibai Kanitkar, the first major woman writer in Marathi,
and Indirabai Sahasrabuddhe who belonged to the next generation
in terms of age and literary phase. A discussion of these two women
novelists raises several interesting issues—the articulation of a modern
sensibility, the value they placed on education, their urge to utilize
it for women's uplift, and their understanding of the concomitants
of education—which together formed their vision of a better future
for women. Also salient are their use of their contemporary male
reformist paradigm in literature as a launching pad and their gradual
development of an independent, feminist paradigm. My principal
argument in this article is that these women's gift to Marathi literature was the concept of gender equality promoted through the con-
duit of fiction. This is the form that 'colonial modernity', induced by
education, assumed in their case.

It must be noted that the gender-related social reform discourse
in Maharashtra emanated from the numerically small Brahmin community, mainly because it enjoyed multiple hegemony. This derived
from the ritually high status of Brahmins coupled with their pre-
colonial political and military supremacy and a traditional monopoly
of education (which was contained in sacred texts). Although some
of this dominance was lost under British rule, Brahmins retained
their social leadership role and interest in education. The other axis
of social reform was caste-related and less visible because of its focus
on the advancement of the lower castes.

A strong impulse for social reform was provided by the new
western-style education, with its in-built policy of nudging the students towards social critique that would prompt them to introspect

upon and rectify social inequities. As education was slow to develop among the non-Brahmin castes, the available written records— authored by both men and women—pertain only to the Brahmin community. This inevitably elitist slant introduced a limitation in terms of broader social change; but at the same time, the upper-caste influence percolated through the rest of the society. Such was also the case in most other regions of India.

The Brahmin dominance privileged gender-related concerns as the focus of social reform, because the community's customs related to women were very coercive, as for example, pre-pubertal marriage for girls, immediate post-pubertal consummation of marriage, and enforced widowhood. An additional and somewhat less embattled site of reform was women's education (Kosambi 2007). Traditional Indian education, which was religious and contained in ancient Sanskrit texts, was reserved solely for Brahmin men, the ritually sanctioned literati; not even Brahmin women could access it. The new, western-style education was secular in content and imparted in the vernaculars and in English. It was available—at least in theory—to all castes and both sexes, but its benefits accrued mostly to Brahmin men whose strict patriarchal norms barred women from it. Men's greatest moral anxiety stemmed from the possibility that education or even literacy would confer upon women the freedom to communicate with men outside the family circle, thus bypassing the strict family control. It was also feared that educated women would lay claim to a measure of equality with their husbands, and neglect the humdrum household chores.

Therefore a conservative backlash to the reformist attempt to promote women's education was quick. As a counter-attack on reformers and as a deterrent to women aspiring for an education, a number of popular plays (the only effective mass medium in a largely illiterate society) were scripted to parody educated, especially English-educated, women. Arguably the most popular of them was *Taruni-shikshan-natika* (A Short Play about Young Women's Education, 1886) which painted a gaudy picture of a few young formally educated women and their activities which would inevitably lead to disastrous consequences ranging from ill health to immoral doings. That the author, N. B. Kanitkar, was the uncle of Kashibai's reformer husband is an indication of the ideological tussle that occurred between the progressive and conservative factions within many extended families.

N. B. Kanitkar was by no means alone in articulating these views; other (male) playwrights and novelists essayed the same theme. But Kanitkar was the most influential because of his open support for the Marathi newspaper *Kesari* which was run by the militant nationalist B. G. Tilak and his promotion of its socially conservative agenda. *The Mahratta*, a similarly conservative sister paper of *Kesari*, advised men not to give their women an English education for fear they would pick up the 'immoral behaviour' including addiction to 'drink and other vices of the West' which Englishwomen were allegedly prone to.[3] For an unclear reason, the English authors who were repeatedly held up as undesirable in this context were Shakespeare, Scott, and Milton. As *Kesari* expostulated: 'If the study of Shakespeare and Scott is going to persuade our girls that everything done by their parents is unsuitable, unholy, and contrary to the *Shastras*, then the sooner Shakespeare and Scott disappear from our homes the better'.[4] But not all women writers knew English; some texts had percolated into their general knowledge through descriptions provided by their reformers, that is, their husbands. Again, the real inspiration to women writers came not necessarily solely from the English classics but also from other lesser known texts, and importantly from their lived experience which enabled sometimes surprising leaps of imagination.

Thus there were startling innovations from the rare nineteenth-century women writers who shared with other women the constricted, home-bound lives and obstacles placed in their stepping out into the public sphere. As Yashodabai Joshi (1985: 5) described it, 'The state of being among us women was that of caged parrots. The only difference was that our cage was somewhat larger than a parrot's...We did not even see the world beyond [our house].' Kashibai Kanitkar deploys the trope of the 'prison-house' to describe this domestic situation. Her most militant outburst against women's domestic suffocation (in 1889) was: 'Incarcerating us within the prison walls of social pressure, bolting and locking the doors, and keeping a strict watch are functions our people perform loyally.' But she follows this outburst with a visible exercise in self-control, realizing that 'we must swallow [our] words quickly before they reach anyone's ears for fear of committing "treason against men", just as our men are afraid of committing treason when they discuss the [British] government' (cited in Kosambi 2008: 70, 72). Kashibai was decades in advance of Indian women who deployed the metaphor of 'domestic colonization'.

Male reformers were aware of 'women's incarceration' and tried to ameliorate it without transgressing the patriarchal limits. Thus Dr. R. G. Bhandarkar defended the liberal agenda of Pune's Female High School in 1891 by saying: 'we do not propose in this institution to make our women learned and teach them to neglect their household duties and take to books. What we intend to do is to make them more fit to discharge those duties and to open a window in the prison-house of a social system through which they may look into the modern world.'[5]

Women's deliberate exclusion from the reform arena was emphasized as their destiny to live in submission. As *Kesari* warned Pandita Ramabai, the sole woman (among a galaxy of men) to appropriate a leadership role in the reform arena: 'In truth it is the task of men to eradicate the evil customs in our society. Women will not be able to interfere in it for many years to come, no matter if they are great *panditas* and have reached the ultimate stage of reform.'[6]

This social milieu renders spectacular the achievement of Kashibai and Indirabai in articulating their feminist agendas and conducting their own parallel social reform discourse through their fiction.

## KASHIBAI KANITKAR (1861–1948)

Kashibai's life reads like a history of the social reform movement.[7] In childhood she was denied an education she yearned for, because women's education was considered suspect, as already mentioned.

In accordance with the prevalent custom of child marriage, Kashibai was married early, at the age of nine. Her husband,

Govindrao Kanitkar, was a bright student with a literary bent and keen appreciation of beauty. His romantic dreams of marriage with a lovely and educated companion were shattered when the wife found for him by the family elders was the plain, dark-skinned, and illiterate Kashibai. He rejected her outright. Having understood that his relationship with her was contingent upon her education, Kashibai taught herself to read and write, with only sporadic help from this temperamental husband. Her efforts were crowned with such extraordinary success that she embarked upon a novel in the mid-1880s. But she was daunted by the superiority of the debut novel of her contemporary, Hari Narayan Apte, which was being serialized at the time. In his effort to encourage her, Govindrao requested Apte to boost her morale through letters. Thus began a sibling-like relationship between Kashibai and Apte which was immortalized in literary legend.

Govindrao had legal training and worked as a lower-level judge, but also displayed literary inclinations by writing poetry and translating into Marathi both *Hamlet* and J. S. Mill's *On the Subjection of Women*. The far-ranging discussions of Govindrao and Apte were a source of knowledge and inspiration for Kashibai who was well-read in Marathi, but had hardly any English. (Kashibai's presence at these discussions became generally known and was frowned upon.) Her increasing success as a writer was a source of pride and gratification to Govindrao, but seems gradually to have aroused spousal jealousy; unfortunately their later years were fraught.

Kashibai's literary career spanned several years and many genres including a biography of Anandibai Joshee, India's first woman doctor, two novels, a review of Pandita Ramabai's travelogue-journal of her sojourn in the USA, and various magazine articles. She started serializing her debut novel *Rangarao* in 1886, but it was disrupted with the demise of the magazine that published it. It was finally published as a book in 1903 (Kanitkar 1931). The novel shows a clear imprint of the male reformist paradigm in fiction (as popularized by H. N. Apte and others): it promotes women's education and late marriage, and even supports the idea of marriage by choice—the man's choice, not the woman's.

All these ideas are woven into the story of Rangarao's life as it unfolds from his childhood as the son of the chief of a small, semi-autonomous principality to his late twenties when he has served several years in the British army, having travelled abroad on duty and also visited England. (This hero was fondly modelled upon Kashibai's brother who was popularly known as 'Soldier Bapat'.)

In a parallel development Rangarao's former college friend Prabhakar educates his two younger sisters and defers their marriages beyond their puberty. This becomes a scandal in their town and the girls as well as their mother meet with public harassment. Unfortunately Kashibai is unable to show the two girls enjoying or imbibing their education and learning to think independently; they pine instead for husbands and marriage. Here we glimpse the author's internal tussle (which she seems to be unaware of) between idealism and realism. Prabhakar himself is consumed with anxiety about finding them husbands and focuses his hopes on Rangarao and his younger brother—to the extent of practically pleading with them—to rescue him from the predicament by marrying the girls (which they do).

There is also a subplot involving Rangarao's married sister and her marital harassment which almost claims her life, although somehow all ends well.

There are some (avoidable) tensions and inconsistencies in the novel, partly because of the hiatus between the first few chapters and its final completion, and partly because of Kashibai's ineptitude in handling the unnecessarily complex plot. The most conspicuous tension is located at the core of Rangarao's, that is, Kashibai's attitude to the colonial state, which was shared by many of her contemporary women. On one level it is perceived as a coercive, exploitative and discriminatory power; on another it is a liberating force for women (and the lower castes) from upper-caste male hegemony. Thus Rangarao grows up detesting the colonial state, but enlists in the British Indian army which is the only avenue for his craving for military exploits. He also valorizes the progressiveness of the British society later in the novel.

Interestingly, the most 'liberating' English text that enjoys centrality in the novel's reformist discussions is Jane Austen's *Pride and Prejudice* which formed part of the college curriculum and had obviously reached Kashibai via her husband. The character of Elizabeth Bennet, her independent views, and her uninhibited expression of those views, ending ultimately in a love match with Darcy, as well as the gender equality all this seemed to imply—these were a source of inspiration for the generation forced into arranged marriages. Rangarao even 'others' Indian society from the vantage point of British society as reflected in the then decades-old novel. Thus an amusing and rather narrowly focused narrative of English domesticity becomes—in an unlikely twist—an emancipatory force which opens, for Kashibai and her fictional characters, the doors of the strictly controlled experiential world of both men and women, and provides a glimpse of the freedom beyond which they aspire to reach out to.

Kashibai's second novel (Kanitkar 1928) *Palkhicha Gonda* started being serialized in 1913, was again interrupted for 15 years. This time a source of inspiration was possibly another English text; not a novel but an ideological text, namely, J. S. Mill's *On the Subjection of Women* (1869).

The novel starts as a playful story about the childhood of two girls: the first-person narrator Manu and her older sister Rewati or Tai. It takes a serious turn when twelve-year-old Tai is married to the scion of a princely state, in ignorance of his being mentally challenged. While finalizing the match Tai's parents have been deceived; their remorse at having ruined their daughter's life leads to their illness and death. But the enlightened Queen Regent encourages the disheartened Tai to receive an education from her older brother and has her crowned at a special durbar. Here again, as in *Rangarao*, Kashibai chooses the locale of a semi-autonomous enclave of an imaginary principality, not directly subject to British rule. Incidentally Manu accompanies her sibling and tries to rescue some of her old friends from their oppressive marriages and help rebuild their tattered lives.

Tai proves to be a liberal and just ruler, and introduces many radical reforms, especially to protect the rights of women. Her Mill-based liberal agenda privileges women's education and employment. All girls are to be educated as mandated by a state fiat, and either a son or a daughter can succeed to a deceased father's job. Also, all married women are entitled to their *stridhan*, or the jewellery given by their parents as a wedding gift (and traditionally appropriated by their marital family). Many women are appointed to key governmental positions. All this results in a utopian society of gender equality predicated upon equal education and employment opportunities. The short prefatory chapter, obviously added later (and absent in the novel's serialized beginning), shows this society in actual operation.

Having achieved her heart's desire, Tai withdraws from all royal and indeed worldly concerns to go in search of spiritual solace along with her husband, Manu, and their older brother. They leave the principality which she has renamed 'The Palanquin Tassel' because of her conviction that she has been a victim of her mother's ambition to achieve a brilliant match for her—by finding a groom wealthy enough to ride in palanquins. Tai has made the best of the situation by wielding power only to achieve the good of her subjects; not for its own sake. She and her siblings have always been detached from worldly advancement.

Kashibai's narrative is an emphatically inclusive, gender-egalitarian utopia (although the actual utopian content is relatively small) in contrast to the gender separatist utopias such as Rokeya Hossain's cheerful short story 'Sultana's Dream' (1905) (see also Chapter 4) which is the first generally acknowledged woman-authored text in this genre in India, or Charlotte Gilman Perkins' internationally known *Herland* (1915). However, as I have argued, 'all three converge at the point of culturally specific articulations of universally experienced feminist desires'. What remains a mystery, however, is how Kashibai conceived an idea of writing a utopia—however partial—considering that the genre did not exist in Marathi, not even in translation.

## INDIRABAI SAHASRABUDDHE (1894–1959)

The inter-generational social distance between Kashibai and Indirabai testifies to the degree of transition in western India. Indirabai was a college graduate, school teacher and headmistress, and enjoyed a companionate marriage. She even engaged in social activism with her husband, mainly during Dr. B. R. Ambedkar's campaign to open the main water tank at Mahad for the town's Dalits, thus crossing the caste divide. She wrote novels, literary pieces, and magazine articles.[8]

Indirabai's first novel *Godavari* (1917) was a close adaptation of the Tamil *Muthumeenakshi* by A. Madhaviah, the renowned Tamil social reformer, journalist, and writer.[9] It reads like a catalogue of various types of oppression that a Brahmin woman could suffer from childhood to young womanhood, and promotes reforms like girls' education, late marriage, and widow remarriage. Indirabai has made a faithful translation, but her skill lies in making the adaptation seem like an original Marathi narrative. Her second novel *Keval Dhyeyasathi* (For the Sake of an Ideal, 1924) was an adaptation of Grant Allen's *The Woman Who Did* (1895). Allen's novel had become controversial in England because it portrays a young woman teacher who lives with her lawyer friend without marrying him, and then, after his premature death, raises her posthumously born daughter single-handedly. Later, when the daughter turns against her unwed mother, the mother commits suicide. This rebellion (even if it failed in the long run) seems to have made a deep impact on Indirabai.

*Balutai Dhada Ghe* (Balutai, Heed This Lesson! 1931) was her third novel, and her first original one.[10] It came immediately on the heels of Kashibai's *The Palanquin Tassel*, and Indirabai's rebellion and militant demand for women's rights at once underscored the divergence of her trajectory from Kashibai's. The novels' protagonist and first-person narrator is Sonu, a young woman who has just finished school and hopes to marry Bhaskar, a friend in the neighbourhood. Bright but poor, he has embarked on medical studies and hopes to marry Sonu as soon as he completes his training and begins to practise medicine. But such a match cannot be allowed by Sonu's wealthy, ostensibly reformist but basically patriarchal father, Baba. Nor is he willing to wait any longer after discovering her small intimacies with Bhaskar—like holding hands and hugging. So Baba arranges a hasty marriage for her with the first wealthy groom he finds, the widower Tatyasaheb.

Sonu is emotionally committed to Bhaskar and finds the notion of another man as her husband not only repugnant but also adulterous. She tries to avoid physical intimacy with Tatyasaheb, until she is finally compelled to give in. But when Tatyasaheb accidentally discovers her intense feelings for Bhaskar, he takes the already pregnant Sonu back to her parents, disclaiming all responsibility. Sonu's parents are stunned, but she is convinced that she is right in refusing to put up with the 'slavery' of a husband who has been foisted upon her. She now tries to propagate through articles and public lectures her ideas promoting a free choice of marriage partner, women's right to divorce, and gender equality in general. When her pregnancy is far advanced, she is confined to the home and Baba brutally incarcerates her in the attic. Here her daughter, Balutai, is born. All through this ordeal, Sonu's only support comes from clandestine visits to the attic from her mother and younger brother, and the occasional, smuggled letter from Bhaskar who shares all her ideas. But after losing Sonu, Bhaskar migrates to Africa to practise medicine and marries an Indian nurse (who happens to be Sonu's friend and now rival).

Tatyasaheb belatedly accepts his daughter and brings her home; this forces Sonu to return to him for her sake and live as his wife, much against her will. But she feels suffocated, pines for Bhaskar, and soon falls seriously ill. She will not be alive to guide her daughter through life's problems, but has documented her entire struggle for women's rights, up to the moment of her early death, in a long letter addressed to her—a letter which, in fact, constitutes the novel. Bhaskar, on a visit to India, happens to meet Sonu on her deathbed and promises to convey the letter to Balutai.

This seemingly straightforward and compact core narrative is embellished with many details and twists in the plot to make it unnecessarily convoluted. But the author never loses sight of her militant feminist agenda and many of her pithy sayings are printed in a bold font, as was common at the time.

The two generations of women novelists discussed here show substantially different mindsets, sensibilities, and imaginaries. This was partly the result of circumstances. Kashibai's life was circumscribed by the normative value system of a conservative extended family, as was common for her contemporary women. Also, she had eked out time from her household responsibilities to educate herself in the face of family opposition. Thus she transcended the limits imposed by a constricted life and lack of formal education; and she eagerly seized every opportunity to broaden her mind. She made the best of the short periods of nuclear family living enabled by her husband's transferable job. There were family excursions to famous sites (such as Ellora and Daulatabad) which she skilfully introduced into *Rangarao*, along with her nationalistic commentary. Wide-ranging discussions, mainly literary, between her husband and H. N. Apte also expanded her literary horizons as well as general knowledge. She also culled information from her family members, especially her soldier brother. Significantly, such informative interludes occurred also in the lives of her contemporary women whose autobiographies are available.[11] But Kashibai's uniqueness lay in weaving them into progressive texts scripted with a literary flair. As she famously said: 'Every family, every home contains a novel; it only needs an observer to see it as one. Anyone who observes it from that perspective will be able to discern it' (ibid.: 181, author's translation).

Kashibai operated mainly within the liberal reformist agenda adopted by her contemporary male novelists. Her two novels promote girls' education so that they can share their husbands' interests after marriage, and postponing the age at marriage to ensure emotional compatibility. This is the romantic ideal that constitutes the happy ending of *Rangarao*. Some years later Kashibai progressed to the idea of a gender-egalitarian society, to be achieved through equal education and employment for women. The idea, however, coexists uneasily with the novel's diegetic reality of unhappy marriages and deserted wives hovering in the background—the reality which cannot be wished away in her utopian society. Significantly Manu frequently expresses her relief and happiness at her own single state in contrast to some of the unhappily married women around her.

Kashibai's second novel was published as late as in 1928, but was the product of a mindset largely formed in the 1880s. This heightens the contrast between her conciliatory tone and Indirabai's militancy in 1931. Neither of the novelists can be seen as a representative of her generation; both women were well ahead of their times. But Indirabai had the benefit of a formal education and women's accepted entry into the public sphere. Thus her agenda spelled outright feminist rebellion. Sonu's conversations with Bhaskar and Baba, as well as her public speeches deploy a language of entitlements. All girls are entitled to a good education to enable them to think independently and make their own choices. Their freedom of thought is to be accompanied by a freedom of action, especially as regards their choice of husband. Arranged marriages constitute 'slavery' given their asymmetrical nature; women coerced into arranged marriages should be set free by making legal provisions for divorce. That Bhaskar fully shares Sonu's ideas and supports her during their meetings and through his letters shows Indirabai's faith in the play by Narayan Bapuji Kanitkar, *Taruni-shikshana-natikaathava Adhunik Taruni-shikshanva Stri-swatantrya Yanche Bhavishya-kathan* (A Short Play about Young Women's Education, or Predicting the Future of Young Women's Education Women's Freedom). This depicts the existence of enlightened men who will help create such a gender-egalitarian society.

Within a few overlapping decades, both Kashibai and Indirabai embarked on a feminist quest: Sarojini Vaidya (1991). Kashibai couched hers in a half-romantic garb using a uniformly persuasive tone; Indirabai was forthright and blunt about her rebellion, and her style was frequently strident. Kashibai's vision of women's entitlements is broad enough to include education, employment, and economic security; but her women—with the exception of Tai, a ruler guided and assisted by her sibling—do not exercise agency. Indirabai's Sonu focuses her struggle on demanding agency for all women in matters touching their lives.

The major women fiction-writers who followed them took feminism for granted and shaped it in their own individual ways.[12] But undeniably their exposure to colonial modernity was mediated by English-language texts—both fiction and non-fiction, some overtly feminist and some ostensibly not amenable to a feminist interpretation. Interestingly the effect of these texts on men and women writers in Marathi was substantially different. Rarely did a man argue for gender equality; for women it was often the end objective. That is why the concept of gender equality was women's gift to Marathi literature. This arguably was the most impressive result of colonial modernity in women's fiction.

## NOTES

[1] The linguistically homogeneous state of Maharashtra was formed in 1960 by combining the Marathi-speaking districts of the former Bombay Presidency (later Bombay state), Nizam's dominions (or Hyderabad state), and Central Provinces and Berar.

[2] These were the dominions of the Peshwa (the Brahmin ruler defeated in 1818) and formed the core of the Bombay Presidency.

[3] *The Mahratta*, 26 July 1891.

[4] *Kesari*, 20 September 1887, my translation.

[5] *The Mahratta*, 11 October 1891.

[6] *Kesari*, 8 August, 1882, my translation.

[7] Kashibai's life and somewhat abridged writings including the two novels discussed here are presented in M. Kosambi, *Feminist Visions* (2007).

[8] This life-sketch and summary of Indirabai's novels is based on Prabha Ganorkar et al., eds, *Sankshipta Marathi Vangmaya-kosh, 1920–2003* (Abridged Encyclopedia of Marathi Literature) (2004): 713.

[9] The novel *Muthumeenakshi* was recently re-translated into English by Vasantha Surya (2005).

[10] *Balutai Dhada Ghe* (Balutai, Heed This Lesson!) 1931/2010; excerpts from the novel are included in M. Kosambi, *Women Writings Gender Marathi Fiction Before Independence* (2012): 127–46.

[11] For these women's autobiographies, see Kosambi, *Crossing Thresholds*.

[12] See Kosambi, ed. and tr, *Women Writing Gender* (2012).

## REFERENCES

Ganorkar, Prabha, et al., ed. 2004. *Sankshipta Marathi Vangmaya-kosh, 1920–2003* (Abridged Encyclopaedia of Marathi Literature), Mumbai: Bhatkal Foundation: 713.

Gilman, Charlotte Perkins. [1915] 1979. *Herland*, New York: Pantheon Books, 1979.

Hossain, Rokeya. [1905] 1993. 'Sultana's Dream', reproduced in Susie Tharu and K. Lalita, *Women Writing in India, 600 B.C. to the Present*, vol. 1, Delhi: Oxford University Press: 340–52.

Joshi, Yashodabai. [1965] 1985. *Amacha Jivan-pravas* (Our Life's Journey), Pune: Vinas (Venus) Prakashan: 5.

Kanitkar, Kashibai. [1903] 1931. *Rangarao*, 2nd ed. Pune, A.V. Patwardhan.

———. 1928. *Palkhicha Gonda* (The Palanquin Tassel), Pune: Ganesh Mahadevani Kampant.

Kanitkar, Narayan Bapuji. [1886] 1890. *Taruni-shikshana-natikaathava Adhunik Taruni-shikshanva Stri-swatantrya Yanche Bhavishya-kathan* (A Short Play about Young Women's Education, or Predicting the Future of Young Women's Education Women's Freedom), rev. 2nd ed., Pune: N.B. Kanitkar.

Kosambi, Meera. 2012. 'Introduction', in *Women Writing Gender: Marathi Fiction Before Independence*, Ranikhet: Permanent Black: 1–77.

———.2008. tr and ed. *Feminist Visions or 'Treason Against Men'?: Kashibai Kanitkar and the Engendering of Marathi Literature*, Ranikhet: Permanent Black: 70, 72.

———. 2007. 'Feminist Utopian Visions'. In *Crossing Thresholds*, Ranikhet: Permanent Black: 193.

———. 2007. 'A Window in the Prison-house: Women and Education in Colonial Western India'. In *Crossing Thresholds*, Ranikhet: Permanent Black: 151–71.

Madhviah, A. 2005. *Muthumeenakshi,* re-translated into English by Vasantha Surya, in *A. Madhviah: A Biography and a Novella*, Delhi: Oxford University Press: 121–86.

Sahasrabuddhe, Indirabai. [1931] 2010. *Balutai Dhada Ghe* (Balutai, Heed This Lesson!), Mumbai: Loka-vangmaya Griha.

Vaidya, Sarojini. 1991. *Shrimati Kashibai Kanitkar: Atmacharitraani Charitra (1861–1948)* (The Autobiography and Biography of Mrs. Kashibai Kanitkar), 2nd ed., Mumbai: Popular Prakashan, 1991.

# 6

## Mukta Salve

### THE EARLY EMERGENCE OF A PROTEST VOICE IN MID-NINETEENTH-CENTURY BOMBAY PRESIDENCY, 1855

Omprakash Manikrao Kamble

Aɴʏ ᴅᴇʙᴀᴛᴇ about a language has to begin by discussing the context and the politics which make the language debates crucial at a given point of time. Be it the national movement demanding independence for the country or the movements demanding separate states, language/s becomes significant in constructing identities and bringing people together. There have been discussions and debates about the dynamics of English as a colonial language, culture and baggage especially in the nineteenth and the twentieth centuries. These debates, interestingly, were getting carved out by the identities and the ideologies of the people. One such context is the mid-nineteenth century when people from the disadvantaged sections of India started voicing their protest against social hegemonies and demanding education, to be specific, English education.

This essay chooses to discuss this context by focusing on Mukta Salve's pioneering essay on the plight of Mahars and Mangs of the

Bombay Presidency, also referred to as western India. It examines Salve's essay as the point of reference to understand the discourse of education and hegemony that became instrumental in colonial modernity. Mukta Salve's essay stands for a significant point in the Dalit movement as well as for modern education in India, which along with it, brought in the different identities into the arena of colonial modernity. Voices and assertions heard through different means occupy a very important place in colonial modernity precisely because the boundaries of hierarchies that became fluid, giving rise to social, economic and cultural mobility by opening up the fields of education, religion, occupation and employment.

It is the thought of change and emancipation that brings the work and writings of some of the personalities in nineteenth-century Bombay Presidency to our consideration. Caste, gender, language, education and religion form a combination of issues that are closely interwoven by such pioneers. Mahatma Jotirao Phule (1827-1890)[1] divides society into Brahmins and Shudratishudras,[2] thus including women under the category of the Shudratishudras as the ones oppressed by religion. His reform brings caste, religion, gender, education and language together to negotiate modernity especially for the upliftment of the downtrodden. Similar is the case with Savitribai Phule (1831-1897) whose writings and work emphasize her commitment towards the issues of caste, gender and education.[3] Added to these is her call to lower-caste people to embrace English which, according to her, was the only means of emancipation and mobility for them. Mukta Salve, their student, is no different from her teachers in weaving these issues together. She laments over the plight of Dalit women, she questions God for making the lower castes religion-less and she interrogates the upper castes about their discriminatory attitudes. She calls out to her people to access education.

Such discussions provide very interesting clues to understand the formation of identities and associations in the times of history making: the nineteenth century, certainly, was making history with regard to the downtrodden people of India apart from the discourse of education and particularly English education. The mainstream nation-building was dealing with languages at one level, that is, English, as the colonial, masculine language of the world, and the regional language as a nationalist, feminine language of the home. But for the marginalized sections of India any language was much more political than what it meant to the mainstream. They did not have the choice to choose a language. Rather, languages chose them in rare cases and abandoned them, prohibited them and punished them in most instances. Hence, language for them was not just a linguistic issue or a nationalist issue but a caste issue as well as an issue of untouchability that was thrust on them for generations.

If we look at all social movements that are led by the backward and the marginalized communities, we find that they have emphasized the necessity and need of education for the downtrodden. The socio-political movement led by Mahatma Jotirao Phule in the mid-nineteenth century Bombay Presidency, and various other movements in different parts of the country have fought for the right to education, whereas the post-independent Dalit struggle is for equal opportunity in terms of education and employment.

In order to understand the emancipatory Dalit struggle in mid-nineteenth century Bombay Presidency, we must refer to history and analyse the socio-political developments during Jotirao Phule's time. Jotirao and Savitribai Phule began their mission of social emancipation of the Shudratishudras amidst socio-political, cultural and religious tensions. The Dalit communities were undergoing severe crisis in terms of poverty, untouchability, lack of education, superstition, violation of human rights, and so on, underwritten by *varnashramdharma*,[4] Bombay Presidency was grappling with severe crisis in terms of poverty, untouchability, lack of education, superstition, and severe oppression. Although the rule of the tyrannical Peshwas had ended with the British defeat of the Maratha Confederacy in 1818, the roots of caste prejudice implanted by the upper castes remained intact.

Mahatma Phule viewed education from the point of view of emancipation for the Shudratishudras and women. He emphasized the importance of primary education and asserted that education was the first step towards social revolution. He firmly believed that the lower castes had the motivation to educate themselves and that they would definitely join the struggle for their emancipation if they were educated. He states, 'Without education wisdom was lost; without wisdom morals were lost; without morals development was lost; without development wealth was lost; without wealth the Shudras were ruined; so much has happened through lack of education.'[5]

The colonial government brought in social reforms in India that did not impact adversely on their political control of the empire. They were not concerned with the hierarchical Indian social system. Some of the missionaries[6] did their best to promote social reforms, but their early attempts of improving the living conditions of the downtrodden were foiled by the dominant caste Hindus as they opposed and condemned the efforts of the British government. The Brahmins were particularly highly critical of the reform agenda of the British and therefore they held and spread the view that 'the colonial government wanted to defile and malign the religious sanctity of the Hindu religion by interfering in their religious matters' (Chole 2000: 24, trans. mine).

Many misconceptions were created by the so-called sanatani/ orthodox Brahmins in order to prevent the Shudratishudras from seeking education. They outrightly declared that only Brahmins should seek education and not the people belonging to the Shudratishudra communities. They did not have the right to do so. Their rigid notions about purity and pollution did not allow others, those who were 'othered' by the varna system, to access education. Taking education in a Christian missionary school was a daunting task for the upper castes. They were very much afraid of the touch of the Shudratishudras.

It is a fact that the social reform movement in nineteenth-century India was led by the upper-caste reformers. There were many who transgressed the boundaries of caste, class and religion by leading movements, by marrying out of caste and by ignoring religion and by converting into other belief systems, be it Brahmo Samaj or Christianity.[7] There were some Brahmins with a reform-ist agenda who supported educational and social cause of the Shudratishudras in western India; for instance, the early reforms in India were all made by the Brahmins, that is, anti-sati move-ment led by Raja Rammohan Roy, a Brahmin who later founded the Brahmo Samaj (1813); and the 1856 widow Remarriage Act by Vidyasagar who was also a Brahmin leading from the front. There were also some Brahmins in the education programme thought up for girls from the mid-nineteenth century. For instance, Jagganath Sadashivji, and Vinayak Bapuji, both were clerks in the Public Works Department, helped Phule in his educational endeavour. Keshav Shivram Bhavalkar taught Savitribai Phule; references of these facts can be found in history. Dadoba Pandurang Tarkhadkar inspected Mahatma and Savitribai Phule school and expressed satisfaction. He was the president of Paramhansa education institute. Bhavalkar, Govande, Walvekar, Karve, Bhandarkar, all established and ran the Paramhansa branch in Poona whose president was Jotiba Phule (Narke 2008: 406).

However, the savarnas who opposed the reform concerning caste and religion were also vociferous as such reforms could drastically affect the preservation of strict *chaturvarnya* system. Brahmanical ideologies linked each and every incident with the religious sanctions of the Hindus, thereby opposing every move of social reform in colonial India. Mahatma Jotirao Phule critically and keenly observed the colonial government and its activities and after a thorough analysis Phule came to the conclusion that the colonial government would do something good for the people.

Phule, who established the first school in all of India for Shudratishudras in 1848 and another school for girls of all castes in 1851, fearlessly expressed his views in his writings. His *Gulamgiri* (Slavery) compares the condition of Shudratishudras with that of 'Negros' in America and dedicates the book to' the Good People of the United States as token of admiration for their Sublime Disinterest and Self sacrificing devotion to the cause of Negro Slavery' hoping that his country people will take this example in the emancipation of their Shudra brothers from the trammel of Brahmin thralldom. He includes women and the castes ranked lower in the caste system including peasant cultivators, labourers, serfs and artisans in the category of shudratishudras. On the cover page of his book *Gulamgiri* is written in capitals ('in this civilized British government under the cloak of Brahmanism exposed by Jotirao Govindraw Fule'). The words he has chosen to use reveal his stand. That he thought the British government was civilized when compared to Brahmanism. Also, he chose to use the word 'expose' rather than 'write' was also strategic.

The Preface of his book *Gulamgiri* is in English and the book is in Marathi. He uses both the languages and decides which language is to be used where. Choice of language becomes one of his tools to counter the caste hegemony. Language becomes an ideology, be it Marathi or English for Phule like it is for the identity movements that were witnessed later. Phule's observations and objections about education can be broadly divided into two, that is, about lack of education and the kind of education that was offered. He emphasized the critical and liberatory education which could dehegemonize knowledge and make it accessible to everyone.

Western India witnessed a severe blow when a certain orthodox section of Brahmins strictly opposed English education and the missionary schools in India as Brahmin boys and girls opposed sitting together with the lower castes in the missionary schools. Phule took a serious note of this fact and resolved himself to start schools for the downtrodden people. Phule wrote categorically to the Hunter Commission, 'The missionary schools, although some of them are very efficiently conducted, do not succeed so well in their results nor do they attract half the number of students' (ibid.: 407).

Although there were a few attempts by the colonial government to establish English-medium schools, they failed miserably in addressing and handling the question of the lower castes. Therefore Jotirao Phule advocated the need to have schools run by their own people, that is, by the downtrodden themselves. By taking initiative in this regard he started schools for the downtrodden for the first time in Pune. Phule comments, 'About 25 years ago, the missionaries had established a female school at Pune but no indigenous school for girls existed at that time. I, therefore, was induced about the year 1848 to establish such schools, and in which I and my wife worked together for many years' (ibid.).

Savitribai Phule faced severe antagonism from the traditional Hindus when she began teaching in the school. They prevented, protested and troubled her. Savitribai underwent severe criticism for her educational attempts for the Shudratishudras. Despite all odds, Savitribai resolved to educate the women and Shudratishudras, taking it as a challenge. A new way of life ushered in western India due to the spread of education and the lower castes got an opportunity to access education to a great extent. In addition to basic Marathi education the lower castes took up basic English education as well.[8] Savitribai appreciated the English language and the English education through her poems and songs. In one of her poems from the collection 'Shreshta Dhan'[9] she valorized English as,

> O Mother English!
> You've offered water to the shudras
> And thus quenched their thirst.
> O Mother English!
> You've broken the animality
> And offered humanity to the Shudras.

> (Ugle 2007: 6, trans. mine)

A fourteen-year-old girl Mukta Salve, who had studied only up to third standard, wrote an essay about the pain and suffering of the Mangs and Mahars, *Mang-Maharanchya Dukkha Wishayi Nibandha*[10] in 1855. This essay was highly praised and appreciated for its intellectual quality and thoughtfulness by the British. This essay has paved the way for the Dalit writings in India today. In this highly philosophical and thought-provoking essay Mukta talks about the pain and the sufferings of the Dalit communities in general and of the Dalit women in particular. Mukta rightly criticizes the Peshwa regime in Poona, she raised her voice against the oppressive *Puneri* culture. Mukta is highly critical of the Hindu religion, the Vedas and the Hindu ways of life. Through her influential essay in Marathi, Mukta not only presents the problems and the hardships of down-trodden people but she also suggests solutions. Mukta Salve's essay is rich in terms of the issues she raises regarding Dalits. This essay could also be looked through different dimensions and perspectives.

   I have looked at this particular essay from a social and political emancipatory point of view. This essay is Salve's revolt against the supremacy of orthodox Hindu society and its cultural practices. The socio-political background in which Mukta grew played a crucial role in her life. Mukta Salve was taught and trained by both Savitribai and Jotirao Phule, hence the cultivation of Mukta's mind happened in Phule's school at such a tender age. In the later phase of her life

Mukta turns out to be highly philosophical and thoughtful person because of the teachings she received at the school. Mukta learnt the lessons of self-respect, dignity, morality and self-confidence at the school level. The education and the knowledge Mukta got was not confined to the four walls of the school, but it was 'education for life', the education was social, political, cultural and historical in nature. Keeping in mind the socio-political context at that time, we can say for sure that Mukta Salve was not only the product of Jotirao and Savitribai Phule's school, but she is the real representative of the entire Shudratishudra communities in western India. In her essay Mukta comes down heavily on the Brahmins; she says, 'The Brahmins think that the Vedas[11] are their inherent property and nobody should read them except them. If at all some Shudra try reading them he would be killed or given harsh punishment' (Meshram 2010: 11).

Mukta Salve's statement recalls a thousand years of suppression of the downtrodden by the upper castes. It reminds us of the tyrannical, unjust, unequal social system of the mid-nineteenth century. Mukta criticizes the whole idea of believing in a religion. She affirms that 'since there is no place for the lower castes in Hindu religion what is the point to be there?' Moving on, Mukta questions God as she inquires, 'The Brahmins behave as per the Vedic religion, the Christians as per the Bible if so then as per what we should behave since we do not know our religion? What is our religion O God? Which religious text should we follow? If the Vedas have come from God, the almighty, then why do only the Brahmins hegemonize them? This is really ridiculous and therefore surprising; even talking about this is a matter of shame! (ibid.)

Mukta lost her faith in 'religion' hence she condemned it. She further mentions the fallacy of religion. From Mukta Salve's powerful and assertive statements we get clear evidence of the fact that Mukta was troubled and tortured by religious bigotry therefore she wanted to set religion aside. Talking about the question of education and employment, Mukta opines that, 'Taking education or pursuing studies was an uphill task for us during the Peshwa regime in Poona. We were treated worse than animals; we were helpless, nobody saved us. If any Mang or Mahar tried to stroll near a gymnasium during the time, his head would be cut by the Peshwas. There was a complete ban on the lower castes to stroll around that area. These were the restrictions for us in Poona. Leave alone the question of education even listening to the Vedas was considered bad and therefore they declared it as a sin' (ibid.:12).

Mukta further argues that the question of employment was another major hurdle for the lower castes. The Peshwa strictly observed the purity-pollution rules.[12] The shadow of Mangs and Mahars was considered a bad omen; nobody wanted to give jobs. The ruthless behaviour of the upper castes psychologically troubled them. Nobody would be ready to give jobs and if there is no job from where and how shall the money come? Mukta admits that at every step on every move the Mangs-Mahars experienced torture and humiliation of various sorts; the low castes were living their lives in wretched conditions.

The tradition of Shudratishudra women's protest that began with Mukta Salve continued through Savitribai to Kumud Pawde.[13] All of them engaged with the issues of social, cultural and political hierarchies and argued vociferously that education was the means to change the social picture of this country. Kumud Pawde's thought-provoking semi-autobiographical essay 'The Story of My Sanskrit' has a similar tone like Mukta in terms of her struggle for education and identity formation. Pawde categorically states in her essay the opposition of the upper castes when she learnt Sanskrit. The point is that Sanskrit and the social group she came from were not acceptable to Indian elites (Pawde 1980: 96).

Just as Mukta Salve questioned and deeply probed the hegemony of the Vedas and the rigidity of the Hindu *Dharmashashtras,* Kumud Pawde also inquisitively asked her father regarding the sanctity of the Vedas and the purity of the *Shashtras.* She says, 'I used to ask my father, "what language are the Vedic mantras composed in?"' He would say, 'They are in Sanskrit, my girl.' 'Is Sanskrit very difficult? Can't we learn it?' My father always encouraged me saying, 'Why shouldn't we learn it?' In this way Kumud's father always encouraged, and motivated her to learn Sanskrit, but her neighbours discouraged her all the time. When Kumud wanted to do M.A., in Sanskrit, her neighbours, college lecturers and the lawyers laughed at her and humiliated her. When they taunted her, Kumud Pawde recollected Savitribai Phule and her relentless struggle for education amidst a highly brahminical, orthodox society.

Passing her examination in Sanskrit and obtaining an M.A. in Sanskrit did not help her getting a job; in order to get a job she had to acquire an additional M.A. in English. Here we can clearly see the politics of hegemony strongly working in terms of languages where English language dominates over a classical language like Sanskrit though it was considered superior at that point of time.

The status, dignity, and the importance of English language as such cannot be sidelined especially when it comes to the translation of any work from its original language to English. Whether it is Mukta Salve or Kumud Pawde or any other regional writer for that matter, when the work gets translated into English, automatically the writer comes into the limelight and gets known to the world.

Mukta was thankful to the British government for ruling India and for the social reforms they had bought in for the lower castes. She says, 'with the implementation of British rule in India the exploitation of the lower castes has stopped to some extent. The social restrictions on the lower castes imposed by the Hindus were lifted. The inhuman tradition of burying the Mangs and Mahars alive at the foundation of buildings has been stopped due to the intervention of the colonial government. The colonial modernity hence truly helped curbing economic exploitation of the lower castes. The Shudratishudras now can move freely in the market place' (Wankhede 2009: 47). This juxtaposition of tradition and British rule reminds one of the way Phule analyses the past and the present in terms of change and looks towards the future.

Mukta Salve writes precisely about the social reforms done by the British in her essay she says, 'All the atrocious acts/deeds were imposed forcibly on Shudratishudras by the Brahmins in the name of God such as burying the Mangs and Mahars alive (and dumping them later into the wells, killing the unborn infants in their mothers' wombs, and so on). All this was curbed due to the intervention of the British. The British government made stringent laws against the social restrictions imposed on the Mangs and Mahars.'[14]

The British mitigated some of the evils the Mangs and the Mahars faced daily. For instance, earlier the Brahmins used to physically harm Mangs and Mahars for no reason; they wanted them to live as they always had, for instance, if some Mang or Mahar wore new clothes, he was alleged to have it stolen from somewhere else, and put in prison, relating this with religious dogma. These inhuman, illogical, barbarous, and irrational deeds were stopped by the British. Mukta Salve therefore rightly remarked that due to the initiation and intervention of the British the Mangs and Mahars could exercise some sort of liberty in almost all walks of life. Mukta asserts at the same time despite all this (changes/acts made by the British) there is no change of heart or mind by the Brahmins; it must happen, hence further in her essay she urges God to give them logic and wisdom so that they would do good to the others at the same time she expressed her gratitude towards the British for showing broad-mindedness and generosity of mind, calling them brothers.

The question of English education was different for non-Dalit women compared to Dalit women such as Mukta Salve because of their different status altogether. English education started after the establishment of the British rule in western India. Through English education the upper castes progressed extensively in society. They started thinking differently or positively regarding English language or education. They believed that if their wives do not seek education they would remain illiterate and thus will be confined to the traditional ways of life and household chores. The prime aim of educating upper caste women was to maintain harmonious relations between men and women. The bhadralok, an upper class, composed of English educated upper castes, in Bengal were liberal regarding women education. They thought that the women would not raise voices against male patriarchy challenging varnashamdharma. Caste rebellion was not really on the rise; but gaining status through 'educated wives' was supported (Omvedt 1990: 9–10).

Famous feminist economist Veena Mazumdar analysed the harmony between husband and wife she remarked that 'education would not necessarily divert women from maintaining their domestic responsibilities; rather their status of being women/aaya (care taker) of the house increased resulting in strengthening their hold of traditional values because women are the best followers of norms'. Therefore Brahmin bhadralok emphasized educating their women because they knew that educating them would not make any difference; they would not raise voice against varnashamdharma or against patriarchy (ibid.: 10).

Many rumours and misconceptions in society regarding education and especially English education were propagated by the orthodox Brahmins. They blamed English people for defiling the Hindu religion with their interference. Rich and affluent people should not strive for education; rather they should enjoy their life luxuriously. They considered religious sanctions a standard, a norm or a parameter to measure everything, therefore, getting educated was considered lowly. They proclaimed that English education brought a bad name to their culture, region and religion. The upper castes deliberately spread this kind of thinking; their motive was to keep the Shudratishudras from knowledge, learning or education of any kind. To emphasize this more vividly Dhananjay Keer brilliantly quotes one of the poets and his beautiful poem in his biography on Mahatma Phule:

> What to do now, how to control these boys?
> Allowing them to go to their schools
> Would pollute/defile them.
> Their entire clan would get maligned
> That is for sure.

(Dhananjay Keer 2008: 13)[15]

Mukta admits that colonial modernity has helped the lower castes in many ways. It was people friendly, progressive in its outlook and in its social bearing as well. *Dnyanodaya* published the following statement after Mukta Salve's open reading of her essay in the school,[16] 'Jotiba Mali, the founder father of schools for low castes girls in Poona had this essay read out by Mukta that is an eye-opener to the orthodox Brahmins in Poona'. It further states 'Now we understood why the Peshwa immediately gave up after his defeat with the British. Now we also know how good the colonial government is for the lower castes.' Colonial modernity propagated values of equality, democracy and liberty in India and this has ushered in a lot of hope in the mind of the Atishudras (ibid.: 48).

It was only after the publication of Mukta Salve's essay in *Dnyonodaya* that people started to discuss openly the attitude of the upper castes towards the lower castes and Atishudras in Poona. Mukta's captivating essay opened up a debate among the British quarters in colonial India. They appreciated the efforts of Jotirao and Savitribai Phule in producing such a confident, daring student like Mukta Salve. Mukta's essay gave voice to the voiceless at that point of time in Poona. Her essay grabbed the common man's attention. Through her enlightening essay Mukta liberated the lower castes in India. Though the common man was not educated at that point in time Mukta's essay became so popular that reached in the nook and corner of the western Indian Shudratishudra society; rather it became the talk of the day, hence, got word of mouth publicity.

Mukta is critical of her own community as well. She points out that it is not only the Brahmins who observe the purity-pollution tandem on the basis of caste but also that this is observed by the lower castes. She says that the Mahars consider themselves superior to the Mangs therefore they hate them. They do not give their daughters to each other in marriage. This is true even today. In a very prophetic manner Mukta guides her community; she urges the Mangs and Mahars to come together under a common umbrella of 'unity'.

*Dnyanodaya* printed and published this essay on 15 February 1855. Mukta Salve aged fourteen, educated up to standard 3, wrote this essay. In Mukta Salve's essay the question of education precedes the question of English. Though it is true it is implicit from one of Mukta's demands to Major Thomas Candy when he felicitated her and wanted to reward her for her outstanding essay on the pain and sufferings of the Mangs and Mahars. Major Candy was the principal of Poona Sanskrit College (later known as Deccan College) and he was associated with early educational reforms in Poona (ibid.).

Waman Meshram clearly stated Mukta's views on education in his thought-provoking book *Mukti: Amhala Dharma Aaheka?* He reveals that Mukta proclaims, 'Sir, don't give us chocolates, but give us a library' (Meshram 2010: 40). This reveals that Mukta Salve was a staunch supporter of the English language, education and modernity in western India.

Mukta Salve is truly a role model and a source of inspiration for Dalit writers and for the Dalit writing that has been produced today. There is a remarkable difference between the then education scenario and now. One can imagine the educational efforts taken by Savitribai and Jyotiba Phule for the upliftment of the Shudratishudra in western India and Mukta Salve is one those students who was taught and trained by them, that too in such a caste-ridden society of that time. That a third-standard educated girl like Mukta could write such a powerful essay itself is a great achievement, given the socio-political turmoil that existed at that point of time.

Today the caste system is operational in society, but not so blatantly. Credit goes to the teaching and the education system which has produced highly conscious and sensitive students like Mukta Salve. Mukta breaks the hegemonized prose format of writing used by the upper castes by writing in a prosaic form and thereby posing a counter attack on them. This is something unique about Salve's essay. Mukta Salve gives a clear-cut evidence of her enormous talent and philosophical bent of mind through her essay. Salve has truly galvanized the entire Dalit discourse by writing this fascinating prose piece, introducing a liberation discourse in Marathi.

It would be apt to conclude this discussion on the text and the context that Mukta Salve represents with a few words from her text: 'Some noble souls have started schools for Mahars and Mangs, and such schools are supported by the merciful British government. O Mahars and Mangs, you are poor and sick. Only the medicine of knowledge will cure and heal you. It will take you away from wild beliefs and superstitions. You will become righteous and moral. It will stop exploitation. People who treat you like animals, will not dare do that anymore. So please work hard and study. Get educated and become good human beings.' These words clearly reveal how the modern education was the only available treatment for the poor and the sick who were treated and exploited like animals. The key to the transformation of the status of the Shudratishudras from animals to human beings, according to her, was in their efforts to gain knowledge by accessing education. She was not referring to 'Indian' education but to British education that was foreign to the Indian caste system in terms of its language, ideology and access.

NOTES

[1] Jotirao Phule (1827–1890), first modern thinker of the Bombay Presidency, father of social revolution; the champion of the Dalit cause; and the founder of Satyasodhak Samaj (Truth Seekers society) in Poona.

[2] Jotirao Phule used the term 'Shudratishudras' for the Shudra (today's OBCs) and the Atishudra (Dalit) communities who are the lowest castes in the caste hierarchy India. Broadly speaking, he included all the marginalized castes and classes, including women in this category.

[3] Poet, teacher, a staunch and ardent supporter of women's education, and a champion of women's cause in mid-nineteenth-century western India, an iron lady. She is the first women who fought and taught for girls education in Pune. She was also the wife of the great social emancipator Mahatma Jotirao Phule.

[4] Refers to the caste system that prescribed rules of the way of living through the different stages of life; also refers to the Vedic system of the goals of life. The social divisions and stages of life, one is encouraged to strive for a balance and harmony of all four goals and not to neglect one in favour of the other. Here used for the caste system that organized castes along a hierarchy with the 'most pure', the Brahmins, on the top, and the 'polluted', the Shudras at the bottom. The 'most polluted', the Atishudras, formed the fifth varna, apparently outside the caste system.

[5] Jotirao Phule, *Shetkaryaca Asud* (The Whipcord of the Cultivators), critiques the exploitation of the peasantry, Shudra and Atishudras by the joint alliance of the British and the Brahmin bureaucracy; Introduction, translated by Gail Omvedt and Bharat Patanakar. https://roundtableindia.co.in/index.php?option=com_content&view=article&id=2892:jotirao-phule-shetkaryaca-asud-introduction&catid=115:dalitbahujan-renaissance&Itemid=127 accessed on 30th April 2017.

[6] See for details 'Intellectuals and Society in Nineteenth-Century India' by Shanti S. Tangri. *Comparative Studies in Society and History,* vol. 3, 4 (July 1961): 368–94.

.7   See for details *History and the Making of a Modern Hindu Self* by
     Aparna Devare (New Delhi: Routledge, 2011).

8    See for related discussions, *Caste, Conflict and Ideology: Mahatma
     Jotirao Phule and Low Caste Protest in 19th Century Western India*, by
     Rosalind O'Hanlon (Cambridge: Cambridge University Press, 1985).

9    A collection of one of Savitribai Phule's poems meaning 'A supreme
     gift'; see M.G. Mali, ed. 1988. *Savitribai Phule Samagra Vangmaya*
     (The Complete Works of Savitribai Phule) (Mumbai: Maharashtra
     Rajya Sahitya ani Sanskruit Mandal).

10   Mang or Matang is a Dalit caste in western India. The Mangs originally
     belong to Nagavansha, an ancient race of North India. This race was a
     staunch follower of Shramanic religions like Jainism and Buddhism. We
     can trace the origin of the Mangs to the Indus Valley civilization; Mahars
     are an important social group within the same region. They are the war-
     rior' caste. There is a military regiment called the Mahar Battalion.

11   Vedas are a large body of texts originating in ancient India. They are
     composed in Vedic Sanskrit. According to Hindu tradition the Vedas
     are not of human agency; they are supposed to have been directly
     revealed and thus are called Shrutis, 'what is heard', distinguishing from
     the other religious text which are called Smritis, 'what is remembered'.
     Mukta Salve's essay *Mang-Maharanchya Dukkha Wishayi Nibandha*,
     published in 1855 is popularly known by the title 'Muktabai's essay'.
     According to some scholars her clan name was Salve; some other
     scholars remarked that in 1855 Mukta Salve was just eleven-years-old
     whereas some others stated she was fourteen-years-old when she wrote
     this essay; but the editor of *Dnyanodaya* mentioned her age fourteen in
     his editorial (Ugle 2009: 16).

12   The concept of purity play a crucial role in maintaining the required dis-
     tance between castes. In pollution the distance varies from caste to caste
     and from place to place. The superior caste tries to maintain their cere-
     monial purity. The notions of purity and pollution are critical to define
     and therefore difficult to understand as this term has different dimen-
     sions. This concept can be understood only in a particular context.

13   Kumud Pawde (18 November 1938) is a prolific thinker and Dalit
     writer. She has contributed enormously to Dalit society through her
     literary writings. *Antasphot* (1980) is her renowned prose piece through

which she has expressed her wider view of Dalit society. It has been translated into English and many other Indian languages.

14 See for a similar discussion see *Challenging The Rules(s) of Law: Colonialism, Criminology and Human Rights in India* edited by Kalpana Kannabiran and Ranbir Singh (New Delhi: SAGE).

15 *Dnyanodaya* published this poem in its issue 19 October 1848; Dhananjay Keer published it (2008): 13.

16 A Marathi periodical published in 1842 mainly for the purpose of the spread and dissemination of knowledge. Mukta Salve's essay *Mang-Maharanchya Dukkha Wishayi Nibandha, 1855* originally written by Mukta Salve in Marathi. The author has not found any translations of this essay in English; therefore he himself did the translations in English as required.

## REFERENCES

Bhole, Bhaskar Laxman. 1990. *Jyotirawanchi Samata Sankalpana*, Mumbai: Lokwangmay Gruha Publication.

Chole, Raosaheb. 2000. *Savitribai Streeratna Krantijyoti Phule*, Pune: *Shabdalaya* Publications.

Dangle, Arjun. 1992. *Poisoned Bread: Translations from Modern Marathi Dalit Literature,* Bombay: Orient Longman.

Dhananjay Keer, Malse, and Y. D. Phadke. 2006. *Mahatma Phule Samagra Vangmay,* Mumbai: Maharashtra Rajya Sahitya ani Sanskruti Mandal Publication.

Gail, Omvedt. 1990. *Jyotiba Phule Ani Stree – Mukticha Vichar,* Mumbai: Lokwangmay Gruha Publication.

Keer, Dhananjay. 2008. *Mahatma Jotirao Phule*, Mumbai: Popular Prakashan.

Meshram, Rekha, ed. 2010. *Mang-Maharanchya Dukkha Wishayi Nibandha,* Aurangabad: Saad Publication.

Narke, Hari, ed. 2008. *Mahatma Phule Sahitya ani Chalval,* Mumbai: Dr. Babasaheb Ambedkar, Mahatma Phule Ani Rajshree Shahu source material publications.

Nerurkar, P. S. 1996. *Phule Ambedkar Dalit Sahitya*, Pune: Sugawa Publications.

Pawde, Kumud. 1980. *Antasphot*, Aurangabad: Anand Publication.

Surwade Vijay, 2002. *Dr. Babasaheb Ambedkaranchi Nivadak Bhashane*, Part One (1920–36), Mumbai: Lokwangmay Gruha Publication.

Ugle, G.A. 2009. *Savitribai Phule: Biography and Criticism*, Aurangabad: Saket Publications.

Waman, Meshram. 2000. *Mukti (Liberation) Aamhala Dharma Aahe Kaya.?* Mukta Salve, Pune: Mulniwasi Publication Trust.

Wankhede, Chandrakant. 2011. *Matang Samajacha Waicharik Warasa*, Nagpur: Asmita Publications.

———. 2010. *Matang Samaj Vicharvedha*, Nagpur: Sandesh Publication.

ADDITIONAL READING

Deshpande, G.P. 2002. *Selected Writings of Jyotirao Phule*, New Delhi: Leftword Publication.

Dirks, Nicholas. 2001. *Castes of Mind: Colonialism and the Making of Modern India*, Princeton: Princeton University Press.

Ghantewad, Digamber. 2015. *Mang-Maharanchya Dukkha Wishayi Nibandha: Mukta Salve*, Cidco, Nanded: Prabhodhan Prakashan.

Hanlon, O' Rosalind. 1985. *Caste, Conflict and Ideology: Mahatma Phule and the Low Caste Protest in Nineteenth-Century Western India*, Hyderabad: Orient Longman.

Moon, Meenakshi. 2002. *Phule Ambedkari Stree Chalval*, Nagpur: Samata Publications.

Shinde, Tarabai, ed. 2009. *Stree-Purusha Tulana*. Vilas Khole, Pune: Pratima Publication.

Thombre, Tanaji. 1991. *Mahatma Phule Yanche Shaikshanik Karya*, Mumbai: Lokwangmaya Gruha Publication.

# 7

# Writing Self

## WRITING FOR OTHERS

Paromita Bose

THE ACT for abolition of the *devadasi* system, by virtue of which, young girls could not be dedicated to Hindu temples anymore, was passed by the Government of India in 1947. One of the most instrumental people behind this act being passed was Dr S. Muthulakshmi Reddi. Reddi was a doctor, legislator and social worker (see also Chapter 2). She was born to a devadasi mother. In her autobiographies titled, *My Experiences as a Legislator* (1931) and *Autobiography* (1964), she talks at length on the ill effects that this system has on society, the gradual regression in terms of health for the practitioners and the absolute necessity for its abolition. I look at these two texts within the framework of 'modernity' and English education and also her attempts to negotiate her position as a doctor and social worker vis-à-vis her identity as the daughter of a devadasi.

> I have been feeling all along and feeling most acutely too that it
> [the devadasi system] was a great piece of injustice, a great wrong,
> a violation of human rights, a practice highly revolting to our

higher nature to countenance, and to tolerate young innocent girls to be trained in the name of religion to lead an immoral life, to lead a life of promiscuity, a life leading to the disease of the mind and the body (Reddi 1964: 64).

Before I close, I will be failing in my duty if I do not record in writing my love and gratitude for those of my Western sisters who made our cause their own, have devoted themselves whole heartedly to the regeneration of the Indian people (Reddi 1931: 232).

Muthulakshmi Reddi graduated from the Madras Medical College in the year 1912. At a time when education was denied to women, she was one of the first women doctors in India who also possessed a brilliant academic record. Reddi went on to become the first woman legislator of India, when she was appointed into the Madras Legislative Council in 1927. Deeply influenced by Mahatma Gandhi and Dr. Annie Besant, she worked towards the welfare of women and children throughout her life. Reddi was the President of the All-India Women's Conference, the first chairperson of the State Social Welfare Board and the founder President of Women's Indian Association. She also began a Cancer Relief Fund and Hospital, the Adyar Cancer Institute and the Avvai Home, a home for destitute women and children. She wrote extensively on issues concerning women, health and children during her lifetime in several periodicals. She was awarded the Padma Bhushan for her service to the nation in 1956.

Reddi's first book (1931) recounts the major bills and resolutions passed during her time. The second gives a detailed account of her personal and professional life. Both the books are written in English. At a time when education was denied to women, Reddi not only spoke and wrote English fluently, but also in doing so set an example for several women to follow.

*My Experiences as a Legislator* begins with a dedication, 'to the loving memory of my late revered mother who was an example of piety, purity and truth'. In her opening chapter, 'How I became a Legislator', she mentions that she did not wish to take up the role of a legislator, owing to three main reasons: firstly, as she was a medical practitioner, she thought that the council work would interfere with her medical profession; secondly, she had just come back from England with a specialization in diseases concerning woman and children and wanted to concentrate on her profession rather than politics; and thirdly, she felt she did not have enough experience of public life. But as the Women's Association pleaded with her, she finally took up this responsibility. Muthulakshmi Reddi was instrumental in getting several legislations passed when she held office and the rest of the book analyses these bills. She was interested in issues concerning women and moved resolutions concerning social hygiene, towards the building of a children's hospital, exemption of fees for poor girls in schools, prevention of child marriage, and reservation of seats for women in municipalities and local boards. However, her main focus was on the situation of the devadasis.

The Anti-Nautch movement began in Madras in 1892. The movement was started by the Madras Christian Literary Association, which was led by Rev. J. Murdoch. He termed the devadasis as 'repulsive and immoral' and put both accomplished and common prostitutes on the same platform. They were also accused of impoverishing and ruining their patrons. A nautch performance was held for the welcome of the Prince of Wales in 1875. However, there was a huge outcry on the proposition of organizing a nautch performance during the visit of Prince Albert Victor in 1890. This crusade against the nautch performance was led by Rev. J. Murdoch who later on went on to publish extensively on Indian social reforms. In a pamphlet issued by The Christian Society, Madras, titled, 'Nautch Women: An Appeal to English Ladies on Behalf of Their Indian Sisters' brought out in 1893, the Christian Society advised the British ladies not to attend these parties and also prevent their men from doing so. Another pamphlet, 'Nautch—An Appeal to Educated Hindus' dealt with the evils associated with nautch like loss of money, disease, bodily weakness, bad influence on one's character, and so on. The only solution provided for the improvement of the society was the abolition of the system.

Social reformers from England took it upon themselves to persuade educated Indians from boycotting these performances. Miss Tennant and Mrs Marcus Fuller were some of the most influential amongst them, who condemned the dedication of girls to temples.

Mrs Fuller, the wife of a missionary in Bombay, wrote in her book *The Wrongs of Indian Womanhood* (cited in Chakravorty, *Bells of Change*, 44): 'We are convinced that if the highest officials in India were to refuse to attend nautches on moral grounds, their action would be an object lesson in moral education to the whole country. Hindu hosts would soon be ashamed and drop the nautch from the programs of their public entertainments'. Both of them also felt strongly that if the higher authorities stopped attending the nautch programmes, it would be a right lesson for other people to follow. As Neville remarks, 'She [Mrs. Fuller] reminded the reformers to keep knocking at the doors of the Viceregal Lodge till the Government took a policy decision against the viewing of the nautch. The persistent efforts of the reformers eventually bore fruit in 1905 when a decision was taken not to provide the nautch entertainment at the reception that was to be held in honour of the Prince of Wales in Madras' (Neville 2009: 121). Muthulakshmi Reddi was aware of these debates and the anti-devadasi movement gained momentum under her able guidance. In her resolution titled, 'Why Should the Devadasi Institution in the Hindu Temples Be Abolished?' she talks about the practice of dedicating girls or young women to temples as a slur on Indian womanhood and a great wrong done to the youth of the country. She advocates the abolition of the devadasi system and suggests that they should be given some land so that they could lead a life of respect thereafter. She blames the temple, religion and people for this 'immoral practice', for forcing children into the profession in the name of religion.

S. Anandhi (2009) quotes from a letter that Reddi had written to Mahatma Gandhi, regarding the devadasi issue.

> Having had the personal knowledge of this unfortunate community and having in the capacity of a medical woman come in contact with all the horrors of a prostitute's life… who would otherwise turn out to be legal and chaste wives and loving mothers and useful citizens… being forced by their dependants to sell their flesh to make out a living… I consider that the saving of even one girl's honour and purity is more than equivalent to the feeding of millions of our people (739).

Mahatma Gandhi in an article published in *Young India*, wrote in her support.

> I heartily endorse the writer's proposal. Indeed I do not think that the proposed legislation will be in advance of public opinion that is vocal and is against the retention of the system in any shape or form. The Devadasi system is a blot upon those who countenance it. It would have died long ago but for the supineness of the public. Public conscience in this country somehow or the other lies dormant. But if some active spirit like Dr. Reddi moves, that conscience is prepared to lend such support as indifferences can summon. I am therefore of opinion that Dr. Reddi's proposal is in no way premature. Such legislation might have been brought earlier. In any case I hope that she will receive the hearty support of all lovers of purity in religious and general social life (Reddi 1964: 68–69).

As Anandhi puts it,

> It was indeed the self image of the essentialised, patriarchal version of Hindu Indian womanhood that would be restored and asserted by abolishing the devadasi system. It was thus, not devadasis but the self image of the Hindu womanhood which was at stake because of the devadasi system. As part of her programme of domesticating and containing devadasis within monogamous familial norms, Muthulakshmi Reddi argued that they should be compulsorily married and those men who were willing to marry them should be encouraged with employment, etc. (740).

She was also of the opinion that since these women were unchaste and immoral, their opinion on the issue was of no consequence as they did not know what was correct or incorrect for them. In response to protests from the devadasi quarters she mentioned, 'As far as the local devadasis' protest, they are all a set of prostitutes, who have been set up by their keepers. How can the Government take cognisance of such a protest? So I would request you not to pay heed to such protests from the most objectionable class of people in society' (ibid.).

Muthulakshmi Reddi faced a lot of protests from the anti-abolitionists. The Devadasi Association of South India and the Madras Devadasi Association protested against such a move. Muthulakshmi Reddi was highly critical of all the counter activities by these anti-abolitionists. They made their stand clear by mentioning that the devadasis were 'a band of pure virgin devotees attached to the ancient Hindu temples. They used to preach religion like the other religious teachers to the common people that resort to the temples for their daily worship. In those days they were held in high esteem and were very well looked after. They would spend their time in doing religious service to the Gods and devotees of the temples as the word dasi signifies. They would follow the procession of Gods dressed in the simplest sanyasi garbs, singing pious hymns suitable to the occasion. This is the history and origin of devadasi.'[1] As Davesh Soneji (2010) mentions, the Madras Devadasis Association had put down twenty points which would strengthen their argument about why this resolution should not be passed. Some of which were that devadasis were not prostitutes, the real purpose of their caste was religion and service, the fundamental principle of their lives was service to God, that the entire community should not be punished for the fault of few, that it was their right to live. They were also of the opinion that what they needed more than the resolution was education and justice. They demanded religious, literary and artistic education which would help them regain back the same position as in the ancient times. It was difficult for them to imagine that at the time when the nation was stepping towards 'an advanced stage of civilization' these devadasis had to fight for their right to live. The devadasis believed that the interest of the country was greater than the interest of individuals and only education could help them attain this greater good. They were also scared of the fact their property rights would be affected as a result of this resolution. Devadasis had large grants of land which were given to them against the services they provided to the temples. This had been with them through generations. They were scared that once the resolution was passed these lands would be taken away from them. Their claim was that this land was a fruit of their honest services to the temple and hence the generations after them should have a right over it.

Another important opposition that Muthulakshmi Reddi faced was from Bangalore Nagarathnamma, a devadasi, who with several others moved to court in opposition saying that there was no relation between performing religious services and prostitution. Nagarathnamma in her resurrection of *Radhika Santwanam*, an eighteenth-century text, written by a courtesan, Muddupalani, had already faced severe criticism from the likes of Veeresalingam (1848–1919) who was considered to be the father of social reform in Southern India. He called the text and its contents obscene (see also Chapter 2). She insisted on the intrinsic value of the text and the skill of Muddupalani as an author, but faced a lot of opposition when she wanted to publish the book and later on fighting a ban that was imposed on the book. She felt that the devadasi system was being evaluated by the abolitionists from a standpoint of western religion and social practise and it was necessary to locate it within its own parameters and then try and reform it. While she did not disagree that some devadasis took to prostitution, and that prostitution was a problem that needed to be dealt with, with utmost priority, she was of the opinion shared with the Devadasi Association of South India, that the entire community should not be reprimanded for it. She was also of the opinion that the bill to abolish prostitution should punish the men responsible for it as well.

It might be of interest to us to note that Reddi's mother was a devadasi who had married an upper-caste Brahmin scholar. In the light of this fact then the dedication for the earlier book becomes very important and so does the fact that nowhere in the two autobiographies does she mention the fact that she was born to a devadasi. Epithets of purity, piety and truth are used for her mother when she is extremely dismissive of the devadasi community, and calls them immodest and unchaste. Apart from this the name of her father is also interestingly missing from both the books. Does it hence hint at the fact that Reddi was extremely caste- and class-conscious? That she is negating a certain past to create a new identity, an identity which is crafted only by her? She speaks very highly of her father, who is an educationist and is instrumental in getting Reddi educated. At the time when women were denied education, it was with the efforts of her father that she managed to study that far. Apart from this, it was her father who gave her lessons in English, something that she mentions in her *Autobiography* that won her several laurels. But at the same time, she speaks of her mother as severely orthodox, who was only concerned about her wedding. She uses terms like 'hysterical' for her mother, apart from complaining about the fact that she was always crying, thinking that she would never get married.

Amidst all this, Reddi's *Autobiography* comes across as a text of self pity. She emphasizes on the hurdles and challenges faced by her, whether it was in terms of her health, education, or even personal level. There are several instances when she talks about the problems she had to face because she had to move from one city to another, because she had to take care of ailing family members, because of the lack of money, and because of her ill health. Also there is constant insistence on the fact that at several occasions what she did and thought were right as opposed to what others felt. The text hence can be concluded to have been cleverly written, where only what was necessary to be published was published. The text brings out her identity as a medical practitioner first and then as a social worker. She was aware of the fact that she had made her mark as a medical practitioner and now wanted some recognition in the field of social work. Hence, in the latter part of her book she only talks about her achievements, perhaps thereby completely moving the focus away from her personal life, which was the main component of the first half of the autobiography. Hence, through this text she projects a certain persona, which might have helped her ideas and ideologies at a later stage. There is a lot of nostalgia surrounding this Hindu identity, where she harps on how things were done in her household in Puddukotah and how they were different in Madras But while constructing this identity nowhere does she mention the fact that she had a devadasi lineage. It is hence not surprising to note that it was this issue that caught her attention the most and she swore not to rest in peace till she had done away with this 'immoral and heinous' system. As Anandhi very rightly points out, Reddi's efforts to abolish the system through legislative intervention was premised on the perception that the devadasis were the 'other'—the unacceptable 'other'—of the ideal Hindu womanhood with its familial ideology.

Devadasi abolition hence stood for the restoration of the idealised womanhood.

The Madras Hindu Religious Endowment Act which was passed in 1926, which termed the institution of dancing girls as objectionable, was amended to alter the relationship between the devadasis and the temple in 1929. The Act mentioned in its objective, 'to discourage the dedication of girls as Devadasis for the service of Hindu temples by freeing lands, if any held by them for such service from the condition of service and making them owners thereof and thereby removing an important inducement for the perpetuation of a system of dedication.' The amendment proposed that 'The bill required that lands controlled by devadasis contingent upon their temple services be deeded over to them and detached from the service requirements. In cases where a devadasi was entitled to a portion of the revenue from land, she would continue to receive this income without being obligated to perform any service' (Jordan 2003: 132). The amendment was proposed by Dr Muthulakshmi Reddi whereby she proposed that

> none of the devadasis currently controlling land or receiving income from land shall be allowed to perform such service in such temple on and from the date on which the land in question shall have been enfranchised or freed from the condition of service in the manner herein before provided (Reddi 1930: 237).

She felt this system was immoral and vicious and the profession was carried out under the cloak of religion which gave it a legitimate standing in society. She was a strong believer of the fact that this system could not be done away with 'unless the educated section of the Hindu community enforces its will upon these backward people'. The Law Member Bahadur M. Krishnan Nair and Mr Satyamurthy criticized the amendment as it had a sweeping statement over the property of a large number of people. The conservatives felt that the devadasi system needed to be protected because it was essentially part of the indigenous Hindu/national culture and it needed to be protected under the colonial dominance. They were not as concerned about the actual state of the devadasis. Also, they felt that the devadasi was always left with the option of performing in any other temple but the one where she was assigned. Reddi took these and many other loopholes into consideration and redrafted it with the clause that the devadasi would receive revenue from land only till the time she is alive and after her death the revenue would revert back to the temple. The amendment was passed and became Act V of 1929.[2]

In January 1930, she presented 'A Bill to Prevent the Dedication of Women to Hindu Temples.'[3] The bill was circulated for public opinion by the government. The government was concerned that the bill might cause public disturbances. The clause that was added in the bill was pretty stern which mentioned that strict penalty and rigorous imprisonment would be granted to a person participating in the dedication of girls to temples. The inability of the government to take a firm decision quickly irked Muthulakshmi Reddi who protested by saying, 'It is beyond my comprehension how European officials coming from a cultured and civilised country could make up their minds to side with those who are for continuing the evil practice' (Reddi 1931). She felt that this bill was necessary to strengthen the amendments which had been introduced earlier by her. Once the voting was done on the legislation, thirty-three people voted for the bill and nine against it. However, as Vijaisri (2004: 245) mentions once the comments were received, the bill was not reconsidered in the Council as Muthulakshmi Reddi had resigned from her post as a protest against the arrest of Mahatma Gandhi on 8 May 1930. The Maharani of Travancore had abolished the devadasi system after having followed the extensive debates around it (Raghunandan 1995: 134–35) and so did the state of Cochin, as mentioned in the *Indian Social Reformer* (October 1930).

The devadasi question was embedded within the larger debate of modernity and Victorian puritanism. The movement was spearheaded by western educated Indian elites and Reddi, being among them and also a medical practitioner, found she was just doubly strengthened in her position on the debate. This framed her argument within the discourse of education and health and hygiene. Her training as a doctor strengthened her position as a social worker, and the English language made her interaction with the legal world easier. So, though her stance with regard to the devadasi system can be seen within the context of reform, it perhaps cannot be ruled out that her participation in the debate also had to do with her identity as the daughter of a devadasi.

## NOTES

[1] This was mentioned about the devadasis by Dr Annie Besant in one of her speeches which was later used by the Madras Devadasi Association to support their demands.

[2] The Act mentioned, 'Provided that where a grant of land has been made to dancing girls or devadasis for the performance of any service whatever in any temple, such inam land shall be enfranchised to the present holder thereof and she shall not be required to perform any service in the temple' (Reddi 1931: 237).

[3] By virtue of this Bill, dedication of Hindu women to temples was declared illegal, the dedicated women were encouraged to get married and there was a penalty assigned for people engaged in dedication of women to temples. 'My object in bringing in this Bill is twofold; firstly to have a law declaring that dedication of girls to Hindu temples is illegal and to prohibit such dedication; and secondly, to punish the persons taking part in the ceremony of dedication…. If the British Government in India have yet undertaken legislation on the point, it is probably out of a tender regard to alleged religious susceptibilities of Hindus. To show that public opinion is in favour of the abolition of the system, and in response to the appeal of several men and women's associations and hundreds of members of the community of Devadasis themselves I have brought forward the Bill' (Reddi, *My Experience as A Legislator*: 243–46).

## REFERENCES

Anandhi, S. 1991. 'Representing Devadasis: *Dasigal Mosavalai* as a Radical Text', *Economic and Political Weekly* 26, 11: 739–46. JSTOR. Web. 12 November 2009.

Chakravorty, Pallabi. 2008. *Bells of Change—Kathak Dance, Women and Modernity in India*, Kolkata: Seagull.

Jordan, Kay K. 2003. *From Sacred Servant to Profane Prostitute*, Delhi: Manohar.

Muddupalani. 2011. *Radhika Santwanam—The Appeasement of Radhika*. Translated by Sandhya Mulchandani, Delhi: Penguin.

Neville, Prem.2009. *Nautch Girls of the Raj*, Delhi: Penguin.

Raghunandan, Lakhsmi. 1995. *At the Turn of the Tide, The Life and Times of Maharani Setu Lakshmi Bayi: The Last Queen of Travancore*, Bangaluru: Maharani Setu Lakshmi Bayi Charitable Trust, Bangalore: 134–35.

Reddi, S. Muthulakshmi. 1964. *Autobiography*. Madras.

——. 1930. *My Experience as a Legislator*, Madras: Current Thought.

Soneji, Davesh, ed. 2010. *Bharatanatyam—A Reader*, Delhi: Oxford University Press.

Subramanyam, Lakshmi. 2001. *Cultural Behaviour and Personality*, New Delhi: Mittal Publications.

Tharu, Susie and K. Lalitha.1993; 1995. *Women Writing in India*, 2 vols, Delhi: Oxford University Press.

Vijaisri, P. 2004. Recasting the Devadasi: *Patterns of Sacred Prostitution in Colonial South India*, Delhi: Kanishka.

# 8

## Reconfiguring Boundaries

EDUCATION, MODERNITY AND CONJUGALITY IN
LALITHAMBIKA ANTHARJANAM'S *AGNISAKSHI*
AND ZEENUTH FUTEHALLY'S *ZOHRA*

Jinju S.

*Man's love is of man's life a thing apart,*
*'Tis woman's whole existence.*—Lord Byron, *Don Juan*

W HEN BYRON wrote these perennial lines early in the nineteenth
century, little could he have foreseen that centuries down the line,
whether or not man's love indeed is woman's whole existence would
still remain a hotly debated and controversial question. Even before
the propagation of feminist demarcations of sex and gender—the
former being defined biologically and the latter culturally—women
across cultures had started challenging the patriarchal hegemony,
directly or indirectly, vociferously or softly, no matter how far and
few between these diverse voices of protest were. One of the key
factors contributing to this gradual but definite upwelling was the
influence of education and, in the case of India, particularly English
education. This distinction has to be emphasized because in India,

in the initial stages at least, English education was largely at odds with a religious/traditional system of learning which was widely prevalent in our land. The education of women met with even stiffer resistance. In the words of Tanika Sarkar (2008: 320), it was considered 'a double repudiation of the husband', being associated with 'immorality and non-conjugality'.

I attempt to analyse critically the way education impacted the lives of women in pre-independence India of the twentieth century through a comparative study of the famous Malayalam novel *Agnisakshi* (1977) by Lalithambika Antharjanam (translated into English by Vasanthi Sankaranarayanan in 1980), and Zeeenuth Futehally's *Zohra* (1951); one of the earliest novels in English by an Indian Muslim woman. *Zohra* is a novel that, despite its pioneering status among Indian Muslim women's writing in English, has been the subject of very little academic study. Save for a 2013 article by Ambreen Hai (2013), there has not been any published scholarly work, excluding book reviews, that discusses the book in its own right. Hai elaborates further in a note to her article:

> Meenakshi Mukherjee briefly criticizes the novel's 'vague adolescent romanticism' (*Twice Born* 55) 'Gandhian idealism,' and 'sentimentality'. R. K. Kaul uses *Zohra* to provide a Muslim framework for Attia Hosain's 1961 novel *Sunlight on a Broken Column*, though the former is concerned with the very different cultures and histories of Hyderabad (in the south) and the latter with those of UP (in the north). Not one of the twenty essays on purdah in Jain and Amin's collection refers to Futehally. There is also no mention of her in histories of Indian English literature such as Iyengar's early magisterial volume or Gopal's excellent recent one, and only a glancing reference in Mehrotra (340).

*Agnisakshi*, on the other hand, has met with considerably more academic engagement from scholars like Jancy James and Meena Alexander, though in this case also the work has been looked at as part of the oeuvre of Antharjanam or Indian women's writing rather than as an exclusive subject of study.

These two works were selected because a comparative analysis of the two has never been attempted before, to the best of my knowledge. The predominant tendency in critical scholarship these days is to compare works with a similar socio-cultural framework to highlight overlapping themes and notable variances. Thus we have numerous studies on the aspect of Islamic feminism, Black feminism, Dalit feminism, Third-world/ Postcolonial feminism, and so on, in literary works. Though it is true that we cannot and should not think of Feminism in the singular if it is to accommodate the infinite heterogeneity of women's experiences, overlooking similarities that cut across regional and religious divides for the sake of emphasizing differences can also sometimes lead to simplistic formulations. This is one of the key motivating factors behind my decision to juxtapose two novels with Hyderabadi Muslim (*Zohra*) and Keralite Brahmin (*Agnisakshi*) female protagonists for the purpose of this study. Despite the spatial, temporal, religious and cultural disparities in setting, *Agnisakshi* and *Zohra* share vital commonalities in terms of a nascent feminist consciousness of the pre-independence era, women's education and women's participation in the Indian freedom struggle, which, I believe, deserve to be brought into focus and studied in detail.

Both novels are set in different geo-cultural locations albeit in the same time period, the turbulent 1920s and 1930s. Devaki, the protagonist of *Agnisakshi*, hails from a Namboodiri (Brahmins of Kerala) family while Zohra, the protagonist of the latter novel, is an upper-class Hyderabadi Muslim woman. Both are relatively well-educated, according to the standards of the time, and have an immense zeal for learning but their marriages pose as impediments in their quest for knowledge. The superstitious belief that educating a girl would lead to her early widowhood was rampant among Hindu families (Forbes 199: 33). Besides, it was feared that educating girls would make them more self-confident and assertive, and less pliant and malleable which, in the patriarchal hegemonic order, would only spell disaster for their marriage.

Zohra's education, though backed by the benevolent support of her father, Nawab Safdar Yar Jung, who feels that she has the potential to become a great scholar or a poet, is vehemently opposed by the women of her household, including her mother and the maids. According to her mother, Zubaida Begum, 'learned girls never settle down happily to domestic life. They pick up ideas from reading unsuitable novels and always think marriage and children can be delayed' (Futehally 1951:11). Zubaida Begum's concern is in tune with the widespread fear at the time that modern education posed a threat to the patriarchal marriage system which thrust women into inexorable, rigid and unbreakable gender roles—that of a wife, mother and daughter-in-law—at the cost of her own personal desires and ambitions. Academic pursuits, since they could not teach a girl how to manage a home, were deemed totally useless and a waste of time, and even an unnecessary taxation on the 'fragile' physical constitution of girls.

Zohra succumbs to the emotional manipulations of her parents and reluctantly agrees to an arranged marriage with a heavy heart. She understands that in the world she lives in, where marriage is considered to be the be-all and end-all of a girl's life, her dreams of nurturing her artistic and creative talents at Shantiniketan or joining Gandhiji in the Indian freedom movement are hardly feasible. Devaki of *Agnisakshi* has also received a liberal education at home from her elder brother P.K.P. Namboodiri, a revolutionary social reformer who is also a staunch champion of women's rights and a fearless crusader against untouchability. It is important to note that the championship of women's education in India during that time period is to be read alongside the growth of the Indian Nationalist movement which required enlightened women supporters to underscore its commitment to democracy, rationality and scientific progress. Under the leadership of Raja Rammohan Roy, there was a concerted effort from Indian leaders to propagate English education in India. In the words of H. R. James (1952: 14), there was 'a newfound desire on the part of the natives of India for a share in the knowledge and training which they discerned to be a large part of the secret of the superior efficiency of the nations from the West, and the source of what was strong and admirable in the English character'.

Devaki finds the transplantation from the progressive environment of her home to the extremely orthodox and stifling atmosphere of her in-laws' place unbearable. She complains to Thankam, her husband's cousin who loves her as his own sister, 'At my Illam, we used to get newspapers and magazines. The shelves there are stuffed with books....Here there is nothing to read except the *Ramayana* and the story of Sheelavathy' (Antharjanam 1980: 33). Sheelavathy is a mythological character, considered to be the epitome of wifely devotion, who was so steadfast in her commitment to her leprous husband that she would even carry him to the houses of prostitutes. It may be noted that the choice of such books which harped on the chastity and wifely duties of a woman, was not incidental but a deliberate though subtle tactic for the perpetuation of patriarchy.

As for Devaki's husband, Unni, he is a gentle and soft-spoken young man who, despite his deep love for his wife, cannot go against religious customs or the wishes of his family elders. He believes that 'for those who are born to the Brahmin caste, life is a prolonged penance' (1980: 66). His life is immersed in the performance of religious duties and the learning of Sanskrit and the scriptures. Religious/traditional learning is visibly accorded an elevated position and English viewed as 'the language of the inferior lot' (ibid.: 53). The orthodox families were yet to welcome the advent of English education, which they deemed to be immoral, and definitely subordinate in status to the 'divine' language of Sanskrit which was considered the highest repository of culture, civilization, religious tradition and learning. Aphan Namboodiri, the head of the family, tolerates Unni's younger brother being sent to school by his maternal uncle, only because he thinks it might be of use to the family in official and legal transactions.

A similar attitude towards traditional/religious knowledge can be seen in *Zohra* as well. Unnie, the old nurse, openly expresses her bafflement as to why Zohra should get modern education—'What is all this studying for? What do you want to do with foreign books? Is not our own knowledge enough for you?' (Futehally 1951: 2). Zubaida Begum is in favour of Zohra continuing her studies in Urdu and Arabic but not in the other subjects. Her husband, though, believes English to be essential as it is the gateway to modern thought. Besides, he points out that all educated young men want their wives to speak English like the memsahibs do (ibid.: 11). Once again, we see every single aspect of a girl's life being linked with her inevitable fate—marriage. Even the moulding of a new, modern, English-speaking woman had, as its end, becoming a source of pride for the husband.

In *Agnisakshi* too, we see this twist of irony. When Thankam's mother wants her daughter to be taught English and brought up in a sophisticated way, it is out of her motherly concern that she may not get a suitable bridegroom without some formal education. Though Thankam's father, the formidable Aphan Namboodiri of the Manampalli Mana, is very much averse to the idea, Unni succeeds in somewhat softening the former's stance.

It is pertinent to note at this point that Thankam is Aphan Namboodiri's daughter from a marriage with a Nair (Shudra) woman and hence is not bound to observe purdah unlike the Brahmin women such as Devaki who have to cover their faces with an umbrella made of palm leaves and be escorted by a maid-servant while going out. Strict purdah and gender segregation often limit the horizons of intellectual exploration and edification available to a woman, and it is no surprise that a Nair girl—who is not bound to observe purdah—going to school met with less resistance from the family and society than a Brahmin woman. One of the primary reforms that people like Devaki's brother, P. K. P. Namboodiri, was rallying for was the upliftment of Brahmin women and the removal of purdah. When the rumour reaches Devaki's in-laws that she had worn a saree and a blouse the last time she visited her own home, they are enraged and forcibly check her box for such items of clothing. The books and papers they find within are burnt in anger and Thankam reprimanded for supplying them to Devaki. The fear that modern education poisons people's minds against religion and tradition is manifested in this act. The belief that education compromised the purdah system and thereby the 'dignity' of the womenfolk, can also be observed in *Zohra*. Unnie complains to Zubaida Begum, 'Why do they have a boys' school almost opposite? Some boys follow the girls' carriages on their bicycles. . . . It is for such fears that we poor folk discourage our girls from learning to read and write' (ibid.: 6).

Tradition and customs cast a pall over the married life of the couples in both the novels. In *Agnisakshi,* Devaki realizes to her great consternation that in her husband's orthodox Brahmin family, marriage is seen merely as a means to be get successors as well as to provide a wedded partner for the completion of certain religious rites. Unni's mother was of the opinion that 'except for procreation, cohabitation even with one's own husband was prohibited. The lives of Namboodiri women should be confined to the precincts of the kitchen and the prayer room. They were only destined to read the *Ramayana* or the *Siva Purana*' (Antharjanam 1980: 32). Even Unni tells Thankam that for a Brahmin, matrimony is not for conjugal bliss but for sacrifice. He says that though he knows his wife is a knowledgeable woman and he wishes to sit and chat in a leisurely manner with her inside the house, he cannot do so as such behaviour would not be acceptable in his orthodox Brahmin household where spousal relationship is deemed to be founded on the necessity for procreation and not companionship (ibid.: 35). When his mad aunt passes away a short while after his marriage, he decides to observe the death rites for a whole year and hence maintains complete sexual abstinence during the period. Devaki's anguish and frustration in marriage are augmented by this turn of events. 'She was like a caged animal, briskly moving hither and thither from the kitchen to the prayer room or to the pond. She would obey the commands of her mother-in-law and do the work meekly. Her leisure was spent in reading in her own apartment or brooding' (ibid.: 40). Having imbibed liberal and progressive views from her eclectic education, Devaki finds it difficult to accept such self-abnegation in the name of superstition and tradition.

When Zohra arrives as a newly wed bride to her husband's home, she is compelled by customs to keep herself confined to the house, fully decked up and entertaining visitors all the time. When her husband Bashir proposes to take her out to meet his friends and their wives, his mother is appalled at the idea of a new bride and bridegroom going out together. Lamenting that young people have no sense of modesty left, she says to her son, 'This is the good that has come out of your English education' (Futehally 1951: 67). The fear that English education would cloud the minds of young men and women, and upset traditional values was a frequently voiced concern.

There is intellectual incompatibility between Devaki, whose heart fervently rebels against the oppressive system of traditions and customs, and the submissive Unni, who is obsessed with performing his religious duties without fail. For Zohra too, the intellectual incompatibility with her scientist husband Bashir, who does not appreciate poetry and art, and also holds views diametrically opposite to her own regarding Gandhiji and the freedom movement, spirituality and social commitment, is hard to digest, in spite of Bashir's all-consuming devotion to her. Bashir, unlike Unni, is very much involved with worldly and political matters, but treats any views his wife might articulate about such affairs with patronising condescension. Gradually, Zohra learns to maintain silence even when her husband spouts controversial views or heatedly argues with his brother Hamid about the futility of Gandhian nationalism though she may herself have strong opinions on the subjects being discussed. A woman was merely supposed to fulfil wifely and motherly duties, be decorative or doting mother at the most, and her intellectual side was never acknowledged or, if at all manifested, appreciated.

The way both women deal with the conflicts in their marital lives is different. The last straw for Devaki is being refused permission to visit her dying mother because of her brother's revolutionary activities. She flings aside all conjugal bonds and rushes off to be with her mother, thus incurring the wrath of the elders in her in-laws' family who write her off as gone forever. She throws off her purdah and becomes a fiery social reformer and Gandhian political activist under the name of Devi Bahen. She asserts that she does not 'represent any particular community, religion or society. I am the representative of the womenfolk who have been subjected to suffering for centuries' (Antharjanam 1980: 70). She is finally able to fulfil partially what she had confided to Thankam once in the early days of her marriage: 'If I were a man, I would give freedom not only to my wife but to all women. I would have sacrificed myself for the freedom of the country and for the ultimate freedom of humanity' (ibid.: 43). However, disillusioned with the political opportunism, greed and corruption that spread after the attainment of India's freedom, she finally becomes an ascetic in search of the Divine, ironically validating Unni's earlier claims in favour of spirituality, as opposed to materialism.

Zohra, on the other hand, is a gentle rebel who can escape the social conventions that bind her only through the ultimate release of death. The mutual love for her brother-in-law Hamid, a love that transgresses all social and religious codes of conduct, throws both of them into irreconcilable mental turmoil. It is significant that her fascination for Hamid is mainly because she finds in him an intellectual companion, a true soul mate that her husband can never be to her. But they choose to keep their love secret and unfulfilled, not wanting to turn their worlds as well as that of their family upside down. Despite her quiet and conformist demeanour, her rebellion towards her doting husband's authoritarian regime and the smouldering regret in her heart at the aspirations she had to sacrifice at the matrimonial altar, do surface at times. When Zohra learns of Hamid's activities as a Gandhian nationalist and his incarceration on breaking the Salt Law, she cannot help musing to herself that she too had once wanted to join the freedom movement: 'Hamid at least had done something, achieved something, while she…? But she was only a woman. She would have gone willingly, leaving the children in the charge of their grandmother, for the duration, but she dared not even breathe a word about it to her husband' (Futehally 1980: 214).

Though the repercussions of the Indian National movement had not been greatly felt in the world of the Muslim aristocracy of Hyderabad[1]–Zohra's world–the educated Zohra was not only aware of all the developments but also ardently supported Gandhiji, who had been able to inspire thousands of young women to cast off purdah and join the freedom struggle. When she finally finds her life's satisfaction in teaching underprivileged children and women at her home, it is not with the wholehearted approval of her husband. He even suspects that Hamid has passed on to her an anti-religious attitude, marking that her evening classes for widows coincided with the evening prayer timings, something which would have been unthinkable to Zohra sometime back. But her gradual increase in self-confidence is revealed in the firm and determined reply she gives to Bashir: 'No other time suited these women, and I would rather help them than sit and pray for my soul, or invoke God, for something that I want badly' (230). When she contracts plague after a visit to a poor, afflicted family and dies, we can only hope that her restless soul found the elusive peace she had been searching for all her life.

As Jasbir Jain (2002: 96–98) has rightly pointed out, tradition and modernity cannot be seen as mutually exclusive polarities; instead, 'they are interlocked in a constant negotiation with each other'. Hence we cannot arrive at a simplistic conclusion that the marital lives of Devaki and Zohra would have been 'happier' but for their education and consequent encounters with modernity. However, one cannot deny the fact that English education, which resulted in the broadening of the mind and greater exposure to alternate ways of perceiving life and the world around them, definitely played a role in sowing the seeds of discontent and questioning in the minds of the protagonists. What their uneducated and secluded mothers or grandmothers would have meekly accepted, they dared to confront. It is clear that the opposition between tradition and modernity, when it comes to the woman's question, boils down to this: 'the female need for choice and personal expression outside the [conventional] roles defined for them'.

Political and social consciousness function as a stimulus to the quest for individuality of both the women protagonists. Zohra's husband even blames her 'newly acquired political views' for the change in her attitudes and actions (Futehally 1951: 230). As Rumana Futehally Denby has rightly pointed out in her Introduction to *Zohra* (ibid.: viii), Zohra's 'political awakening and emotional flowering' are inextricably linked, and her personal struggle for self-expression is paralleled by India's growing desire for independence). Similarly, in *Agnisakshi*, we see Devaki telling her brother-in-law who had come to call her back to her husband's home that it was not possible for her to be the old Tethikutty, carrying an umbrella and walking with bent head. She asserted that she would continue attending meetings and addressing crowds and would not observe untouchability. She expressly stated that she would go back only if her husband was ready to accept her conditions as she did not wish to bring conflicts into the family. However, patriarchal norms of social and marital life were not as yet capable of accommodating this strong woman who loved freedom more than life itself and who realized that if the society was to be free, the country too should taste freedom. As Lalithambika Antharjanam poignantly puts it, 'Devaki Manampalli did not have a nest to return to. She had grown too big to be contained in a nest' (1980: 86). Thus we see that both Devaki and Zohra—intelligent, strong and courageous in their own right— fell victim to a patriarchal system against which they fought in their unique ways. They were martyrs to an ideology that is best summed up in Devaki's words: 'A woman is not a mere idol or a wooden doll' (ibid. 47).

## NOTE

[1] Hyderabad was founded in 1591 by the Bahamani Sultan Muhammad Quli Qutb Shah as part of the Golconda Sultanate. In the seventeenth century, the Golconda Sultanate along with Hyderabad was merged with the Mughal Empire under Aurangzeb and viceroys of the Mughal empire were put in charge of the Deccan state as it was far from the administrative centre of the Mughals. Rao and Thaha (2011) write:

> As the Mughal Empire began to disintegrate, during the eighteenth century, the Viceroy of Deccan, Mir Qamaruddin, who was given the title of Nizam-ul-Mulk Asaf Jah by the Mughal emperor, asserted his independence in 1724 and established the Asaf Jahi dynasty. During the rule of Nizam Ali Khan Asaf Jah II, the capital was again shifted from Aurangabad to Hyderabad in 1769, reviving the importance of the city (189–90).

They also note that the Nizam of Hyderabad was the first native ruler to sign the Subsidiary Alliance with the British and the Nizams remained loyal to the British throughout the Raj, while being opposed to the Indian National Congress that was viewed as a Hindu party. Therefore it is no surprise that the Indian struggle for freedom led by Gandhi did not make waves in Hyderabad or affect the complacently opulent lifestyles of the majority of the Muslim aristocracy there, represented in the novel by the families of Zohra and her in-laws.

114 *Jinju S.*

## References

Anatharjanam, Lalithambika. [1977] 1980. *Agnisakshi,* translated by Vasanthi Sankaranarayanan, Trichur: Kerala Sahitya Akademi.

Forbes, Geraldine. 1999. *Women in Modern India,* Cambridge: Cambridge University Press.

Futehally, Zeenuth. [1951] 2004. *Zohra,* edited by Rummana Futehally Denby, Delhi: Oxford University Press.

Hai, Ambreen. 2013. 'Adultery Behind Purdah and the Politics of Indian Muslim Nationalism in Zeenuth Futehally's *Zohra*', *MFS Modern Fiction Studies* 59, 2: 317–45. Project MUSE. Web.

Jain, Jasbir. 2002. 'Evolving Traditions, Retreating Modernities: The Reworking of Women's Locations', *Writing Women Across Cultures,* Jaipur: Rawat: 96–98.

James, H.R. 1917. *Education and Statesmanship in India: 1797–1910,* London: Longmans Green.

Rao, Neena Ambre, and Abdul Thaha. 2012. 'Muslims of Hyderabad: Landlocked in the Walled City', in *Muslims in Indian Cities: Trajectories of Marginalisation,* edited by Laurent Gayer and Christophe Jaffrelot, Delhi: Harper Collins: 189–211.

Sarkar, Tanika. 2008. '*Strishiksha* or Education for Women', in *Women's Studies in India: A Reader,* edited by Mary E. John, Delhi: Penguin: 320.

# 9

# Securing Pass Marks

## EDUCATION FOR WOMEN IN THE EARLY MODERN KANNADA NOVEL

Nikhila H.

## INTRODUCTION

*RECASTING WOMEN: Essays in Colonial History* (1989), published more than a quarter century ago, marks a watershed for the study of woman/gender in the colonial period. From those essays, and particularly from the Introduction to the volume, I draw upon three general points in order to help understand how education, or rather the discourse of education for women, worked out during the colonial period: *(i)* a new kind of femininity was constituted during colonialism in tune with the forming of a new kind of patriarchy; *(ii)* the femininity so constituted would secure women within their upper/middle-class boundaries, thus obliterating earlier forms of sociality and interaction among women across castes/classes, and make modernizing and democratizing processes antithetical to each other for women; *(iii)* again, during the colonial period, particularly with respect to women, change was explained (away) as continuity, so that even what was new was seen no more than a perpetuation of the old.

While these provide broad brushstrokes, the specific line that I will be etching in the present essay is what education meant for women in the colonial period. I would be doing this by tracing the debates, discussions and pronouncements on the subject in the early novels in Kannada. The closing decades of the nineteenth century saw women's education become visible in the Kannada context in more senses than one. As in other parts of colonial India where it was a part of the social reformist project, here too it became an issue that was to remain in the public eye at least for the next four to five decades. Again, as elsewhere, education for women in the Kannada context, rather than being a singular or stand-alone agenda, was tied up with the modernizing aspirations of castes and communities, their desire for upward mobility and forming new relations of sociality. Reading and writing novels, were a part of this process of modernizing; novel reading and writing turned into activities geared towards staging an argument for and disseminating a discourse on women's education.

Education for woman took on a demonstrable and performative dimension. In order to make herself recognizable, the woman had to secure certain mark(er)s—marks that visibly distinguished her from others, and also marks that pronounced her place in a hierarchy of merit. The marks distinguished the educated woman from other women, but also made her (to be perceived as) more worthy than other women, and sometimes other men around her. Here I must clarify that 'English education' did not always mean education in English; rather it connoted the modern system of teaching-learning, which more often than not for women happened in Kannada.[1] Since the closing decades of the nineteenth century, one is more likely to come across terms such as *stri shikshana* (which connotes women's instruction, training or cultivation), *shikshitha hennu* (which refers to a woman who has had such instruction, training or cultivation), and *Odiruva hudugi* (meaning, a girl who has read, where 'read' in past tense connotes both the skill of reading and the transformation that such a reading has wrought) in Kannada discussions than references specifically to an education in English for women. In the following sections, I will look at how debates on education for women invariably became debates on gendering, and served to constitute a new femininity.

## THE DATA SAMPLE

I will primarily look at a sample of four early novels in Kannada, *Indirabai: Athava Saddharma Vijayavu* (Gulvadi Venkat Rao 1899), *Indira* (Kerur Vasudevacharya 1908), *Sadguni Krishnabai: Uttama Gruhini* (Shantabai Neelagara 1908) and *Nabha* (Nanjanagud Tirumalamba 1914).[2] Two of the authors, Venkat Rao and Kerur Vasudevacharya are male, and two, Shantabai and Tirumalamba are women writers. Gulwadi Venkat Rao regarded by Kannada literary historians as the first known writer of the social novel in Kannada (*Indirabai*), belonged to the Saraswat community, which constituted an upper-caste minority in South Canara, and the novel is written in the backdrop of the reform of the Saraswat community, particularly with respect to widow remarriage. Kerur Vasudevacharya belonged to a Vaidik family in Bagalkot, which is in present day north Karnataka, was educated in Belgaum, Bombay and Pune, and was a practising lawyer in Bagalkot when his first novel *Indira* was published in Bijapur, and would then go on to edit several newspapers and weeklies such as *Sachitra Bharata* and *Shubhodaya*. Nanjangud Tirumalamba was considered as the first Kannada woman novelist till Shantabai Neelagara's novel *Sadguni Krishnabai* was found. While not much is known about Shantabai, it is said that her family had settled in Maharashtra on account of work, and Shantabai herself had received higher education and was the principal of a girls' school. Tirumalamba of Nanjangud in the Mysore region, a child widow in a Brahmin family, was a novelist, a journalist and a publisher, starting her own publishing house, Satihitaishini Granthamala, and editing the periodicals *Karnataka Nandini* and *Sanmargadarshi*. The novels chosen for the present study happen to have come from different Kannada-speaking regions which were under different political arrangements/units—Madras Presidency, Bombay Presidency and the princely state of Mysore.

It goes without saying that all the four protagonists, Indirabai, Indira, Krishnabai and Nabha, who lend their names to the respective novel's title, are educated women. A curious point about the mode of narration in these novels is that while we see all these four women characters saying and doing things, and undergoing trials and tribulations, we rarely see them reflecting, going over their choices, trying out alternatives, being in a state of confusion or going through the joys and pains of the process of learning-unlearning. We do not know how these women saw themselves or how they understood what was happening to them through the process of education. It is as though these women characters are evacuated of all interiority. The third person narrative mode in all the novels adopts an objective narration, not describing the thoughts or the inner musings of the protagonists at any point. The narrative treatment is reminiscent of the expressionistic style where individual characterization is dispensed with and character types expressing basic issues and conflicts are created. The setting in the novels is often symbolic and is not defined in terms of specific place and time. For instance, we are never sure exactly when and where the story of Indirabai unfolds; the characters are representative of ideas. We do not get a glimpse of the inner conflicts and confusions of the protagonists with the exposure to new ideas and new modes of thinking; instead these conflicts are exteriorized as conflict between the woman with education, and the one without, as in the case of Indirabai and her mother. Was it because this was the widely prevalent novelistic technique or mode of narration of the times? Or, are we to assume that the protagonist's thoughts were almost completely geared towards refuting, justifying, responding to what others were saying about her speech and actions? Or, was it that in the case of women, education did not or, at least was hoped, would not alter their thought processes, make available new cognitive structures, bring transformation in modes of knowing? It is hard to say what exactly was at work in these novels, but the cumulative effect of this narrative style is that we can see what education made of the woman, but we never get to see what she made of education, or rather what the narrators/authors/reformers thought that she made of education.

## THE WOMAN QUESTION IN THE EARLY
## NOVEL IN KANNADA

In recent years there has been a resurgence of scholarly interest in the early modern novel in different Indian languages, which has also given rise to efforts to translate these novels into English, and make them available to a wider readership. This resurgence of interest has been especially in the context of discussions of nation and modernity, and the early novel, particularly the social-realist novel, has emerged in these studies as a primary genre in 'narrating India' (Ramakrishnan 2005). Padikkal (1993: 237–38) sees the early novels as indicative of the quest of the English-educated upper caste for a new social identity, a new nation and a new community. Discussing the early modern novels in Kannada, and seeing parallels with the early novels in other Indian languages, he points out:

> A woman is the central character in all these novels, and is usu-
> ally presented as the object of reform. Not only in their titles, but
> in content as well, the nineteenth-century novels foregrounded
> women and the 'Woman Question'. In doing so, these novels were
> constituting the ideal Indian woman as virtuous/heroic/submissive.
> As part of the emergence into modernity, the novels created new
> men and women, and new relationships between them (232).

Jayasrinivasa Rao's essay (2011) looks at virtually all the novels taken up in my study, among others, to trace their social reformist themes. Looking at the prefaces written by the novel's authors, he says that their literary attempts were imbued with their moral purposes, but notices a difference between male and female reformers:

> The entire burden of maintaining the social equilibrium falls on
> women and the anxiety (and sometimes anger) that the society
> will fall apart if women are educated and acquire the confidence
> to assert their identities is not confined only to male reformists
> and dissenters. Women reformers also expressed similar sen-
> timents, but even when they were calling for reforms, they also
> dealt carefully and tactfully with these anxieties to prove that the
> fears were illogical (23–24).

While I agree with these studies that the social reformist discourse as well as other competing and conflicting discourses of the times can be traced through the debate in the novels, and that the novels foreground the woman question, I would like to clarify that I am not looking at the genre of the novel here as any special source or as the most important site where the question of woman and education was raised. It is simply that the novels allow me to see how 'education' got translated for women in the Kannada context, that is, it helps me to look for the markers of education that emerged in the colonial period, and to some extent to understand why these markers became acceptable, or how they were made acceptable to the Kannada public.[3]

## LANGUAGE, GENDER(ING) AND EDUCATION

Discussing the differential trajectories that the novel took in English and in the Indian languages, Meenakshi Mukherjee (2000) says that knowledge of English was a gender-specific skill, that debates in the social reform movement in the nineteenth century revolved around what and how much should be taught to women, rather than whether they should be taught English at all, in the Bengali and Marathi context, and that a sizeable proportion of the readership of the novel in Indian languages was women (19). Shefali Chandra in her articles (2009; 2007) and in her dissertation (2003) has consistently argued that the differential function of English and Indian languages and their differential sphere of operation are tied to the axis of gender. She has argued that English became a masculinised domain, while its feminization and indigenization happened through and for women. Looking at the Marathi context, she delineates the sexual division of the linguistic sphere in the colonial period—the constitution of femininity and masculinity, as well as sexuality that was tied to casting Marathi and English in particular ways. Nita Kumar (2007), eschewing the widespread notion of education prevalent in discussions of the colonial period as a pedagogical project carried out in schools and formal sites of learning instituted by the British system of education, turns her attention to the role of home language learning, classical learning and to the sites of non-formal education, such as indigenous school and home, and nurturers such as mother and her surrogates in the making of the native intelligentsia. She argues that because of what she calls 'plural education' of this intelligentsia, 'the construction of the "new" as opposed to "traditional" was not intellectually problematic ... It was logical to use a new epistemology to reinterpret familiar facts, or to fit in new facts into a familiar epistemology' (107). The whole chapter where she makes this argument titled 'Languages, Families, and the Plural Learning of the Nineteenth-Century Intelligentsia', however, assumes that the receivers of education were men. Would the same explanation hold for the process at work for women?

These studies gesture towards a neat divide between the world of education in English and education in Indian languages, which can also be mapped on the axis of gender. In this essay, without going into the kind of education that women received in Kannada, *as opposed to English*, I am looking at what was considered appropriate for women in the name of modern education which, more often than not, came to them in and through Kannada. How were women expected to transform themselves through the new modes of learning being instituted ostensibly for their benefit? How were they expected to make visible its impact on themselves? These are the questions that I address in the rest of this essay.

## CONSTITUTING THE MARKERS OF EDUCATION IN KANNADA/GRADUATING INTO A NEW DOMESTICITY

Even before Ramakanta—who is to later marry Indire in Vasudevacharya's novel (1908) *Indira*—knows her, he recognizes certain marks in his very first meeting with her, and they are enough to make the educated young man become favourably disposed towards her:

> There was not a trace of sensual excess or indulgence in the speech and actions of this young lady. Her simple nature, purity

of practice, large-heartedness came through even in the few
words that she spoke. However as it was getting dark, and as she
had covered her head with a shawl, Ramakanta could not clearly
make out her beauty and charm (70).[4]

Nowhere in the paragraph extracted are we told that Indire was educated. All that we are told is what makes her agreeable to Ramakanta.
We get to know what education is only by the indexical marks in the
woman. We see here that the marks of education on Indire stand
out even in the enveloping darkness.

I enumerate below some of such distinguishing marks of the
educated woman, marks that became acceptable and desirable for
any woman to have:

> *Odu* or reading as a mark of education;
>
> *pariksheyalli jaya, hatasaadhane*, or passing examination, deter-
> mined achievement as a mark of education;
>
> *vidya-abhyasa, dinachari*, or practice, putting into practice as writ-
> ing a diary, routine, habit and behaviour, discipline, systematic
> method, as a mark of education.

Firstly, 'Odu' or reading, that is, silent engagement with books came
to be an early marker of education. To begin with, reading itself was
perceived as dangerous for women probably because *(a)* there is
no outward expressive (i.e. spoken or sung) dimension accompanying reading; and *(b)* there is no intermediary for explication of the
written/printed word, though this activity of reading was conducted
generally at home in the domestic space. For example, if we take
Indirabai in the 1899 novel of the same name (Rao 1899/1962), her
first brush with education, so to speak, is through her neighbour
Sharade who is learning in a school for young girls, whose house
Indirabai visits in order to read books such as *Stridharma neeti,
Aesopana neeti kathegalu, Panchatantra,* and *Satyavati charitre.* As
we can see from these titles which emphasize *neeti*, which could
roughly be translated as morals or values, the books that she was
reading are those which are training her to be a good woman. So

the act of silent reading could go along only with the cultivation of ostensibly good morals and values for women.

When Indirabai's parents come to know about her reading, they see forebodings of ill times for her because of her reading books printed by 'mlechcha padriyaru' (the outcaste Christian priests), and warn her. But Indirabai defends herself spiritedly saying, 'Does reading spoil one's caste? I haven't read anything so far that will destroy/spoil my caste, and all that I am reading teaches women how to behave with their husband and others' (118-20). When her mother says that she can learn all this at home, Indirabai says that nobody made the attempt to teach her, nor did she learn all this at home. When her mother tells her that reading the books at home such as *Krishnana Balaleele* or *Radhavilasa* is more fruitful, Indirabai asks her how it would be so, and that reading her books and uttering Krishna's name can quite easily go together (ibid.). Later when she becomes a widow and is one day reading a book called *Neetikathegalu* ('Moral Stories') borrowed from the same friend Sharade, her mother chides her severely for going against her elders' wishes by wearing a blouse, combing her hair and reading books, suggesting that they are all equally forbidden. When her mother asks Indirabai, of what use the books that she is reading are, Indirabai says that reading these books makes the mind and character pure. When the mother asks her if it is not pure now, Indirabai says that now we can only see others' shortcomings but not our own. When the mother persists with her questioning, asking her if reading books by the mlechchas is necessary for this, Indirabai's reply is, 'Whatever the books advocate or teach, apply not only to those whom you call mlechchas, but to any human being; for example, "do not steal" is a value for not only mlechchas, but for everyone' (152-54). Through this whole discussion between Indirabai and her mother, we see Indirabai's attempt to win her mother's approval for her actions; we can see that in doing so reading becomes defined by and confined to whatever keeps her within the boundaries of caste and gender. What was new and unsettling to begin with was the new mode or activity of reading. Earlier in the novel, there are references to girls being taught to read in order to sing songs or shlokas. The new mode of reading which did not have an oral expressive function, where one read for oneself, as it were, seems dangerous because the contents are not manifest or known to those around the reader. Later on Indirabai's parents invite a guru to read out from Shrimad Bhagavad Githa, *Bhaktivijaya, Dasasevamritha* outside her door to bring her to her senses after she has locked herself in. What seemed dangerous at least to her mother about Indirabai's new mode of reading was that it did not require such intermediaries to explicate the written word.

Still later, when Indirabai has come back after her matriculation examination to Amrutharaya's house (the latter acts like her foster father in the novel, giving shelter to Indirabai who had left her parental home), he tries to find out what she is thinking by looking at the books that she is reading when she is away from her room; he finds that she is reading books like *Grihanirvaha Karya* ('How to Carry out Household Duties'), *Stridharmaratnakara* ('The Treasure Trove of Stridharma'), *Paakashaastra* ('Culinology'), and so on, and concludes that the time is ripe to broach the subject of re-marriage to Indirabai. Here we see that Indirabai is reading books related to domestic duties, and those that will help her to fit into the new domesticity that was getting constituted at that time. Whatever Indirabai reads now only serves to provide her an added justification for the role that she is set to perform in the household.

In Kerur Vasudevacharya's novel *Indira* (1908/1984), when Indire is asked what she has read lately, she replies that she has read *Hindu Dharma ani Sudharana* by Professor Gole in Marathi. What she reads is made known to us at different points ostensibly to give us an idea of what she is like, and what her values are. Once we are told that Indire is reading Bankimchandra Chattopadyay's novel *Vishavriksha*; another time, we are told that she is reading the paper *Induprakash*. Yet another time, we are told that she took up a book titled *Praachina Hindustana* by Romesh Chandra Dutt to read. As opposed to what Indire reads, we have another character in the novel called Natesha, portrayed in general as quite an undesirable character, whose reading is said to have comprised such 'books as *Satyarthadeepike* ('The Gospel of Truth') and *Punarvivahabandana* ('The Bond of Remarriage', probably a book advocating widow remarriage) printed by the Christian missionaries, books condemning the Aryamatha. Aryan religion, that is, the Vedic religious practices by the Lingapanthis (the Lingayats who established themselves as a separate religion against Vedic Hindu practices) and vulgar novels and plays' (79). We see here that Indire reads only those books that affirm and uphold the Hindu religious and caste order and that is what makes her desirable, whereas Natesha who reads those books and materials that challenge, or go against this order is represented in the novel as quite an unsavoury character.

Indire's suitor, Srikanta, whom her father wants her to marry, but whom she does not want to, claims that he has read Herbert Spencer, Mill and Bacon, a claim which Indire is quite sceptical of, but simply chooses to tell him that she has not even heard these names. Srikanta is portrayed in the novel as a shallow braggart, and reading these English works or even claiming to have read them, makes him superficial, undesirable and unsuitable to Indire. Another character, Kamale, in the same novel in another instance is reading *Subodhapatrika, Vrutthantha Manjari, Sudharaka Epiphany*. I am not sure what exactly they connote, but they would have communicated to the then readers why Indire (through what she reads) is to be regarded as far superior to Kamale.

So we see here that reading, and reading with discrimination comes to define a woman's character. Reading was thought to be a means of strengthening her moral values and helping her attend to her domestic calling more sincerely. The act of silent reading, scanning the page with one's eyes, sitting with a book in hand would become a visible mark of education, and it would also become a desirable mark of femininity for the woman. The terms 'Odiruvavalu', 'Odiruva Hennu' (a well-read girl), mentioned earlier, would come to stand for the educated woman in Kannada.

A second mark of education in Kannada is *pariksheyalli jaya*, or *hatasaadhane*, that is, education as overcoming hurdles and emerging victorious in the exam. After Indirabai becomes a widow and is severely ill-treated at her parents' home, her reform-oriented guardians Amrutharaya and Jalajakshi send her to a distant town to study, and the novel describes her period of study thus:

She gave her full mind to her lessons without being distracted by anything else. She learnt her lessons well and pleased her teacher, Anandibai, by repeating the same to her, wrote frequently to Amrutharaya about all the subjects that she was learning, went on learning more and more, emerged victorious in all the exams given to her, and in two years' time she took the Matriculation exam and stood first in her school in the exam (Vasudevacharya 1984: 206–07).

Here we see that learning her lessons becomes a way of pleasing her teachers and elders. So much is the premium placed on a woman appearing favourably to those older than her and having authority over her, that pleasing them becomes the end of education. Also, after passing the examination, Indirabai receives much appreciation from people in her home town, and this prepares the ground for her marriage to the educated son of Amrutharaya and Jalajakshi, indicating that passing the examination becomes a qualification for securing a good match.

In the novel *Sadguni Krishnabai* by Shanta Neelagara (1908/ 1996), Krishnabai's father takes up the task of teaching her at home. But after his death, her brother sends her to a tutor to distract her from her grief, and there she learns her lessons so well that she wins the approbation of the teacher and leaves the other children far behind, provoking their jealousy. She solves mathematical problems even as they were being given by the tutor, often earning jibes from her classmates as to why any learning was necessary for a girl. Later when she joined the Zenana Mission Girls' School, she was far ahead in her lessons than the other girls there, and began to receive independent lessons from the principal, even winning appreciation from an American teacher who visited the school. An important event in the novel is when she is publicly feted for her performance in the examination, which is also the occasion where her family receives her marriage proposal. The occasion is described thus:

> Today is the fifteenth of November, the day when those girls who passed in the exam would receive their prizes from the

Governor's wife. High-ranking officials belonging to different castes, lawyers, doctors, businessmen, many European, Parsi and Hindu women had arrived for the programme. Though the auditorium was huge, it was packed to capacity on that day. The girls of the school came dressed in accordance with their caste norms, and wearing expensive jewellery. Since Krishnabai had secured a first class and stood first, she was to receive a gold medal and also many prizes that day, and so she was suffused with happiness. The programme began at five in the evening with the reading of the school report. Then there were a number of speeches in favour of women's education, and then a few students sang songs in English and in Indian languages. Soon the school principal came to where Krishnabai was seated, took her to the Governor's wife, made her sing a beautiful song in her melodious voice, which was much appreciated by the assembled audience. The Governor's wife was also very happy and she praised Krishnabai immensely (11–12).

In these descriptions, we can see that doing her lessons well, coming up with a good performance in the examinations somehow becomes a vindication of all the past difficulties and suffering for the woman. Winning the approval of the teachers, winning public approbation is an end and becomes the justification for the study. Doing well in school becomes a way of ensuring her continuing her formal studies, which could be terminated at any point by family members. There is a premium placed on the woman's performance in the examination, and becoming successful in it also stands for gaining merit and winning other battles of life for her. And importantly, her accomplishment in the examination also becomes a desirable qualification for securing a good match.

In the novel *Nabha* by Nanjangud Tirumalamba (1914/1992), the heroine Nabha continues her lessons in her uncle's house with his sons, but soon leaves them far behind in her lessons. When one of the sons, Ramananda asks her admiringly about the secret of her accomplishment, she says that it is on account of her *hatasaadhane*, the determination to achieve, a quality that women have (45). We see here that determination to do well in studies becomes a characteristic, a mark of womanhood itself.

*Vidya-abhyasa*, or being seen practising her learning every day through a systematic routine was yet another marker of education. For instance Nabha's daily routine is described in detail in the novel:

> She would get up early in the morning every day; after attending to her bath and other daily work, and assisting in household tasks, she would take up her learning practice (vidya-abhyasa). Along with her brothers, she would undertake the assigned practice of English learning, and recitation from Sanskrit and Kannada books. Later in the presence of the guru there would be recitation from such books as *Tatvabodhamruta*, *Sitamahatme*, *Sanatacharitre* and *Vishnupurana*. Besides these, at Ramamani's (her aunt) insistence, she also learnt a little embroidery and craft-making (46).

Indirabai's daily routine after she goes back to Amrutharaya's home on finishing her Matriculation exam was not that different from Nabha's:

> Every day after getting up at dawn, washing her face and having her bath, she would spend one or two hours reading and writing, before going to the kitchen to supervise the preparation of the various dishes by the cook. After lunch, she would spend some time discussing various topics with Jalajakshi before sitting to read and write, or sometimes do embroidery work with colourful threads (Rao 1962: 209).

This daily routine is noticed by Amrutharaya and his wife who remark appreciably that Indirabai does not waste a single moment of the day (210).

Krishnabai's practice of learning even after her marriage is again described in detail:

> Though Krishnabai had to take on a lot of household work, she did not give up her regular practice. These days Sanskrit and Painting became her favourite subjects. Bavusaheb (her father-in-law) appointed a Shastri to teach her Sanskrit. The translations and essays in Sanskrit and English that she wrote were scrutinized and corrected by Madhavaraya (her husband)

himself. Krishnabai had kept aside a notebook, where, every day she wrote about the day's important events and about her learning practice (Neelagara 1984:17).

Also, as we can see that in the case of Krishnabai and Nabha, they practise both Sanskrit and English, indicating that the practice of English learning will not be at the cost of Sanskrit, or that English would not replace Sanskrit. We see here that it is this disciplined practice of a routine that is seen as a mark of education. In *Sadguni Krishnabai* we see the systematization of this practice when Krishnabai is residing at her sister's place, and she prepares virtually a timetable and a curriculum for educating her nieces and nephew. In fact a significant portion of the novel is spent in elaborating how she put them into a systematic learning routine. So following a set routine, practicing lessons, maintaining an orderly day-to-day record come to be the visible markers of education. The point is that in all these instances this practice of learning is carried out at home, and becomes very much a part of domestic routine.


IN LIEU OF A CONCLUSION


My attempt in this essay has been broadly two-fold: *(i)* to disaggregate the term 'education' into what came to be its markers in Kannada; and *(ii)* to show how pedagogic work became coterminous with the work of gendering in the novels. We see the meanings that education takes in the Kannada context *(a)* reading what is appropriate for a woman, that is, that which will not affect or disturb caste, religion and gender boundaries, and which will prepare the woman for the new domesticity being instituted in the times; *(b)* passing examination and securing good marks, that is, study geared towards performing well in the examination; *(c)* being regular, disciplined, punctual and practical, so that education becomes a rote learning experience through practising repeatedly what is taught, rather than independently thinking and reflecting.

Though men were in the forefront of women's education for large measure, education for woman seems to have been secured on two conditions: That it would be 'surficial', that education would mean securing visible markers—recognizable marks of differentiation and order of merit. That the 'pass marks' would ensure that the educated woman would just graduate into the new domestic arrangement, and that the marks will not become a passport to the world of men. Anticipating that these marks might be seen as threatening the gender system or gender order, much of the narrative's work in the novels goes in ensuring that the sphere of functioning of men and women remains separate; in allaying fears of crossing the gender boundary; in putting the educated woman on view and showing her performing better than she had earlier in her own sphere; and in not turning into a threat for men in their sphere.

## NOTES

[1] Here it may be noted that I am not making the distinction between English and Kannada along the lines of English standing for modernity and Kannada for tradition. To the new pedagogical model that was instituted during colonialism, I have given the name 'English education'. This does not necessarily mean instruction in English, or direct contact with ideas in English. I am saying that modernity through education came to women through a Kannada sieve. Kannada too was modernizing itself in the process (rather than remaining as a static repository of tradition). The question of how/whether the colonial modernity instituted through English, and the modernity instituted through Indian languages were different is certainly important, but that kind of a comparative analysis is not what I am undertaking in this essay.

[2] These novels and some others were read for discussion in the Early Modern Kannada Novels Reading Group comprising faculty members and research scholars of the EFL University, University of Hyderabad and Osmania University, among others, that met periodically over a six-month period in the EFL University from March 2011. I am grateful to the Reading Group members for sharing the source material and for the discussions. I also thank Tharakeshwar V.B. for extended discussions.

³ For instance, Uma Maheshwari's (2001) chapter titled 'Kannadada Modala Kadambarigala Samajika Hinnele' (The Social Background of the First Kannada Novels) draws our attention to the debates happening in the magazines and journals of the period on women's education.
⁴ All translations from the novels here and in the rest of the essay that follows are mine.

## References

Chandra, Shefali. 2009. Mimicry, Masculinity, and the Mystique of Indian English: Western India, 1870–1900', *Journal of Asian Studies* 68, 1 (Feb.): 119–25.

————.2007. 'Gendering English: Sexuality, Gender and the Language of Desire in Western India, 1850–1940', *Gender and History* 19, 2 (Aug.): 284–304.

————. 2003. 'The Social Life of English: Language and Gender in Western India, 1850–1940.' Ph.D. diss, Department of History, University of Pennsylvania.

Kumar, Nita. 2007. *The Politics of Gender, Community, and Modernity: Essays on Education in India*, Delhi: Oxford University Press.

Maheshwari, Uma. 2001. *Idu Manushiya Odu: Kannadada Modala Kadambarigalu–Ondu Streevadi Adhyayana* (Early Kannada Novels: A Feminist Study), Puttur: Shivarama Karantha Adhyayana Kendra, Vivekananda College.

Mukherjee, Meenakshi. 2000. *The Perishable Empire: Essays on Indian Writing in English*, Delhi: Oxford University Press.

Neelagara, Shanta. [1908] 1996. *Sadguni Krishnabai: Uttama Gruhini*, Bangalore: Kannada Sahitya Parishat.

Padikkal, Shivaram. 1993. 'Inventing Modernity: The Emergence of the Novel in India', in *Interrogating Modernity: Culture and Colonialism in India,* edited by Tejaswini Niranjana, P. Sudhir and Vivek Dhareshwar, Calcutta: Seagull: 220–41.

Ramakrishnan, E.V., ed., 2005. *Narrating India: The Novel in Search of the Nation*, Delhi: Sahitya Akademi.

Rao, Gulvadi Venkata. [1899] 1962. *Indirabai (Athava˙ Saddharma Vijaya)* (Kan.); *Indirabai or The Triumph of Truth and Virtue: A*

*Novel in Kanarese* (English Title), Mangalore: Kannada Prapancha Prakashana.

Rao, Jayasrinivasa S. 2011. 'Rewriting Social Reform—The Early Phase of the 'Social' Realist Novel in Kannada', *Language in India*. 11 (Jun. 6): 13-27.

Sangari, Kumkum and Sudesh Vaid, eds, 1989. *Recasting Women: Essays in Colonial History*, Delhi: Kali for Women.

Tirumalamba, Nanjanagud. [1914] 1992. 'Nabha'. *Hitaishiniya Hejjegalu: Nanjangud Tirumalamba Avara Sahityada Vaachike,* edited by Vijaya Dabbe, Bangalore: Department of Kannada and Culture.

Vasudevacharya, Kerur. [1908] 1984. *Indira*, Mysore: Usha Sahitya Male.

# 10

# Women and English Education in Coorg/Kodagu

## A DISCUSSION OF ALTERNATE MODERNITIES DURING 1834–1882

Sowmya Dechamma C. C.

KODAGU, IN KARNATAKA, known as Coorg in its anglicized version, was annexed by the British as a separate province under the Madras Presidency by a proclamation dated 7 May 1834. Based on the Lewis Rice Report (1882) we now know that three schools were established in the same year, two Anglo-Vernacular schools in Mercara, now Madikeri, and in Virarajendrapet (now Virajpet) and one Kannada school in Hatgatnad. Lewis Rice, Director of Public Instruction, authored and compiled the Report under the orders of the then colonial government. Until 1857, the state of the schools left much to be desired for, with hardly any instructors and very little pay for existing instructors. It was only after the new scheme of education in 1857 that some semblance of regularity came into being. The one Anglo-vernacular school in Mercara was under the Basel Mission and there were twenty government schools in the province. The primary tasks of Rev. Moegling, the erstwhile headmaster of the

Mercara school were *(i)* proselytizing of Coorgs; *(ii)* the instruction of the youth of Coorg; and *(iii)* the creation of a vernacular literature in Canarese (Kannada), although Coorg spoke Kodava among other languages. However, it was doubted whether Rev. Moegling would be allowed to function as the headmaster for the fear that his proselytizing mission would carry on to his educational efforts. In 1860 after Rev. Moegling had to leave India due to ill health, Mr Richter took his place and under his efforts, printed books were first introduced in the schools of Coorg and there was regular payment for instructors. The missionary school in Madikeri was later taken over by the government.

These efforts were spurred by the letter written and signed by more than fifty headmen of Coorg. Here is the part of the letter that is available:

> We, the undersigned headmen of Coorg, being the representatives of our countrymen beg most respectfully to lay before you what is now uppermost in our minds, and what appears to us of the greatest importance for the welfare of our people.
>
> Through the noble generosity of the late lamented Chief Commissioner, General Sir Mark Cubbon, KCB, the blessing of education has been extended to us six years ago, though at the time we did not appreciate as to its possible effect. But the influence of the established English school at Mercara, its steady progress, the temperate, judicious, and devoted manner in which it has been carried on for the last six years, together with the encouragement from the successive Superintendents, have disarmed all our fears, and we most earnestly desire that all our children should be benefited by the instruction there given.
>
> The great influx of European settlers into our country makes the education of our children appear doubly necessary to our minds, since our own ignorance renders our intercourse with the planters most difficult, unsatisfactory and disadvantageous.
>
> The peculiar circumstance, however, that Mercara, though the principal town contains but a few Coorg houses, enables only a limited number of Coorg boys to attend the school. To remedy this disadvantage, we have resolved to collect amongst ourselves

a sum of money sufficient to build and endow a boarding house for about one hundred boys. The Coorg officials and pensioners are ready to contribute half a month's pay, which, together with the subscription of the farmers, will amount to about Rs. 6,000/-. This is all we can do for the present, but we earnestly wish that our daughters should also receive some education, and for them we would have to build a similar house.

Mr Richter, the present head master of the Anglo-vernacular school, who has conducted it for the last six years and our entire confidence, has not only given the first impulse to this movement, but declares himself with his esteemed partner most willing to carry out the proposed plans; and as they have hitherto acted as father and mother towards our children, we have not the least hesitation in confiding them also for the future to their paternal care. The inner arrangements of the boarding-houses, however, would be managed by our own people (Rice 1882).

My essay attempts to look at how and why at a time (the mid-and late nineteenth century) English education even to boys was questioned by mainstream nationalists such as Ishwar Chandra Vidyasagar, Bankimchandra Chattopadhyay and Swami Vivekananda (Pani and Pattnaik, 59), Coorgs/Kodavas as a community came forward willingly to educate their sons and notably daughters. I also propose to look into how this system of education worked differently for different communities and genders. What do reports and statistics have to say regarding the education and 'progress' of girls from different communities that inhabited Coorg? How was progress understood in relation to English education? How can we understand this within or beyond the framework of colonial modernity and anti-colonial nationalism? What notions of gender did English education inscribe into the existing ones of the community?

In forwarding the petition, the superintendent and the commissioner of Mysore and Coorg wrote very supportively, obviously tinted with 'oriental' bias: 'I beg to bear testimony to the genuineness of the people to progress in knowledge, their readiness to make sacrifices in the cause' wrote Captain Campbell, the superintendent (Rice 1882, 4–5). Mr Bowring, the Commissioner, wrote: 'It has rarely happened in India that a whole race has come forward in this manner, putting aside traditional prejudices, to meet half-way the earnest wish of their rulers that they should educate themselves, and it is especially remarkable among mountaineers in this country, as the hill races are generally far below those of the plains in their acquisition of knowledge' (ibid.). After these petitions and recommendations, Kolovanda Kariyappa who was the first pupil to enrol in the Mercara English schooling in 1856 (then against the wishes of the headmen) offered to erect the girls' boarding house at his own expense. Subsequently, many Anglo-Vernacular schools were started across Coorg to act as feeders to the Mercara school (ibid.: 2).

Somewhere around 1875 an attempt was made to start a boarding school under a European mistress but only day scholars could be obtained and the mistress fell ill and resigned, ending the efforts for an all-girls school. But as the records (ibid.: 12) show, girls continued to go to mixed schools. Schools were opened for Muslims in 1872. In 1877, education for coolies of the coffee estate was enquired into and the Coorg Planters' Association (constituting only British planters) favoured it. But, Coorgs were against opening schools for Holeyas (then called untouchables) and jungle tribes (adivasis) given their 'no settled status and no land to cultivate and given their wandering nature'. In 1879, some Bettada Kuruba children applied but do not appear to have joined. In 1879, with 6 English schools, there were 306 boys and 1 girl. In the remaining 56 school across Coorg, there were 2,697 boys and 304 girls (this being in the primary section). There was one middle school with 119 pupils and one high school with 38 pupils in Mercara. There was no college in Coorg at this point. The only girls' school was the aided Roman Catholic school at Virajpet, run by nuns for the native Christian Konkani girls. In the Basel mission school in Anandapur, many were girls mostly converts from Holeyas, the untouchable caste (ibid.: 15).

All the government schools, especially the *nad* primary schools were well attended by girls almost up to one by eight of its strength. The report mentions that the girls went to the same schools as their brothers and relatives, passed through the same classes and course of study and generally remained unmarried to a later age than is common among Hindus. It is worthwhile to mention the paradox that the school that was exclusively established for the girls in 1872 did not have many takers. But most schools that were not really intended to be mixed gender schools ended up having girls as pupils. It should also be noted that there were hardly many mixed schools in Victorian England. This is also true for schools meant for untouchables. The small number of lower castes, who went to school, went to 'regular' schools and not schools that were exclusively meant for them. In 1882, out of 21,000 children of school-going age, nearly 4,000 went to school. This included children belonging to different communities and castes. A quote from the section of the Rice report titled 'Female Education': Female education so far as the Coorgs are concerned, presents fewer difficulties than in many parts of India, owing to the absence of prejudice on the subject and the later age at which girls are married. The attendance of so many girls in the boys' schools is an exceptional and pleasing feature, and exerts, it is believed, a good influence.' Most boys belonging to the Coorg community and one-sixth of the girls from the community were attending school by 1882 when Lewis Rice wrote the report.

How do we understand alternate modernities through the subject of female education from sections of the report? The task/method is not easy, especially because this work does not look into narratives by women but looks into the letter written by headmen belonging to the community and records kept by the colonizer. The women here were not anglophiles, they were not elite, were not educated nor had access (and did not require this access) to the power of knowledge as framed by the British or by the brahmins. A small section of Kodava women might have been daughters of well-to-do farmers but we have no access whatsoever to their own stories. Their stories and narratives are mediated through men of the community to some extent and largely by the colonial official, record keeper, ethnographer, and of course, folklores that are not of concern here.

What is the unit of modernity that we are talking about? For our purposes, the unit of modernity is the small community of Kodavas/Coorgs. The British thought of Kodavas as offsprings of Kshatriya men and Shudra women, a theory which like many others on the origin of Coorgs leaves much to be proven. Nevertheless, Coorgs were and still are outside the Hindu frame of religion because of their non-brahminical practices, and this partly explains their zeal towards 'English' education (note that the report mentions how girls are not bound by prejudices that plague Hindus, early marriage being one). Although not belonging to the Hindu fold, Kodavas are now included in the Other Backward Classes. It also needs to be noted that though patrilineal, divorce was in practice among Coorgs and remarriage for divorcees and widows were/are customary. Practices of sati, purdah, child marriage, and widowhood that British and reformers considered barbaric—thus justifying education as a mode of reform—did not simply hold for many communities like Kodavas. Therefore, unlike the nationalists in other places who had to work against the idea of oriental decadence to build a superior culture of their own, making women central to their nationalist scheme of things, for the Kodava, the burden of proving—'our tradition was great'—simply never existed. In a culture where tradition was embedded with the materiality of existence, tracing a past that was superior to that of the British, and to preserve that past despite its encounter with newer ways brought in by the British—was an anxiety, which Pandian (2002) has brilliantly articulated, did not exist for communities outside the nationalist elite. Contrary to this, we see in the reports that during the period 1834 to 1881 girls (and their families) sought and had the same course of study and subjects as the boys. What is noteworthy is that the critique against English in Bengal in the mid- and late nineteenth century and other regions of cultural power came from within the circle of the elite English-speakers, while in regions like Kodagu, the critique was at least visibly absent and support for English education came from within the community—in ways of partially financing it, encouraging it morally, and so on. The tension, if any, was not about the corruption of Kodava minds by 'outsiders' or about the caste being spoilt, but the distance girls and boys had to travel to school/live away from home in harsh climatic conditions.

As far as I am concerned here, alternate modernities are practices that communities negotiate—practices existing with newer practices that they encounter. The tensions between these existing and newer practices are much studied as conflicts between tradition and modernity. The resolution of tension between tradition and modernity, between the public and the private, between the material and the spiritual, between the exterior and the interior/domestic, now known to us as colonial modernity, is fraught with gendered and casteist notions of the binaries involved. For communities such as the Kodava and many other backward and lower castes, the dividing line between what was public and the private, what was exterior and interior was very thin if not non-existent. Dilip Menon (2006) has discussed how tradition that was considered spiritual and hence superior to the material world of the West was not accessible to the backward and lower castes. Although Dilip Menon's argument is agreeable to an extent, 'accessibility' of tradition of the upper castes leaves no tradition of their own for the lower castes. It suggests that there was one tradition, which some could access who barred others from accessing it. For communities like the Kodava, lives revolved around small-scale agriculture, gathering, and hunting which in turn was largely dictated by the harsh weather of the region. The labouring communities had no choice but to involve everyone in the household for all kinds of work without strict divisions of labour on gendered lines. This is true for most backward and lower castes for whom labouring either for themselves or for the upper castes blurred and erased the binaries of the outside and the inside. What one may construe as tradition was built around the practicalities of life that could maximize productivity in some form or the other. Lives that were in no ways certain led to fluid notions which were open to newness, minimizing conflict with outsiders.

It is in this context that we need to locate the letter written by the Coorg headmen (Rice 1882: 4) requesting the British to open a school for girls as well. That there were no takers for the all-girls school and girls went to schools meant for boys also indicates notions of gender that were less rigid and more open. In Pandian's words, what this implies to the nationalist binaries of spiritual and material is this—that subaltern groups consciously unsettled this binary between spiritual and material, inner and outside thereby questioning the modernity of the upper-caste Hindu who spoke a language of modernity by claiming caste in the language of spirituality (2002: 1737). Also, the manner in which this spirituality of the upper-caste nationalist elite encoded in a gendered sphere is called to question from the ways in which Kodava girls participated in the sphere of education, making it a public that was desirable to all, a public where presence of genders and communities propelled a move towards modernity very unlike that envisioned by the nationalist elite.

Another aspect of this modernity (unlike colonial modernity) is that it works in a space that is not characterized by the anti-colonial debates C. P. Hull and Robert Elliott whose books on coffee in the early 1860s mention how the people of Kodagu and people of Karnataka (then Mysore) had hardly heard of the 1857 revolt. This absence of anti-colonial wave went along with a loyalty to British in years to come that led the British to wave-off the license to possess a gun for Kodavas, a privilege that is held even today. Debates between orientalists and anglicists remained unknown. There were no newspapers in Kodagu until the late 1800s. The nationalist struggle did create some flutter in post-1920s, but there are no records of this struggle for freedom colliding with colonial policies on education and other matters. Kodavas to this day have been sneered at for being very English (especially for their love towards English language, for being 'traditionally' pork eaters, for their mannerisms that do not fit within caste-Hindus) for being 'modern' and I remember when studying in Mysore in the mid-1990s the cultural capital of Karnataka, my Mysore friends were warned not to befriend the 'fast', 'modern' (an euphemism for promiscuous, cultureless) Kodava girls. This modernity, following Pandian, I argue is 'one step outside modernity' thereby making it one step ahead of the upper-caste modern. A modernity where gender-community participation is seen as undesirable, a modernity that sought to separate exterior and interior—relegating women and caste to the spiritual possibly perceives modernities without these binaries as the undesirable modern. This modernity, however undesirable, in fact precisely undesirable since it unsettles hierarchies of gender, caste and communities, and moves forward to a modernity that is more or less equally participatory, in matters of accessing English education is what makes it one step ahead of upper-caste modernity particularly during the period when Rice wrote his report. The period 1834–1990 in the history of Kodagu has been prominent for its representation by the Europeans as a period in the history of colonial rule that saw little or hardly any anti-colonial struggles. Most colonial records and ethnographies and gazettes make no mention of any community's anti-colonial struggle. Non-Kodava and Kannada historians writing in Kannada have focused on the 'little' histories of anti-colonial positions and struggles in Kodagu roughly from around 1900–1947, in which the visit of Gandhi to Kodagu in 1932 stands out. While these two contradictory positions are understandable from their own locations, I wish to question both these positions. I argue that the relationship of Kodavas, the prominent community of Kodagu, has neither been as smooth as the colonizers liked to believe nor has been as nationalist as charted out mainly by non-Kodava/non-Kodagu historians. My attempt is to show how the narrative of nationalism has always been associated with anti-colonial struggles which are in turn associated with the tensions between modernity and tradition. My argument at this point is that while this meta-narrative of anti-colonialism and nationalism may hold good for the national elite during colonial and post-colonial times, for the backward and lower castes, colonial modernity meant a different thing altogether.

There are many questions that need elaboration and require separate attention in this context: What did progress and reform mean for the people of Kodagu in the colonial context and how did it differ from that of the mainstream? From what we have seen above, reform and progress meant a participation in a sphere via school education, participating in a manner that enabled communities and genders. Given the fact that education was supported by Kodavas belonging to different classes, it is a space that Kodava claimed as a space for their politics. Especially because the subject of nationalist reform and colonial reform, as many studies point out, has been 'the Hindu woman', and because gender identities and gender relations, like any other practices or ways of life in the context of Kodagu are outside the framework of Hindu, and being altogether digressive from what is known from the nationalist point of view, we need to understand modernity in such contexts as the Kodavas.

Unlike the questions of revivalism and reform that has characterized studies like that of Partha Chatterjee concentrating on responses to colonial modernity in the context of nationalism, responses to colonial modernity in domains like Kodagu where revivalism did not play a role need attention.

Also since Kodavas, the prominent community in Kodagu, and their relation with other minorities in Kodagu has been problematic, we need to look at how colonial modernity redefined the relationships among communities in Kodagu. This is to a certain extent inseparable from the 'coming' of coffee plantations to Kodagu, introduced by the British.

The dynamics of modernity, then, turn out to have different effective histories in different institutional sites, even in the same historical period and for the same people. This phenomenon cannot be understood as uneven development, because it is not simply a problem of different time lags or uneven dispersion over space. Rather, it becomes necessary to suspend the totalizing structural contrasts between the modern and the pre-modern and focus instead on localized, contingent and often transient changes in actual practices (Chatterjee 2008: 325).

The path of modernity in the context of India is not an easy one to chart. As pointed out earlier, this is precisely because modernity though associated with colonialism and usually referred to as colonial modernity for our purposes here, cannot be conceptualized under one model or framework. And as Chatterjee elaborates, we need to look at modernity in its 'localized, contingent and often transient changes in actual practices'. There is also the need to understand colonial modernity and modernity as being negotiated by the coercive power of the nation-states and other agencies or that of the colonizer in the colonial context. Prominent projects of reform associated with colonial modernity and nationalism consolidated the hegemonic order of brahminism in one form or the other. While as Vasudha Dalmia clearly demonstrates revivalism in the same context is mostly seen in opposition to modernization. My framework for colonial modernity in Kodagu seeks to question this polarity between revivalism and reformism, and tradition and modernity. Because,

> The traditional/modern polarity used to establish the distinction between the indigenous and the alien was a part of the self-expression of those who sought to depict their tradition as standing firm against the pressure of change. (Dalmia 1997: 5)

Again as pointed out earlier, this kind of polarity between tradition and modernity, and between revivalism and reform held true only for the upper castes, whose position in the traditional order had begun to be questioned from various other positions. For the lower castes and for communities like the Kodavas whose practices was firmly rooted in material conditions (unlike brahminical order's dependence on spiritual superiority which was inaccessible to the lower order), the question was *not* to stand firm and establish their spiritual superiority as against a material West. Neither was the lower castes' response to colonial modernity characterized by the imagining of the nation, courtesy Benedict Anderson. As Dilip Menon (2006) points out, for the lower castes, before the nation was imagined, free and 'modern' individual, families, and homes had to be imagined. Along with the imagining of the 'modern individual', these minority communities also had to imagine a community of their own, especially so because, for centuries together, they had been ruled both politically and culturally by Hindu communities. Therefore the rhetoric of anti-colonial nationalism would be of little help for us to understand how these individuals and communities imagined and actively constructed identities of their own during colonial times. Without falling into the trap of defining a community as static—because this would lead to the assumption that 'there is coherence of interests, actions, and values within these communities—which binds together the actions of individuals and engenders fixed identities (Menon 2006) and caste), what might help is to look into how the Kodava community and its constituent individuals negotiated colonial modernity to interests that best suited their needs. Drawing from Menon, community here is looked into in terms of resistance to the existing, unequal social order. This would enable us to critique nationalism's notion of a wider community of Hindus devoid of differences within and outside its fold. Following Aijaz Ahmad (1994) about how the discourse of nationalism has determined discussions on identity and cultural forms in the context of colonial and postcolonial India, I would argue that we need to look at these formations beyond the discourse of nationalism and anti-colonialism. Though it appears simplistic, for Kodavas modernity ushered through colonialism is a very powerful signifier towards 'progress' and how it works towards 'desired (happy) story-endings (Osella and Osella 2004 40)'. My understanding of backward and lower castes' response to colonialism and modernity is also drawn from and based on Ambedkar's critique (1979–2003) of the nationalist movement, which by its emphasis on modern education and by its strong anti-caste ideology, deviated from the major reformers of the period including Gandhi's.

If this is a modernity that can be understood not necessarily as anti-colonial, not framed by nationalist debates of the time, but as mobility involving no or less tensions between different kinds of practices, it is also a modernity that empowers. Alok Mukherjee's study (2009) argues that 'the gift of English' to the brahmanical classes helped consolidate and further empower their hegemony in newer ways'. To communities like the Kodava, the gift of English, I would argue, worked in many ways. It countered the dominant modes of brahminical knowledge—although this mode was not very prevalent in Kodagu, the countering offers us newer ways of understanding education from domains away from the nationalist mainstream. The gift of English and English education also gives us alternate notions of existing practices of gender and how those notions can lead us conceptualize communities, notions beyond the anti-colonial, nationalist framework. Needless to say, English has also been empowering to backward and lower castes, as argued by many, giving them spaces of knowledge and mobility. Being largely the first local community in Kodagu to be educated, it also consolidated the Kodavas' hold over other lower castes as mentioned in the 1882 Rice Report. This combined with the coming of the coffee plantation in Kodagu leading to the requirement of new labour, leading to and new class/caste relations, which take us to a field that is yet to be looked into.

REFERENCES

Ahmad, Aijaz. 1994. *In Theory: Classes, Nations, Literature*, New Delhi: OUP.

Ambedkar, B.R. 1979-2003. *Collected Works*. vols. 17, Mumbai: Department of Education, Government of Maharashtra, 1979-2003.

Chatterjee, Partha, 2008. 'Critique of Popular Culture,' *Public Culture* 20, 2: 321-44.

———. 1997. 'Community in the East.' Presented in the 22nd Word Congress of the International Political Science Association, Seoul, August 1997.

———. 1989. 'The Nationalist Resolution of the Women's Question.' *Recasting Women: Essays in Colonial History,* edited by Kumkum Sangari and Sudesh Vaid, Delhi: Kali for Women: 233-53.

Chinnappa, Nadikerianda. 1924. *Pattole Palame*, Bengaluru: Kannada Pustaka Pradhikara.

Dalmia, Vasudha. 1997. *The Nationalisation of Hindu Tradition*, New Delhi: Oxford University Press.

*Karnataka State Gazatteer: Kodagu District*. 1993. Suryanath Kamath (chief editor), Bangalore: Government of India.

Menon, Dilip. 2006. *The Blindness of Insight: Essays on Caste in Modern India*, Pondicherry: Navayana.

———.1994. *Caste, Nationalism and Communism in South India, Malabar 1900-1948*, Cambridge: Cambridge University Press.

Moegling, H. 1855. *Coorg Memoirs: An Account of Coorg Memoirs and of the Coorg Mission*, Bangalore: Wesleyan Missionary Press.

Mukherjee, Alok. 2009. *This Gift of English: English Education and the Formation of Alternative Hegemonies in India*, Hyderabad: Orient Blackswan.

Osella, Caroline, and Filippo Osella. 2004. 'Once a Upon Time in the West: Narrating Modernity in Kerala, South India', *Culture and Modernity: History Explorations,* Calicut: Calicut University Press.

Pandian, M. S. S. 2002. 'One Step Outside Modernity: Caste, Identity Politics and Public Sphere', *Economic and Political Weekly* 37, 18 (4 May): 1735–41.

Pani, Susmit Prasad, and Samar Kumar Pattnaik. 2006. *Vivekananda, Aurobindo and Gandhi on Education*, New Delhi: Amol Publications.

Rice, Lewis. 1882. *Report on Education in Coorg: 1834–1882*, Calcutta: Indian Education Commission. Government of India.

Ritcher, G. [1879] 2002. *Gazetteer of Coorg*, New Delhi: Low Price Publications.

# 11

# Nation, Ideal Womanhood and English Education

## REVISITING THE FIRST TULU NOVEL, *SATI KAMALE*

Yogitha Shetty

*'All forms of consensus are by necessity based on acts of exclusion.'*

–Chantal Mouffe[1]

NINETEENTH-CENTURY INDIA has drawn a significant amount of scholarly attention principally on account of the subcontinent's encounter with colonial modernity, and the emergence of nationalism during the last quarter of the century. Colonialism, in general, and the modern apparatuses it brought along, in particular, elicited diverse responses from different communities across the subcontinent. In an ambivalent engagement, the colonized elite on the one hand reaped fruits from the colonial machinery, and on the other, attempted to reinvent 'the' tradition so as to fashion a 'modern', national subject of a particular kind of nationalism.

This essay attempts to study the dominant 'Hindu' nationalist sentiments as narrated in the first Tulu novel, *Sati Kamale* (1921, published in 1936) by S. U. Paniyadi while contextualizing it within the significantly transforming ethno-linguistic minority region of South Canara[2] in the beginning of the twentieth century. *Sati Kamale* is a treatise of the anti-colonial nationalist project, and a critique of the colonial modernity brought chiefly in the form of English education to the natives. I problematize the nationalist project of Paniyadi, which blankets the heterogeneity prevalent among Tuluvas, Tulu-speaking inhabitants of 'Tulunad' or 'Tulu-country,' under the all-encompassing garb of anti-colonial, dominant nationalism. Meanwhile, an account of the advent of modernity through English education brought by the Basel missionaries, and the subsequent rise of nationalist awareness among some sections of Tuluva society follows, as a trajectory, to imply the complex nature of the ambivalent engagement with colonial modernity.

RECONFIGURING THE SOCIETY

The then South Canara, Udupi and Kasargodu districts of the coastal region of Karnataka were brought under the Madras Presidency in 1799 with the defeat of Tipu Sultan.[3] With the enactment of the Charter of 1833 which permitted Christian missionaries to enter India, the Basel Evangelical Missionary Society came to the country in 1834 and set up its first station in the coastal city of Mangalore. Its purview of activities gradually spread to other parts of southwest India, making it the most important missionary outpost of the Basel Mission (Shetty 2008).[4] The Mission established its first school in 1836 in Mangalore, and went on to set up different kinds of institutions like Parochial Schools, Catechist Institution (theological seminary), Canarese and English Schools, Canarese School for girls in 1856.[5] Boarding houses which, in addition to proselytizing into Protestant Christianity, also served in supplying catechists; Christian masters to the missionary schools and native workforce to colonial government offices, thereby disciplining the bodies to fit into 'modern' institutions like the factory, the school, the government offices, and so on. The Mission introduced a printing press in the region in 1849, and Industrial Institution, acquainting people with new professions, was founded in 1850. The wide-ranging activities of the Basel Mission in South Canara effectuated significant socio-religious restructurings of Tuluva society. It re-contoured the existing mappings of caste, class and gender hierarchies, engendering new constituencies in the much-altered society. The pedagogic strategies and the educational institutions of the Basel Mission (the means of constituting and defining new forms of community) intersect, under-mine, re-form and collude with existing forms of community in the region' (ibid.: 512).

While the presence of the Basel missionaries induced an irre-versible restructuring of Tuluva society in general, a cursory study of the composition of different kinds of schools set up by the Basel missionaries in South Canara with a specific focus on the Brahmin caste could open up sufficient instances to understand how the upper caste maintained a dichotomous relationship with the western edu-cation brought by the missionaries. This ambivalent engagement of upper castes with colonial modernity is discussed later while dealing with the subject of modern education as addressed in *Sati Kamale*. The focus on the Brahmin caste and its negotiation with western education is of particular significance within my concerns as both the author of *Sati Kamale* is a Brahmin and the nationalist ideology his novel espouses is dominant Hindu in nature.

In addition, browsing through the history of major communities in South Canara like Bunts[6] and Brahmins throws ample light on the newly-awakened consciousness about the necessity of modern edu-cation for their youth, which further nurtured the cause of nation-alist consciousness among the native population. In his detailed study on the Bunt caste, Surendra Rao records that 'the educational renaissance in the district in which the Bunts participated was so pas-sionate that by 1925 there was even an opinion that South Canara indeed needed a Tulu University' (2010: 210). This impulse to set up a Tulu University in the region by some dominant sections of the region needs to be viewed with the backdrop of emerging nation-alistic fervour among them. The anti-colonial nationalism that was gearing up in some other parts of the country had its impact on some groups of the southwest coast as well. Growing community awareness which also contributed to national consciousness was evident in the way many associations like Bunt Sangha and Upasana Sabha[7] were built. Many instances of reconverting the Christian converts into the 'Hindu' fold have been noted. A branch of Arya Samaj set up in Mangalore in 1918, the Theosophical Society established in Mangalore in 1901, the Home Rule League established in 1917, and the tremendous appeal these had for the upper-caste Brahmins and the higher non-Brahmin castes like Bunts explain the mobilization of nationalistic ideals among a certain section of Tuluva society. The ideas of National Education and women's education brought with Mrs Annie Besant's two visits to Mangalore further strengthened the cause of indigenism in the region.[8] After Gandhi's visit to Mangalore in 1920, these groups participated in the movements and Swarajist Party activities, subscribing to the Gandhian Swadeshi ideals of national education, popularization of Hindi, revitalization of Hindu religion, *deshi*[9] clothes, eradication of untouchability, and so on.[10]

It is within this setting of the nationalist project and religious reform in the South Canara region, in the early twentieth century that I proceed to place and analyse the first novel published in Tulu language, *Sati Kamale* by S. U. Paniyadi. However, a theoretical frame that situates such an artistic expression within a larger cultural discourse is necessary for an imminent critique. Such an account of the works, by social scientists and cultural critics, is outlined here to engage with the first novel in Tulu language.

## FRAMING WITHIN FRAMEWORK

In his much acclaimed study of the rise of nationalism among Bengali bhadralok, Partha Chatterjee (1993) explains this seeming contradiction by pointing at the bi-level categories of 'inner' or 'spiritual' and 'outer' or 'material.' He argues that nationalism in the colonies 'produced a discourse in which, even as it challenged the colonial claim to political domination, also accepted the very intellectual premises of "modernity" on which colonial domination was based'. While the privileged colonized class acknowledged the supremacy of colonizers in the 'material' sphere, it struck a 'strategic compromise' by adopting 'a dichotomous, even schizophrenic, consciousness' (Menon 2006) while retreating into the 'spiritual' world of language, family, religion and women. Tanika Sarkar (2001) well qualifies this in her analysis of the late nineteenth-century Bengali Hindu middle class's turn towards Hindu cultural indigenism and nationalism, and its reappearance in the form of Hindutva ideologies in contemporary postcolonial India, particularly after the demolition of Babri Masjid in 1992.

While Chatterjee's study helps us to move away from the eurocentric views of nationalism as 'a set of modular forms' co-opted by the East in imagining the nation (as propounded by Anderson in his celebrated work *Imagined Communities: Reflections on the Origin and Spread of Nationalism* in 1983), his claims that the 'material-spiritual' formula is 'a fundamental feature of anti-colonial nationalisms in Asia and Africa' has been problematized by later scholars (Menon 2006; Guru 2011; Pandian 2002) in recent times. The boarding house examples that Chatterjee draws from Bipinchandra Pal's memoirs[11] while explaining the inner/outer duality displays is, in fact, a dichotomy between 'inner' domain of upper-caste Hindus and the 'outer' world of subaltern sections of the society. Both Pandian and Menon insist on shifting the locale of discourse from the dominant, singular 'national community' to the marginalized sections; from the diametric categories of nationalism and colonialism to the oppositional dialogues of dominant nationalism with the subaltern articulations which would reveal alternative imaginations of the nation, and 'deviant' engagements with colonial modernity at large. As Menon says, 'If we place the experience of the subordinated castes at the centre of our understanding of colonial modernity, we are faced with the unresolved dilemma of belonging' (112). The clearly defined domains of interior/exterior, spiritual/material crumbles when the arena of analysis is expanded to include the marginalized, hitherto relegated constituencies as well. When colonial modernity produced discontent among the dominant elite—in the inner domain in particular—under the sweeping air of nationalism, the marginal sections of the society negotiated with the colonizers on their own terms. To quote an example, a group of Kodavas, a linguistic minority community in Karnataka, wrote a letter to the colonial officials around 1860s endorsing English education as an essential aspect of Kodava life, thereby paving the way for an alternative modernity as against the anti-colonial nationalism that was prevalent at many places in the country, anachronous at that time (see Chapter 10). Similarly in 1868, a petition signed by 34 people in Mangalore was submitted to the German missionaries requesting them to reopen the Brahmin girls' school and to appoint Europeans as teachers. Hailing missionary education in their petition, the supplicants also gathered a donation 297 rupees to the Mission.[12]

With this background, while analysing the novel *Sati Kamale* within the framework of Chatterjee and Sarkar's formulations on nation and nationalism, the essay also critically analyses the homogenizing tendency that effaces out the 'little traditions' and subaltern subjectivities from mainstream discourse.


THE NOVEL, NATION AND WOMAN


The late nineteenth and early twentieth centuries in India have been an era of academic interest along with the emergence of nationalism, print culture, formation of community consciousness and the establishment of new constituencies/public spheres of articulation. The period also witnessed the rise of new literary genres of expression like the novel. The novel form stepped in neither as a mere imitation of the western genre nor did it create a rupture into the traditional forms of narration already available here. While examining the 'synthesis of the borrowed literary form and indigenous aesthetics as well as cultural expectations' that comes to inform the genre of novel in India, Meenakshi Mukherjee (1985: 18) also points at the contemporary socio-political scenario which contributed to the emergence of the novel form. Her prominent work *Early Novels in India* (2002) is a project to study 'the complex configuration behind the emergence of the new genre (in different Indian languages) and locate it in the intersecting webs of social, cultural and economic changes taking place during the colonial era' (2002: vii). The rise of dominant nationalism and the consequent engagement with colonial modernity is one of the chief aspects which informed the production of novels in some Indian languages including Tulu. To qualify this in Dilip Menon's words, 'The late nineteenth century in India saw the fortuitous coincidence of the first stirrings of nationalist sentiment as well as the emergence of a new artefact of the imagination—the novel' (2006: 73). With the two interpretive frames: imaginings of the nation and the formation of colonial modernity, Menon, by his reading of the Malayalam novels of the subordinated caste groups, adds a third one—'fashioning of the modern self and new forms of community' (ibid.: 75). The early novels addressed a turbulent present, engaging with questions of self, community and society, particularly relating to ongoing debates about the role of women, and this explains for many early novels being eponymous with their heroines. One among them is the pioneering Tulu novel *Sati Kamale*.

The first novel in Tulu, *Sati Kamale* written by Srinivasa Upadhyaya Paniyadi,[13] could well be seen as a treatise on the then existing indigenous discourse, and an elucidation of the formation of national identity through the dichotomy of space, gender in the Indian national project of the nineteenth century. While propagating the Gandhian principles of the Swadeshi movement, it launches a scathing attack on the English educational apparatus brought about by the colonizers. The novel is replete with references, discussions and debates surrounding the issues of nationalism and ideal subjecthood, attempting to create a different set of youth who devote their life to the cause of the 'motherland'. The symbolic function of ritual embodied in the mystical notion of female virtue and power appended by indigenous/*deshi* education is the predominant ideological undercurrent in the novel. A synopsis of the major episodes bringing out the most relevant themes of the novel is provided.[14]

The eponymous novel is centred on the protagonist Kamale who is a personification of resistance to the alien/colonial forces translated in the form of westernized *deshis* like Narayanaraya. She is a female counterpart to the self-declared soldiers like her husband, Umesha, who fight against the colonial forces at a larger level. The locus of their struggle—Madras and Mangalore in the case of Kamale and 'far off' Calcutta in the case of Umesha; home in the case of Kamale and the world outside for Umesha—Umesha against the British colonizers and Kamale against the westernized-oriental-gentlemen like Narayanaraya. This already indicates the two realms of resistance that the nationalist project envisaged for the purpose, based chiefly on the dichotomy of home/world and woman/man.

Drawing from the formulations of Chatterjee, the two domains of 'the outer' and 'the inner' or 'the material' and 'the spiritual,' one can debate the location of women within dominant Hindu nationalism of the later nineteenth and early twentieth centuries in India. As the outer domain was influenced, controlled by the colonial culture, the nationalist project turned to reiterate its control of the cultural realm (chiefly embodied in the forms of home, family, women and spiritual life) making it the sanctuary of resistance to foreign control. Home in its essence must remain unaffected by the corrupting influences of the material world, and women being its representation must protect the high ideals of chastity, purity, conjugal love and sacrifice. The female body was a site of resistance to the alien/colonial powers, and women assumed the dual roles of 'Heroic Women and Mother Goddesses'. To quote Sarkar (1995),

> The Hindu woman's body, hemmed in with scriptural ritual, was imagined as a pure space that escaped the transformative effects of colonisation . . . the woman's body, having passed through the grid of Hindu ritual exercises, therefore alone remained, for these Hindus, the site of an existent freedom as well as the future nation (186).

Similarly, the emphasis laid on the notions of female chastity and purity by the upper-caste Brahmin author Paniyadi in the novel *Sati Kamale* echoes the gendered spirit of the time. The emancipatory project of nationalism appropriates the inviolate, acquired space of woman's body in its scheme of things. Kamale's one vow that compels Umesha to marry her, is the preservation of her chastity, and the 'last' letter that he writes to Kamale also is an unconditional attempt to reaffirm the same. While authoritatively charting a role for Kamale, Umesha writes,

> Forgoing all the worldly desires, I am ready to sacrifice my life for the cause of the nation, if the need may arise. I have married you trusting the promise you have made. Here! Beware! I am one among those heroic men. You should also be a heroic woman. In case of my death, at attaining age, you should also serve the country. Do not long for worldly things. There should not be a shred of taint on your chastity. You should sacrifice your life for chastity and celibacy. Do not think for a minute of sleeping with another man. With that very thought your chastity will come to an end. Beware! Kame!... Don't be deceived, *don't be spoiled and do not spoil...* (emphasis mine)(24–26).[15]

The vehement fervency associated with the speech of Umesha also gets reverberated in Kamale in her unrelenting debate with adversary Narayanaraya about various 'evils'/issues of Hindu society like widowhood, remarriage, chastity and patriotism. Through the heroine, the author interposes to endorse child marriage for females; celibacy for men; chastity for women and monogamy for men; the crucial role of women in men's lives, and so on. Denouncing the opposite sex as 'monkeys being marionetted by women' she says, 'If you need Swaraj, set your women right first . . . Rajput kings became warriors only because of Rajput women' (48). The entire debate that Kamale launches here and also the public speech she delivers while setting the western clothes ablaze is aimed at instigating 'manliness' in men, thereby spearing them for the cause of a homogenized Hindu nation. At two or three instances in the novel, the author in the disguise of the protagonist emphasizes the moral resistance strategies of women and refuses to admit that women could ever be raped/sexually abused without their consent. Kamale says, 'I never would believe that the chastity of women could be ruined by men without their consent. If a woman has the urge to retain her chastity, she could drive the men away like dogs' (46).

As an exemplification of this, Kamale assumes the violent self-image of goddess Mahakali when she is sexually confronted by

Narayanaraya. She is presented with a dagger[16] by her husband to protect her absolute and unconditional virtue which becomes a unifying tool in the dramatic reunion of the couple in the final pages. Woman/inner domain is a sovereign territory refusing to allow anything foreign to intervene, and more significantly this onus of protecting the essential identity and spiritual quality of the national culture rests with the women. Women like Kamale are the custodians of the 'inscape' of the nation as imagined by the Hindu cultural indigenists. Kamale becomes a tool to construct the nation's sovereignty over the crucial domain of cultural hegemony, and citizens like Umesha who sacrifices his life for the cause of the nation, sidelining all other worldly desires. Umesha with 'Vande Mataram' in his mouth is a symbol of the 'Hindu imaginary of disciplined, warlike, chauvinistic nation-builders reared on a pedagogical apparatus of martial, scriptural and nationalistic values' (Sarkar 1993: 6).

Conjugality within the alternative order of home is 'conceived as an embryonic nation' (ibid.: 39), which is set as a dichotomy to the materialistic values of colonialism. Kamale and Umesha's unconsummated, non-consensual spiritual love upholds the ideals of a lifetime companionship which grows even in the absence of the companion is underlined by Kamale in her debate with Narayanaraya. For fifteen long years Kamale lives the life of a widow to the outside world, nurturing the hopes of reuniting with her husband one day. Alone in the room, each night she wears her marks of a married woman, caresses the image of her husband, sings *shlokas* from the Bhagavad Gita and the patriotic song of 'Vande Mataram' according to his parting instructions. She adopts and propagates the life of willed chastity, austerity and sacrifice, belonging to her husband in the spiritual, transcendental world, also thereby escaping from 'foreign' domination. The novel ends in reinstating the indissoluble minor marriage of Kamale-Umesha facilitated by the nationalistic symbols of dagger and 'Vande Mataram' on the 'pristine' Himalayan mountains. As Sarkar aptly summarises:

> Hindu nationalists…argued that non-consensual Hindu marriages could, indeed, be more loving than the Western pattern of courtship…In the Hindu case, a lifetime of togetherness

beginning with infancy guaranteed a superior and more certain compatibility…While the entire system of non-consensual, indissoluble, infant marriage was to be preserved intact and inviolate, each aspect of the Hindu marriage needed to be written as a love story with a happy ending (40–41).

## THE NOVEL AND EDUCATION

While Paniyadi's novel, written during his sojourn in Gujarat, subscribes to the prevalent anti-colonial discourse of the time, it spares no chance to denounce the English education made available by the colonial masters. Both the heroine and direct authorial intervention at many places in the novel ascribe all evil developments in the then contemporary society to the westernization process brought about by foreign education. In one such authorial aside this excoriation of the imported culture comes in its most unjacketed words:

> On the whole, our country is in a regretful state. The number of people learning our knowledge has decreased. It lacks encouragement. People have been lured by western education and civilization. We are now left with nothing. Everything is gone. We have already dubbed gods as stones. *Shastras* have been disposed off as Brahmins' composition to earn their livelihood. *Deshi* clothes have become signs of poverty. Vernacular languages signify savagery. Hindu denotes servants. Everything is gone with only one scene left here—Whites becoming priests in conducting the *shraddhavivaha* rituals, at least as an enactment. When will our people open their eyes? Only God can answer! (28).

In an elaborate Swadeshi speech that the protagonist delivers while burning western clothes in the public, she attributes the erasure of justice and freedom in society, destruction of the social fabric of 'Hindustan' to an alien education system. Narayanaraya's brutal act of poisoning his innocent wife was also identified with the vile language of English. Although the novel speaks for the cause of women's education, it is selectively prescriptive in advocating *deshi* education alone, embodied in the form of Sanskrit learning, an invocation of

Vedic civilization. Kamale has made a conscious choice of pursuing a B.A. in Sanskrit which, according to the author, has facilitated her understanding of temporal, worldly duties. But ironically enough, the institution of English education that is denied to others in the novel is readily made available to Kamale (a graduate, speaking English), her father-in-law (a lawyer by profession) and her husband, Umesha (a graduate from Calcutta). The novel constructs a dichotomous portrayal of westernized slayer Narayanaraya on the one side and the virtuous, Sanskrit-read, self-abnegating 'sati,'[17] Kamale on the other.

The heteroglossic conflict prevalent within the upper-caste brahminical negotiations with colonial modernity, specifically in relation to western education, is reflected in the novel *Sati Kamale* as well. The Sanskrit-educated, 'Vande Mataram' reciting protagonist Kamale, her husband, father-in-law are clearly the beneficiaries of modernity, modern means of education made available by the westerners since the mid-nineteenth century in the Tulu region. These characters who launch a scathing attack on western education symbolized by English are themselves recipients of the same modern education. This is indicative of a contradiction between the historical relationship of Brahmins like Paniyadi to western institutional education and the nationalist ideology he espouses.

A study of the Basel Mission Annual reports sheds sufficient light on this dichotomous historical relationship. After the experimental period of around two decades, the Basel Mission Report of 1852 records that a majority of scholars or pupils to the Higher Educational Institutions called as 'English Schools'[18] comprised of Brahmins in Mangalore. The 'English Schools' with highest Brahmin students was also the most popular among different kinds of Schools maintained by the missionaries. To quote from the 1852 Report:

> These schools, in which, besides the English language, most of the higher educational branches of study are attended to, have been hitherto numerously attended, and seemed altogether in a promising state.[19]

Although this school was open to all children of the region, a look at the 1850 census of students of the English Schools informs us that a majority of the boys who attended were Brahmins. Among the total of 157 students enrolled, Brahmins alone consisted of 98, amounting to 62 per cent while Protestants, Roman Catholics, Mussalmans (the spelling used in Basel Mission Reports) and other castes together numbered only 59. In addition, although their presence in the Canarese Schools with Kannada medium was also on a higher side, in aggregate it was merely 45 per cent. As early as 1837 a school for Brahmin boys with a Brahmin teacher was started by the missionaries and 1855, a school was set up for the Brahmin girls with wives of missionaries Lehner and Griener as their first teachers (ibid.: 549). And, the earliest high school for girls established by the indigenous society in Mangalore was the Canara Girls High School by the Gowd Saraswat Brahmins in 1896. Thus, the Brahmins were not only the earliest in reaping benefits of English education but also were the majority to do so. As Shetty (2008) says,

> The communities that had established themselves as superior in caste hierarchy were also the first to avail of the new opportunities made possible by the colonial institutions and missionary education (543).

While such an institutional interaction led to a 'cultural hybridization,' creating educated, westernized upper-caste representatives, the process was not devoid of internal tensions. Many Basel Mission Reports record cultural objections raised by the Brahmins towards heterogeneous caste configuration of Missionary Schools. The spatial organization of these Schools were unheeding to caste regulations governing the prerogatives of privileged caste, and this resulted in many exodus of the Brahmin students, albeit to return later. Despite fear of conversion and infringement of caste rules, the Brahmins continued to reap from English education; the chief intention was getting government jobs. This trajectory of upper-caste encounter with western education when placed in contrast to the tirade launched against English education within the spatial enclosure of Paniyadi's novel, the contradictions of upper-caste engagement with colonial modernity, its inherent contradictions are unwrapped for the reading publics.

## THE INVISIBLE 'VOICES'

While we have analysed the Hindu ideologically-driven nationalist selfhood that Paniyadi invokes in the novel, it is also essential to discuss the thorough disavowal of caste in the entire Swadeshi paradigm that he generates. The crux of the novel—Kamale's discussion on the blemishes of Hindu religion with Narayanaraya—ironically is completely mute about one of the biggest stigmas of the subcontinent's society: caste. Debate between the two revolves around various issues like child marriage, celibacy, widowhood, remarriage, sexual abuse of women, Swaraj, and so on, excluding caste, and thereby delegitimizing the language of caste in both political and cultural sphere (Pandian: 1737). Caste remains 'the Other' of and outside the fold of nationalist project which silently inscribes itself as 'upper' caste. 'Caste always belongs to someone else; it is somewhere else; it is of another time' (ibid.: 1735). The self-fashioned 'nationalist self' represses caste in the public sphere, expunges it from the paradigm, denying it any audibility at all. 'The derivative and the desi… hesitate to engage with the local but show an extraordinary urgency to confront the imperial State in the colonial configuration of power' (Guru: 39).[20]

Further, the uncompromising moral resolve of safeguarding the sanctity of her marital status 'Sati' Kamale displays in the novel could also be critiqued from the standpoint of an ideal Tuluva woman presented in one of the major oral narratives of *Siri Paddana* in Tulu region.[21] The ideal womanhood invoked in the 'text' of the Siri oral song, unlike the Sati envisaged in the novel, doesn't enter the masculine world either as 'a heroic mother, chaste wife or celibate warrior'. Faced with the disloyalty of her husband, Siri curses him, pronounces divorce and walks out of his house, leaving the village behind in cinders. Moving on, Siri also remarries another man bearing a female child from this wedlock. The paragon of chastity and womanhood emphasized by the patriarchal Hindu-self in the case of Sati, doesn't find any significance in the mythical and ritualistic world of Siri, an integral part of thousands of women in the Tulu region. One of the Siri women offering her corporeal/mediating services to the deity for more than four decades reiterated,

It is only because Siri married again, the tradition of remarriage became a part of Tulunad and its social system. It is only because Siri cursed (her first husband), and went ahead to marry again that it got incorporated into our caste culture. No second marriage, if not for Siri![22]

Regardless, the Hindu nationalist imagination espoused in the novel doesn't deem it fit to incorporate a 'defiled' body like Siri in its scheme of ideal citizen for the impending nation. The nationalist invocation of Vedic/Aryan civilization homogenizes the differential experiences under the garb of mono national community. The overarching all-Brahmin world of *Sati Kamale* refuses to admit the existence of heterogeneous non-Brahmin voices that could cause rupture to the all-subsuming normativity of Aryan civilization/'Indian Tradition'. All-pervading 'Vande Mataram' subsumes the innumerable 'folk' forms of *paddana, kabita, sandi, obele*[23] which are part of the day-to-day existence of Tuluva life. Kamale in her rigorous devotion and asceticism—and in reclaiming her husband from 'death'—is modelled, as mentioned earlier, after Savitri in an intertextual reference to *Mahabharata*'s episode of 'Savitri and Satyavan.' The much prevalent narrative of *Siri* that has permeated deep into a large section of the Tuluva psyche is, in fact, an insufficient 'history' to fit into the nationalist project of Paniyadi. 'Nationalization of tradition' (Vasudha Dalmia quoted in Blackburn 2003) banishes 'folklore' as 'too native, too redolent of backward traditions, to be capable of assuming the public mantle of a political nationalism (ibid.: 16).'

Placing this novel in contrast to the Malayalam novel *Saraswativijayam* (1893) will challenge the anti-English tirade that it has set forth. Written by a Tiyya Vakil Potheri Kunhambu, *Saraswativijayam* aimed at depicting 'the plight of the suffering creatures (Pulayas)' advocating modern education as the chief remedy out of this distress. 'Education is the greatest wealth' says its epigraph, 'the pragmatic and robust alternative of empowerment through colonial education' (Menon: 124). Although, still oscillating between the worlds of colonial modernity and tradition, 'the blandishments of colonial modernity meant much more to him [Kunhambu] than the doubtful solace of tradition' (ibid.: 121). Identically, the absent articulations of non-Brahmin communities in *Sati Kamale* could have perhaps revealed alternative imaginations of the nation and colonial modernity offered to them. I qualify this with an example: one of the projects of the nationalist agenda 'Temple Entry' of Harijans and *Harijanoddara*—a Gandhian attempt to assimilate Dalits within its hegemonic framework—of which the author in discussion, Paniyadi, was an active member (more than a decade after he penned the novel) evoked an unassuming response from the community in question. An anonymous letter from a Billawa community member, considered lower in the caste hierarchy, was published in the newspaper *Swadeshabhimani*, 28 October 1932, rejecting the 'reformatory' offer as a strategy with some ulterior motives, and that there was no need for the Billawas to enter 'Other' temples. This alternative subaltern thought should be considered 'outside' the framework of *deshi* that the mainstream nationalist discourse offers to us, one of them being *Sati Kamale*. Finally, recasting of 'other,' subaltern discursive practices and alternative modernities to the centre stage may not lend itself for an easy, lucid study of the 'modern self'.

## NOTES

[1] Chantal Mouffe quoted in Pandian (2002).
[2] 'South Canara' was the colonial name of the coastal province of the present-day Dakshina Kannada, Udupi districts in Karnataka, also including Kasargodu district, now in Kerala. The term 'Tulunad' is often used to refer the region with Tulu as lingua franca. Unless otherwise used in quotations in this paper, I retain the colonial spelling of 'South Canara.'
[3] A ruler who had overthrown the Wodeyars of Mysore to occupy Mysore, Coorg, South Canara and some other parts of the then Mysore kingdom, founding a new kingdom, becoming an implacable enemy of British expansionism. An alliance of the British with the Nizam of Hyderabad and the Marathas defeated his army in the battle of Srirangapatnam, 1799, where Tipu Sultan was killed and his children exiled to Calcutta.

⁴ In this paper, information about the Basel Mission and its activities in South Canara is chiefly informed by Parinitha Shetty (2008).

⁵ However, girls started going to schools for the first time in 1843 itself, as recorded in the Basel Mission Report of the same year. The object of this endeavour was to render the girls good Christian wives and mothers.

⁶ It is said that as early as 1865, Timma Shetty started a school at Karnad near Mulki. To quote Rao (2010), who provides the major source of information on the Bunts: 'By the end of the nineteenth century the Bunt preference for modern education was clearly registered in schools. They followed with alacrity the early lead taken by the Brahmins and Christians.' The Bunt Sangha, which had come into existence in 1907, built hostels to accommodate the Bunt students from distant regions, and the Mutual Help Association built by the Bunts of Mumbai also supported the cause by extending financial help. In the first two decades of the twentieth century, many elementary and primary schools, secondary schools, etc., were established at different places with generous donations from the landlords and prominent persons of the group. Nitte Mahalinga Adyanthaya joined the Edinburgh University in 1912 to pursue B.Sc. becoming the first Bunt to travel abroad for higher education, and this community also recorded its first woman graduate in 1924 who later took up the cause of setting up institutions for girls in the region.

⁷ A society set up by the Saraswat Brahmins incorporating many Brahmo Samaj doctrines in late 1870s. It was started as a counter-association to a branch of the Brahmo Samaj in Mangalore (1870) which held its meetings at Arasappa's house (he was a Billava by caste). The Brahmins found it uncomfortable to gather at a 'low' caste house, and hence this society was set up which later came to be called as the Brahmo Samaj of Mangalore. 'Thus the Brahmo Samaj was transformed from a broadly critical movement led by an untouchable, to one of limited goals under control of the Saraswat Brahmans of Mangalore' (Kenneth W. Jones quoted in Rao 2010).

⁸ Also, National Education Week was celebrated in 1918, and donations were raised for *Rashtriya Balika Shikshana* and National Education Fund during this celebration.

⁹ Tulu and Kannada word for 'indigenous;' Unless used in quotations, I retain the phonetic transcription of *deshi*, not *desi,* to remain closer to the way it is used in the novel.

[10] While on the one hand, the anti-colonial resurgence among certain sections like Brahmins and Bunts in South Canara was a result of the national movement at the larger level, the colonial government's policies on the other hand also contributed to the growing uneasiness among these groups. The colonial administration had brought about many changes in the social and political spheres of life. By the end of the nineteenth century, the administrative machinery had mandated the Patels (village headmen) to pass an examination in order to possess charge of villages. While on the one hand, these sections gained material prospects in their affiliation with the colonizers, on the other, under the same rule, the erasure of prestige associated with being the landed gentry (*guttu*) in the society for generations created annoyance towards the ruling government. Bunts Sangha passed many resolutions demanding the government to make the post of Patels hereditary.

[11] Bipin Chandra Pal (1858–1932), a leader of Swadeshi movement in Bengal; his memoirs: *Memories of My Life and Times*, Kolkata: Modern Book Agency, 1932; digitized, University of Michigan, 2006.

[12] Ramanatha Kotekar (2011: 64).

[13] The 'Tulu movement' which gained momentum for two decades (1920s and 1930s) in Tulunad was spearheaded by S.U. Paniyadi, a Saraswat Brahmin, in Udupi. Although short lived, the movement gave rise to a heightened sense of linguistic identity among a certain educated class of Tuluvas. It derived its inspiration, and in turn, contributed to the nationalist demand at a larger level.

Although the Tulu movement's call for the chiselling out an independent Tulu statehood didn't materialize amidst the dominant presence of unification of Kannada state, Paniyadi's contribution in raising awareness among Tulu intelligentsia about a distinct Tuluva identity is unparalled in Tuluva socio-political history. It calls for a full-length monograph on its own.

[14] The novel commences with an insight into the mind of Narayanaraya who intends to marry a 25-year-old widow Kamale. The heroine of the novel, Kamale is a student of the nearby Mary College in Madras. Author intervenes to narrate the story of the protagonist. She was happily married to Umesha at the age of 10. The groom immediately leaves for Calcutta to join the national movement against the colonizers. The parting vow (similar to the one they had exchanged before marriage) that Umesha

gets from his wife is to remain chaste all her live and to serve the cause of the country if he sacrifices his life in the anti-British struggle. After some days, Umesha is declared dead in a newspaper. Not entirely convinced of her husband's death, Kamale nurtures the hope of reuniting with him one fine day, and this belief leads her to live the life of a widow to the world outside, whereas every night she embraces the life of a married woman (by wearing all the markers of a wife) waiting for her husband's return. Treading on the nationalist path led by her husband, Kamale also gets involved in the Swadeshi movement in Madras. At the same time, she also thwarts the advancements of Narayanaraya, rebuking him for his westernization. But unmindful of Kamale's detestation and still nurturing the hopes of marrying her, Narayanaraya poisons his village-bred wife. His motive to remarry Kamale is ruined as she walks out of her home to an unknown distant land. In the climax of the novel which is set in the Himalayas, Kamale gladly reunites with her ascetic-turned husband Umesha.

[15] All English translation of extracts from *Sati Kamale* are mine.

[16] Also symbolic of the penis.

[17] Kamale attains the mythical name of *Sati* (from the myth of 'Savitri and Satyavan' from *Mahabharata*) after cursing a sanyasi—who tries to seduce her—into blindness in an ashram near Haridwar. Deriving from the referential myth of 'Sati Savitri', as in the myth, even she reunites with her husband at the end.

[18] In 1852, there were two 'English Schools' set up by the missionaries, one in Mangalore and the other in Calicut.

[19] Shetty (2008: 518).

[20] Gopal Guru (2011) points at the three discourses surrounding the idea of India: Derivative, Desi and Beyond creating alternative imaginations of the nation. The first 'derivative' which fashions itself on the modular form of nationalism as developed in the West; the second 'desi' which creates the West as a negative reference point, and the hegemonic discourse assimilating the heterodox intellectual traditions; and the third 'beyond' suggesting a 'parallel problematic' to the first two nationalist thoughts.

[21] The song of Siri, or *Siri Paddana,* sung primarily by women in the fields during paddy transplantation is considered to be a major epic in Tulu. It is the story of three generations of women—Siri, her daughter Sonne, and

twin granddaughters Abbaga and Daraga and the tragedies that befall them. The song of Siri is also a referential script for the Siri ritual, a mass mediumship practice that takes place annually (between January to May) in many places of Tulu region. *Siri Paddana* is significant to this essay as the protagonist Siri emerges, in many ways, as a contrast to 'Sati Savitri' of *Mahabharata*. Siri in her rebellious spirit, divorces her husband who had an illicit relationship, and enters into a second marriage later. She curses the husband to go begging and also burns down the maternal palace that was occupied by the kinsfolk. Siri is evoked by thousands of non-Brahmin Tuluva women during the annual rituals, considering her as an empowering force against the multi-layered exploitation against women existing in society.

[22] In the interview conducted on 16 March 2014 at Shambhulingeshwara Temple in Daregudde in Karkalataluk of present Dakshina Kannada district.

[23] Different forms of songs sung during paddy transplantation, during the annual *Buta* rituals in Tulu region.

## REFERENCES

Blackburn, Stuart. 2003. 'Introduction,' in *Print, Folklore and Nationalism in Colonial South India*, Delhi: Permanent Black.

Chatterjee, Partha. 1993. 'Whose Imagined Community?' in *Nation and Its Fragments: Colonial and Postcolonial Histories*, Princeton, NJ: Princeton University Press.

Chaudhary, S. C., et al. 1985 *Survey of English: South Kanara District*, Hyderabad: Central Institute of English and Foreign Languages.

Guru, Gopal. 2011. 'The Idea of India: Derivative, Desi and Beyond', *Economic and Political Weekly*, 46, 37.

Kotekar, Ramnath. 2011. Billawarumattu Basel Mission: Ondu Adhyayana, Mangalore: Sai Sundari Seva Trust.

Menon, Dilip. 2006. *The Blindness of Insight: Essays on Caste in Modern India*, Pondicherry: Navayana.

Mukherjee, Meenakshi. 1985. *Realism and Reality: The Novel and Society in India*, Delhi: Oxford University Press.

———. ed. 2002. *Early Novels in India*. Delhi: Sahitya Akademi.

Pandian, M.S.S. 2002. 'One Step Outside Modernity: Caste, Identity Politics and Public Sphere', in *Economic and Political Weekly*, 37, 18.

Paniyadi, S. U. [1936] 2009. *Sati Kamale*, Ujire: Vishwa Tulu Sammelano.

Rai, Viveka, et al. eds, 2007. *Tulu Sahitya Charitre*, Hampi: Prasaranga, Kannada University.

Rao, Surendra B. 2010. *Bunts in History and Culture*, Udupi: Rasthrakavi Govinda Pai Samshodhana Kendra and World Bunt's Foundation Trust.

Sarkar, Tanika. 1995. 'Heroic Women, Mother Goddesses: Family and Organisation in Hindutva Politics', in *Women and the Hindu Right*, edited by Tanika Sarkar and U. Butalia, Delhi: Kali for Women.

———. 2001. 'Introduction', in *Hindu Wife, Hindu Nation: Community, Religion and Cultural Nationalism*, Delhi: Permanent Black.

Shetty, Parinitha. 2008. 'Missionary Pedagogy and Christianization of the Heathens: The Educational Institutions Introduced by the Basel Mission in Mangalore', *IESHR* 45, 4: 509–51.

# 12

## Between Langue and Parole

### THE FORKED ROAD TO DEVELOPMENT

Jasbir Jain

LANGUAGE SIGNIFIES in itself more than mere communication and interaction. Philosophers, linguists, anthropologists and sociologists have researched on both: language as well as the processes of its acquisition, growth and evolution. There is no way it can be treated as a matter of mere convenience or a skill to be learned mechanically. When Ferdinand de Saussure in *A Course in General Linguistics* made a distinction between langue and parole—language represented by its internal rules and projected in writing and the spoken language of the people—he perhaps never for a moment imagined that the two could hail from entirely different worlds in this age of globalization. But this becomes an evident reality when we discuss language learning in the context of rural India or of the deprived sections of society. A host of problems crowd the mind: English is not the language they speak at home or in their social and market interactions. They do not think or conceptualize in it, do not dream in it, do not make love in it or sing lullabies to their children in it. There may be other problems such as an absence of access to home supervision for school-going children, or to newspapers or other light, non-prescribed reading material, or the malady of malnutrition, or the inability to take out study time from their other duties and responsibilities. I could go on enumerating them all along the way. English is also not the language of their entertainment. Humour and irony are closely interwoven with culture and may not always be the same in another language, and as such they are likely to miss out on the nuances of language especially if they learn it for utility purposes.

Besides this schism between langue and parole, English has had a very complex relationship with India down the years on account of the educational policies of the colonial regime and later the claims of individual regions and their education policies. There has been a constant tussle between political policies and economic/employment needs for about 400 years at the most. It has a history of being an imposed language and of necessity, proceeding to become simultaneously the language of protest, exposure and of communication with the outer world. We picked up the crumbs from the master's table and made it our weapon, our road to freedom. Paradoxically, both political policy and strategy (I make a distinction between the two as they work differently—one is public and openly spelt-out, the other is hidden and works through subterfuges) have been divided over the issue of language. We have alternated between English, Hindi and regional languages as the medium of instruction. In addition we have an economic division strewn all over our schooling system, and are torn between the demands of globalization and our cultural needs.

English may be the mother tongue of a small educated population and some other communities, a language spoken at home, and one used for social interaction as well as for conceptualization. It comes easily to many of us of an earlier generation who have been brought up on English nursery rhymes, fairy tales and Bible stories as also to those who have studied in English-medium schools, but not so easily to others who have missed out on those adaptive processes resulting in a huge social and classroom divide. Toru Dutt and others like her had almost an English upbringing and were exposed to English music, Irish or English teachers and other media of learning, but they constituted a small percentage.

Does it imply that learning a language is a cultural transference or a simultaneous habitation of two cultural worlds? Language is neither a tool, nor a mere medium, and its survival and continuity are dependent on many factors such as political and social power as well as creative use and production of ideas. Meanings have significance as well as a history; they grow, evolve and change when influenced by environmental and cultural changes. In our own times we are witnessing the slow erasure of Urdu in India, when an increasing number of Urdu speakers are unable to read it. This is the case with many other languages in India when their speakers shift to other locations. Language has played a major role in identity politics and nation-building, and yet again a country's language may or may not have an international presence. Today's requirements have shifted the primacy to economic considerations of power and visibility as much as to the gender/class hierarchies which need to be addressed in this context.

In language learning or in according it primacy, a political decision in itself is never enough. Pedagogical methodologies and suitable texts are equally important. We have experimented with various strategies such as direct, structural and drill methods, translation, bilingualism, basic vocabulary and a host of others. To be honest, none of them has fulfilled our expectations or met our requirements. For decades now NCERT has struggled with textbook materials in an attempt to introduce familiar contexts. Each of the above methods has had negative fallouts. A grip over the grammatical rules does not lead to a fair grasp of reading or writing skills, not to mention fluency in speech. Limited vocabularies are like a tight clamp over the cranium, where ideas struggle for words. C. K. Ogden (1930) prepared a list of 800 words as Basic English and we, in India, tried the same with a list of 2000 words in the late 1970s and early 1980s. But what about the results? Orwell, during his years in the BBC resented the limits placed on the vocabulary where third world colonies were concerned. It implied 'problematization' of the issue in the context of totalitarianism and the colonial learner. It is related to both— freedom of expression and the freedom of thought. If one does not have the words, ideas remain locked in silence. With fresh editions of reduced vocabulary, thought processes were being curbed. It was a process of censorship: a restriction on all generations of thought, ideas and freedom. In the years following the Second World War, Chomsky's *Cartesian Linguistics* (2009) raised the possibility of universal structures. Initially accepted, it was soon to be questioned and criticized and later Chomsky himself shifted his stand.

One of his critics, often bypassed by linguists, was George Steiner who addressed the issue of language in several of his books. His *Extraterritorial* is entirely devoted to the language revolution. Steiner's treatment is part literary and part philosophical. He raises questions of language learning, of being polyglot, of languages surviving despite being un-housed and also comments on the formative influence of languages on culture and generation of ideas, literary approaches and on human life. In fact in 'The Language Animal' (1971a: 110–34) he draws attention to our common experiences which we do not even think about when speaking of language such as memory, the sense of the past, present and future, the ability to dream—all of them are the products of language and as such acquisition of any second or third language should create some of these possibilities for the learner whether man or woman, possibilities which require getting under the skin of the language in order to reach to culture.

In India we have also experimented with English as a library language and looked upon it as a tool. But no language lends itself to any such routing of knowledge. Similarly, learning language in order to be employed in the call centres or BPOs or just as computer typists can never be an isolated task. None of these surface skills is likely to lead to creative output unless they are enhanced over a period of time by a better understanding of the language. They will merely create workers who can use English for minimal purposes with no space for a genuine exchange between mother tongue and English or any other foreign language. This form of enslavement is a setback for both the individual and the society. This applies to all learners, though in our social environment in the subcontinent women are easily at a disadvantage regarding opportunities, freedom, time and leisure and even socialising.

Yet, the scene is not so dismal. One is often surprised by the linguistic ability of people who have had the minimal of schooling and learning opportunity. Where and how do they learn a new language? Is it that they become proficient when thrown into these new waters and an English-speaking working environment? A whole range of migratory populations quickly learn to speak the language of another region, country, or location when seeking business or employment in that area. True, it may remain at the noun plus verb stage for a long time. But in businesses such as medical representation and marketing, in business houses and similar other establishments, English is picked up with some measure of success as a matter of necessity. It is obvious that the foremost reason for learning another language is the need to do so. All other reasons such as competition, motivation, aptitude and opportunity align themselves behind it. Empowerment interfaces with this need while equality in terms of gender is not necessarily a direct cause and does not provide a direct motivation.

How do we fare as a nation where the question of caste/class equality and gender equity are concerned? For centuries we have accepted a hierarchical caste system as well as a hierarchical gender relationship. For the most, we have accepted it silently, often unquestioningly, at both political and personal levels, with occasional protests, often indirect, as in the case of the Bhakti women poets, through religious conversion as in Pandita Ramabai's case, through the wisdom of educated husbands, such as Jotirao Phule and Govind Rao Kanitkar and at times through a religious fervour and the need to express. Rassundari Devi in the nineteenth century learnt by observing her son being taught and imitated the letter formation in the plate of rice she was sifting through. It was an added task along with her household chores. The missionaries, especially women missionaries, contributed a great deal to the education of women. The 1883 Report of the Indian Education Commission admitted that when the British obtained possession of the country, 'a section of the female population was educated up to the modest requirements of the household life' (Jain 1997: 51). Education was considered a part of religious training, but this again applies to the upper-class families.[1] Legal struggles for rights led to the famous Rukhmabai case where Rukhmabai defended her right to say no to a child marriage where she had had no voice.[2] When we deliberate the issue of English-language learning and women with a specific reference to Dalit women, we come across similar difficulties in language learning as in upper-caste women, only with one major difference: caste and its consequent social sphere. If Dalit women are to learn English with the idea of equal participation in social, public and political life, they have to overcome the mindset of caste prejudice in addition to all the other difficulties. Before proceeding any further I feel the need to debate a couple of issues and open them out for further discussion: firstly, Why Dalit? Secondly, Why women? Thirdly, Why English?

Beginning with the last first, evidently the English language adds to both work and class mobility. It carries with it an aura of sophistication, a social presence and, at times, arrogance. It enables migration not only within the country but also abroad. Subsequently a whole range of jobs outside the mere routine become available, such as those of translators, announcers, interpreters, event managers, and other public positions. But more than all else it is the sophistication that the language has come to be associated with—a sophistication which should be a part of any educational system no matter in whichever language it is delivered. Definitely it does achieve some kind of social bridging. Many of us who have worked with young students know how difficult it is to bridge the gap between two different school systems based on different language mediums. It is much easier to handle a single group. But a mixed group opens out a totally different kind of challenge, provided the teacher is able to tame the English-knowing group to a level of friendship with the other. More than language it is classroom management, faculty and pedagogy that are to blame for widening the gap.

Next: why women? I believe, primarily because they are doubly disadvantaged, and their schooling is considered peripheral to the well-being of the family or of society in general. Even in middle-class families, in cases where resources are limited, the male child gets preference, but increasingly women are also being encouraged to join professional courses. Caste plays a role at the entry point on account of reservations but this does not necessarily continue in curriculum related matters. They are looked upon as prospective mothers, as appendices to their men, and are responsible for household chores. Government's schemes for the girl child and for the women students have brought about some change in literacy figures. But the sprouting up of private institutions often negates these schemes. The gender inequity is the result of a mindset—of the majority of men of all categories including teachers, lawyers and public servants and of women who are tradition-bound, ritualistic and afraid to take up cudgels for a cause. Despite all this, English learning has increasingly become a necessity supposed to open out magic doors to class (and caste) mobility, education and economic opportunity. A certain degree of prestige is attached to and it also happens to be a link language and gives a semblance of unity to the nation.

This in itself is a much larger issue where caste, research methodology and market forces come together and where political reservation policies also need to be reviewed. Today, in the twenty-first century, we are still contesting the issue of caste. Both Gandhi and Ambedkar, despite their different strategies, failed. Education and job reservations with the Mandal commission recommendations thrown in have not really made much difference except in economic and political terms. Caste hegemonies and hierarchies still continue to exist, though power structures are fast changing with Dalit participation in politics, which leads to their bargaining power in economic, social and political terms; their numbers give them this power. The term, however, is also engaged in enlarging itself to include feminist struggles. Our progressive ideas do not go far enough. At some point, these terms need to be reinterpreted and recast and mindsets changed both through the efforts of the privileged classes and through improving the self-image of the Dalits. The situation can improve only when we lift our minds a little above caste locations; even though the negative role of khap panchayats and the hullabaloo attached to inter-caste unions continue to haunt us through all shades of modernity. One way of rising above this is to liberate the Dalit from being perceived as a reserved category, but with the political advantage that caste gives them as a vote bank it is unlikely to happen in the near future. So, are we then in a no-improvement zone, or are there other ways? The onus lies with political leadership and the privileged. The legal provision exists in the constitution in our Fundamental Rights; moreover the initiative has to come from the Dalits themselves, just as women have fought their own battles albeit with male support. Caste labels continue to be problematic and confine identity construction in a larger society and at some level, obstruct the accessibility to equality, especially in social discourse and residential facilities. 'Vernacular' is another such term—educationists, almost without exception—even a theorist like Homi Bhabha (2001) and a creative writer like Lakshmi Kannan (2016) use this term. They are unable to avoid it as this was the term used by the British for Indian language schools, but it is unfortunate that the legacy has gone so deep as to bracket our own languages with the vernacular, giving them an inferior status. Amongst its several meanings such as the mother tongue; the language spoken by ordinary people; one which doesn't need to be learnt or is not imposed, it is also described as a dialect and one spoken by slaves and natives. 'Verna' is a Latin word and refers to slaves born in a master household. Vernacular includes slang, implies subordination in rank and status, and has a colonial connotation for us; the African-American slaves' language is referred to as vernacular; even when applied to architecture it implies domestic architecture.[3] To set the word 'vernacular' against English as a category, establishes hierarchy and implies subordination. English is now recognized as one of the Indian languages but it does not have a history of being a classic language while several of the so called vernaculars are long-standing literary languages. To change our mindsets, we need to change the way we look at things, and how we describe them. We need to change our terminologies or at least deconstruct them. We need to rethink its application to Indian languages. Similarly, all poor or oppressed people do not belong to the scheduled castes and likewise all scheduled caste people are not, or are no longer, poor—else we would not have had such a term as 'creamy layer'. Those who are participants in power may have reached those positions by their own efforts, and however low the percentages, they are in positions of political, administrative and industrial power. Hence the simple equation of Dalit with caste has no longer the same validity as it had fifty years ago except that the term denotes a shared historical condition.

The agencies that have been working for this change have been several—social movements, political leadership, alternative action and, more than all else, self-motivation. One more reason—though somewhat controversial—has been religious conversion (Webster 2001). Christian missions played both a positive as well as a divisive role. Their contribution to education and to health services has been creditable. People thought of educating girls and women before the missionaries did but the missionaries opened out the school system to the lower castes. The Baptist Zenana Mission recruited women teachers and though it began with Brahmin and Kayastha girl students, 'by the late 1830s... these schools were utilized entirely by caste girls... by the daughters of cobblers and sweepers' (Carpenter, vol. 1: 137). And the schools set up by Savitribai Phule, Pandita Ramabai and some others were being established at the same time. The missionary activity in western India was not as extensive as in Bengal and Madras, though in Travancore and Baroda the rulers were aware and initiated action on their own for women's education in addition to other agencies. We cannot leave out the Parsis, Jews or self-educated women. Reformist societies also took initiative in this direction. The Buddhist and the Jain nuns were learned (though not in English) and some have left their diaries behind. In fact, the high literacy rate and facility in English in the hill areas of the North East, the plains of Punjab and other states of India has been enormous. But increased wealth on part of the convertees has now led to a greater segregation than ever before as in the case of converted Sikhs who have built their own religious houses and the Christians in Kerala where separate colonies are being set up by the lower caste convertees as against the earlier Brahmin convertees of the sixteenth century. Through this move they are making a political statement of their economic and political power. The women in these households are impacted in their educational pursuits by the rest of the environment in the state. In Kerala the literacy levels are higher than the rest of the country, one of the many reasons for which is the effort of the missionaries who paid attention to the convertees. This includes both men and women. Unfortunately, even within the Church Mission there is a continued discrimination against convertees. Both Bama in *Karukku* (2000) and Sister Jesme in her autobiography (2009) have discussed this at length leading one to ask what the price of conversion is. Several decades before them—nearly half a century, we have Mulk Raj Anand's Bakha who realises that there is continued discrimination. Both equality within the mainstream and solidarity amongst Dalits for a political gain have eluded the oppressed. In the midst of all these complexities one needs to have a closer look at multiple aspects of development. Amartya Sen (1979) has asked the question 'Equality of what?' I would like to supplement it with the query 'What kind of development?' Development works at more levels than one. True, economic development is the base of other developments, but it does not necessarily lead to increased awareness or growth of the individual consciousness, or a change in the mindset and least of all to production of ideas. The last is one of the most important issues if men and women from the Depressed Communities are to develop their subjectivities and agencies and participate more fully. English education for women has become a gateway to gender equality and to the enhancement of their employment opportunities. It helps to improve their status both socially and economically. The various reasons for this have already been enumerated above and we are quite aware of the trend that has overtaken us.

The automatic location of local interests in the general idea of globalization does not work. Often they move in opposite directions (Touraine 2004). Globalization focuses on economic and, in limited measure, on ecology; but political, individual and identity interests do not necessarily coincide with its agenda. Globalization has been brought about by the technological revolution which is both an instrument and an agency. And the steamroller tendency of technology results in multiple erasures. We are witness to a large-scale shift in social and political institutions such as education, marriage, family and even the nation state. It is even more worrisome that this shift is neither linear nor unidirectional. Since the 1980s a growing conservatism in social structures is also visible. The objectives of development—whether those of the society or the individual—are being constantly thwarted. Today perhaps the world is far more unequal and divided than ever before. The restlessness born of these divisions, the revolutions, encroachments, terrorist onslaughts and the neo-imperialist tendencies are all an evidence of

this. Somewhere or the other war or violence is afoot all the time.
Steiner in (1971a) writes,

> We are also beginning to suspect that certain patterns of *anomie*,
> of anti-social and anarchic conduct are related to verbal inade-
> quacy, to the inability of the grammatically underprivileged to
> 'branch into' society whose codes of communication an idiom of
> values are too sophisticated (95).

In another essay (1971c) 'Of Nuance and Scruple', he argues
that our silences are also attributable to it. Human beings have
forgotten the art of communication, hence the importance of language, and the need to acquire it not as a mere skill to be used
externally but as one which connects with the internal mental
activity. Capitalism, like imperialism, frowns at the underprivileged
'other' of both genders. It has no hesitation in erasing it. In the final
instance it is a question of values and ideas of the underprivileged,
no matter whether men or women, and whether nations or their
margins. If they are to work towards some kind of a shared world,
languages are essential for both values and ideas. Values need to be
preserved to ensure the quality of human life and ideas are the base
of questioning and the necessary change towards modernity. They
equip us to meet the challenges of the outside world on our own
terms. Nothing second-hand or borrowed ever serves the purpose.

There is no denying the fact that literacy provides a base, that
in order to build upon it we need money, books, time, motivation
and good teachers. In India multi-pronged efforts are afoot and all
of them together have made some dent. A country-wide experiment
has been made by setting up community schools since the beginning
of the twenty first century. The 93rd Amendment of the constitution
made education a fundamental right. Stipends and scholarships are
available for the underprivileged. The Right to Education is being
implemented in some measure and mid-day meals are being provided. Literacy rates have gone up in the decade between 1991 and
2001, no matter how slowly. The 1991 Census showed a literacy
rate of 52.21. In 2001 it was 65.38 percent, though a huge gap still
remains between men and women. In Rajasthan, Scheduled Castes
have a rate of 52.2 percent while the national average stands at 54.7

per cent. The literacy of Dalit women still remains dismally low with high drop-out percentages. But the encouragement lies in the fact that it nearly doubled in the decade of the nineties. This literacy rate is largely based on the learning of the mother tongue. There is no separate data for English language literacy. But literacy in itself is not education. It does not make an aware human being. It only opens the door a wee bit. In no way are the objectives met. The number of dropouts and the gender-ratio both are alarming and are indicators that the idea of development with its increased materialism and accompanying erosion of values, and language-learning entangled as it is in the web of the 'reluctant teacher' and the 'reluctant learner', need to be examined and consequently changed if the objective of education is to be an effective equality. The 1986 Education Act for the first time used the term 'equality' in the context of women, going beyond the earlier policy and political statements that educated women made better mothers and improved the quality of life. The recognition of equality as an objective, however, has still not, even after a quarter century, gone deep enough in our minds or our educational approaches. It is so comfortable to fall back into conventional positions, whether located at home, the family or the classroom. Activism continues to be guided by the old guard. The middle-class women in universities are somewhat indifferent to feminist concerns.

Education is and has always been a social project, involving multiple agencies but the two most important people remain the teacher and the learner. They together are capable of surmounting the problems created by other limitations. Women's education was earlier thwarted by child marriage, a practice which still continues in several parts of India. I have noticed, however, that Dalit women remain unmarried longer then the middle-class rural women, where social respectability and purdah play a greater role. The Dalit parents get the girl engaged but not married while they are wait for some dowry money to accumulate (my reference is to Rajasthan). Now more than ever before the factor of personal motivation of the woman learner has become important. The challenges are many. I present some case studies where efforts to educate the girl child have not succeeded despite monetary help and the push by the mothers.

## CASE NO. 1

Nalini, a young Dalit girl, was sent to school at the age of six. She would slip away from the school and refuse to learn. Blaming the Government Primary School, the mother removed her and admitted her to an English-medium school, along with Nalini's two younger brothers. After a year the school asked that they be withdrawn as they were unable to keep pace with the other students. They were then admitted to a Hindi-medium private school where they are studying at present but the girl, now fourteen, is only a year ahead of her much younger brothers, and only in the fourth class. Although she appears to be smart, she is not eligible for any professional course such as nursing.

## CASE NO. 2

Ria Mandal's education is supported by an activist right from her childhood years. She has entered the ninth class this year but she barely scrapes through, and her results have shown deterioration every year. In this case it is the environment which is to blame because they live in a one-room tenement where cooking also takes place, a TV is mostly on, and her father is an alcoholic. She has a mobile, but strangely enough is not allowed to play with her school friends. Her mother also works as a domestic help in other people's houses. In this case there is status snobbery within the lower class. The necessary environment and counselling required are missing or unacceptable to the parents.

## CASE NO. 3

Naina, a grown woman, slim and good looking, mother of two children, and expecting her third, is very good at massaging, pedicure and other such things but cannot be sent to a polytechnic institute for a beautician's course as the minimum qualification for admission is the twelfth class certificate.

Men are also equally handicapped because they do not study beyond the fifth or the eighth class. If they acquire a skill they may get employment as cooks (in domestic households, and not hotels) or drivers (not as mechanics, either because they are not eligible for admission to the qualifying courses for entrance to these services, or do not have the initiative to seek apprenticeship (as mechanics). This indicates not only a lack of opportunity but also of motivation. Of course there are exceptions and there are both men and women who have risen above their problems. Many women have struggled to get educated or move out of an unhappy marriage, but despite these exceptions, spreading awareness and raising motivation levels still remain a major problem. At times, even when they receive monetary help and encouragement, they are not motivated enough to pursue further studies/qualifications. A handful of success stories do make us proud but they do not allow us to be complacent about the education scenario of the Dalits, particularly women.

The success stories go to prove that the task of educating them and facilitating the learning of English is possible but extra efforts have to be made in raising their self-motivation and improving the social and familial environment. Caste prejudices still run high. The upper caste has objected to Dalits being employed as cooks for the mid-day meal kitchens. Even fully qualified Dalit women have had difficulties in placement in educational institutions and other middle-class jobs. The writer Bama confided in me in a private conversation that despite her education and her teaching job in a respectable Roman Catholic School in her township Uthiramerur near Chennai, she has to face social discrimination. When her permission was sought whether this could be made public, she further elaborated that she was unable to get a water connection, had to collect water from public pump and her maids were threatened if they worked for her. This still continues to be the social environment— one of the major hurdles in raising the motivational levels. But education holds the promise of a better life and earning potential. Bama is a Tamil writer, knows English, has travelled abroad for literary conferences, and has a place for herself in the literary world. What she misses is the community life in her neighbourhood. Languages, other than one's own, open out additional windows for communication so that the voice can go across.

I have tried to give both a theoretical framework for language learning and the difficulties that lie ahead as well as some pedagogical approaches that can help. Democracy and freedom require greater participation of all classes and genders for the proper protection of our rights, if we are not to be caught up in enslavement of different kinds. And for this communication and contestation across cultures, the learning of English is essential. We need to be bilingual and trilingual in order to make our presence felt so that we are neither Rushdie's 'translated' men (or women) nor the professional translator who creates a bridge, but instead have the agency to translate ourselves and be comfortably at home in more than one language. The task of learning is difficult because of the gap between home environments and the conditions ideally required for learning a language not one's own.

This in itself is a daunting task, difficult and enormous. Medium of instruction inevitably gets linked with economic status and home background. Meera Lal, a senior consultant at the Indian Institute of Economics at Hyderabad, observes (2010) 'An increasing number of researchers strongly advocate the use of mother tongue or home language as medium of instruction in early stages of education' (17). But the problem remains as to how we learn, what we learn, who teaches us and how and whether or not it is ideologically enthused. If it is ideologically enthused, another issue becomes important: how and to what extent are we morally equipped and responsible for working through it. This is an issue—the one of moral responsibility— which we have not trained ourselves to think about. It also raises the question of authority. Those in positions of planning are the ones to decide but are their decisions based on neutrality, lack of condescension and long-term futuristic vision? Are they seized with the idea of shaping independent minds capable of thinking and making choices? And those of us outside the power structures, the implementers, the field workers; do we find the time and energy to make an intervention wherever possible? Education has never been and never will be a simple task. The human element involved throughout is enormous. Mastering a language not in daily use in their homes and lives, for Dalit women, is indeed forked. An all-out effort both at social and governmental levels alone can help bridge the gap between the two—English and the home dialects. It is both a pedagogical and a social challenge which faces us and requires major environmental shifts. But there is hope in the few success stories where education has helped Dalit women to enter middle-class jobs as nurses, computer typists, shop assistants, teachers (both at university and school levels), researchers, lab assistants, writers, poets and many more. All of these jobs may not be related to their command over English, but many are. The inspiration exists; it is ambition that needs to be stirred to match the potential with the dream.

## NOTES

1. For details see 'From Listener to Reader' in *Feminizing Political Discourse* (1997): 47–57.
2. For more details see Jasbir Jain, *Indigenous Roots of Feminism* (2011): especially Chapters 5 and 6, 172–267.
3. Refer *Shorter Oxford Dictionary* (in 2 volumes) and http://www.dictionary.com/browse/verna

## REFERENCES

Anand, Mulk Raj. 1935. *Untouchable*, New Delhi: Orient Paperbacks, 1970.
Bama. 2000. *Kurukku*, trans. Lakshmi Holmstrom, Chennai: Macmillan.
Binde, Jerôme, ed. 2004. *The Future of Values: Twenty-First Century Talks,* trans. John Corbett (and Brian Verity for Derrida's essay), New York: Berghahn and Paris: UNESCO Publishing.
Bhabha, Homi. 2001.'Unsatisfied?: Notes on Vernacular Cosmopolitanism', in *Postcolonial Discourses: An Anthology*, edited by Gregory Castle, Oxford: Blackwell, 38–52.
Carpenter, Mary.1868. *Six Months in India*, 2 vols. London: Longman, Green & Co.

Chandra, Sudhir. [1998], 2008. *Enslaved Daughters: Colonialism, Law and Women's Rights*, New Delhi: Oxford University Press.

Chomsky, Noam. 2009. *Cartesian Linguistics*, Cambridge: Cambridge University Press.

Devi, Rassundari. 1999. *Amar Jiban* (My Life), trans. Enakshi Chatterjee, Calcutta: Writers Workshop.

Jain, Jasbir. 2016. 'Negotiations with Faith: Conversion, Identity and Historical Continuity', *Dalit Literature in India,* edited by Joshil Abraham and Judith Misrahi-Barak, New Delhi: Routledge, 93–107.

——. 2011. *Indigenous Roots of Feminism: Culture, Subjectivity and Agency*, New Delhi: SAGE.

——. 2011. 'The Nineteenth Century and After', in *Indigenous Roots of Feminism: Culture, Subjectivity and Agency.* New Delhi: SAGE, 172–216.

——. 2011. 'Articulating the Self', in *Indigenous Roots of Feminism: Culture. Subjectivity and Agency*, New Delhi: SAGE, 217–267.

——. 1997. 'From Listener to Reader', in *Feminizing Political Discourse: Women and the Rise of the Novel in India*, Jaipur: Rawat, 47–57.

Jesme, Sister. 2009. *Amen: The Autobiography of a Nun,* New Delhi: Penguin.

Kannan, Lakshmi. 2016. *The Glass Bead Curtain*, New Delhi: Vitasta.

Lal, Meera. 2010. 'Education: The Inclusive Growth Strategy for the Economically and Socially Disadvantaged in Society'. Internet 1–22. http://www.dise.in/downloads use0%200f%… Also in *Challenges of Education in Twenty-first Century*, New Delhi: Deep and Deep.

Ogden, C.K. 1930. *Basic English*, London: Kegan Paul, Trench Trubner.

Orwell, George. 1949. *Nineteen Eighty-Four*, Harmondsworth: Penguin, 1962.

Pangaria, Ashok, '*Matrbhasha Mein Shiksha Faidemand*', *Rajasthan Patrika* 6 December 2011. Jaipur edition.

Sen, Amartya. 'Equality of What?' Tanner Lecture on Human Values (Stanford University, 22 May 1979). http://www.uv.es/mperezs/into-poleco/lecturecomp/Distribution— Consulted 24 Dec. 2011.

Steiner, George.1971a. 'The Language Animal', in *Extraterritorial: Papers on Literature and the Language Revolution*, Harmondsworth: Peregrine: 88–109.

Steiner, George. 1971b. 'Extraterritorial' in *Extraterritorial: Papers on Literature and the Language Revolution,* Harmondsworth: Peregrine, 14-21.

———. 1971c. 'Of Nuance and Scruple', in *Extraterritorial: Papers on Literature and the Language Revolution,* Harmondsworth: Peregrine: 22-31, vol. 1, New Delhi: Oxford University Press.

Touraine, Alain. [1975] 2004. 'Reconstructing Culture', in *The Future of Values,* New York: Berghahn; Paris: UNESCO: 154–158.

Webster, John C.B. 2001 'The Dalit Situation in India', *International Journal of Frontier Mission* 18.1 (Spring), 15-17.

West, W.J. 1987, Introduction, *George Orwell: The War Broadcasts,* Harmondsworth: Penguin, 13-68.

# About the Editor and Contributors

## EDITOR

**K. Suneetha Rani** is Professor, Centre for Women's Studies, University of Hyderabad. Her areas of interest are Cultural Studies, New Literatures in English, Translation Studies and Dalit Studies. Among her many publications are: *Australian Aboriginal Women's Autobiographies: A Critical Study* (2007); *Dweeparagalu*, an anthology of Sri Lankan women's short fiction translated from English to Telugu (2008); *Flowering from the Soil: Dalit Women's Writing from Telugu* (2012).

## CONTRIBUTORS

**Somdatta Bhattacharya** is Assistant Professor, Department of Humanities and Social Sciences, BITS Pilani. Her areas of interest are Urban Cultural Studies, Indian Writing in English, Popular Culture and Digital Humanities.

**Paromita Bose** is Assistant Professor of English, School of Humanities and Social Sciences, Mahindra École Centrale, Hyderabad. Her areas of interest are Indian Writing in English and Translation, Cultural Studies, Gender Studies and History of Dance in India.

**Sanjukta Dasgupta** is Professor, Department of English, University of Calcutta. She is a critic, translator and poet. Among her published works are: *The Novels of Huxley and Hemingway: A Study in*

*Two Planes of Reality* (1996) and *The Indian Family in Transition* (co-edited, 2007).

**Sowmya Dechamma C.C.** teaches at the Centre for Comparative Literature, University of Hyderabad. Her teaching and research interests include Indian Literatures, Translation Studies, Minority Discourse, Kodava language and Cultural Discourse.

**Nikhila H.** is Professor in the Department of Film Studies, EFL University, Hyderabad. Her recent publications are on multimodal translations between different Indian languages and studies on literary translations from Kannada to English.

**Jasbir Jain** is Honorary Director, Institute for Research in Interdisciplinary Studies, Jaipur. Among her publications are: *Theorizing Resistance* (2012), *The Diaspora Writes Home* (2015), and *Forgiveness: Between Memory and History* (2016).

**Omprakash Manikrao Kamble** is a PhD scholar in the Centre for Comparative Literature, University of Hyderabad. His research interests include Dalit Studies, Afro-American Literature, and translations.

**Meera Kosambi** who died in 1915, was a distinguished scholar who wrote on various subjects ranging from feminist history to urban ecology. Among her many books are: *Crossing Thresholds* (2007), *Returning the American Gaze: Pandita Ramabai's 'The Peoples of the United States' (1889)* (2003), *Gender, Culture, and Performance: Marathi Theatre and Cinema before Independence* (2014), and *Dharmanand Kosambi: The Essential Writings* (2013).

**Jinju S.** is Assistant Professor of English at M.E.S. College, Nedumkandam, Kerala. Her research interests include Minority Discourse, Subaltern and Postcolonial Studies, Feminisms, and the writings of Orhan Pamuk and Elif Shafak.

**Yogitha Shetty** is currently pursuing doctoral research at the Centre for Comparative Literature, University of Hyderabad. She is also a

Doctoral Fellow at the Centre for the Study of Developing Societies, New Delhi. Her areas of interest include Mnemonic-Cultures, Religion and Tulu language and culture.

**Alladi Uma** retired as Professor in the Department of English, University of Hyderabad. Her research interests include African-American Studies, Indian Writing in English, Translation, Comparative Literature and Women's Studies. She has published extensively in these areas.

**C. Vijayasree** who died in 2012, was Professor in the Department of English, Osmania University, Hyderabad. Her areas of specialization were Postcolonial Literatures and Women's Writing. Her publications include: *Mulk Raj Anand: The Raj and the Writer* (1998), *Suniti Namjoshi: An Artful Transgressor* (2001) and the edited volumes *Writing the West* (2004) and *Nation and Imagination* (2007).